FREAKSHOW

FREAKSHOW

*Misadventures in the
Counterculture, 1959–1971*

ALBERT GOLDMAN

Cooper Square Press

First Cooper Square Press edition 2001

This Cooper Square Press paperback edition of *Freakshow* is an unabridged republication of the edition first published in New York in 1971. It is reprinted by arrangement with Spritzgun Productions, Inc., and the Estate of Albert Goldman.

Designed by Kathleen Carey

Published by Cooper Square Press
An Imprint of the Rowman & Littlefield Publishing Group
150 Fifth Avenue, Suite 814
New York, New York 10011

Distributed by National Book Network

Library of Congress Cataloging-in-Publication Data

Goldman, Albert Harry, 1927-
  Freakshow : misadventures in the counterculture, 1959-1971 /
Albert Goldman.—1st Cooper Square Press ed.
      p. cm.
  ISBN 0-8154-1169-3 (paper : alk. paper)
    1.   Popular music—History and criticism. 2. Popular culture—
History—20th century. I. Title.

ML60 .G59 2001
781.64'0973—dc21

2001028420

⊖™ The paper used in this publication meets the minimum requirements of American National Standard for Information Sciences—Permanence of Paper for Printed Library Materials, ANSI/NISO Z39.48–1992.
Manufactured in the United States of America.

For Sharon Spencer Maljkovic

Preface

MY INTEREST in popular culture dates from a day in 1955 when I picked up a couple of dusty old shellac records by Benny Goodman and carted them home as souvenirs of my youth. I had loved Benny Goodman the way any kid did growing up in the late Thirties and early Forties. I loved the way his needle-sharp clarinet cut with surgical accuracy through the hot sweaty flab of a swing band. I loved the squirting, spritzing, high-nozzle velocity of his style. His impatient, imperious attack. His trick of getting in there and getting out before you could get him in your sights. What difference did it make if he looked like your high-school English teacher? Benny was thrilling.

Could he still thrill me in 1955? After the big war? After the deep freeze of the late Forties when I studied Aristotle at the University of Chicago or the Age of Cultural Aspiration in the early Fifties when I studied with Lionel Trilling and Jacques Barzun at Columbia? When I was a child, I swung like a child. But now that I was a man, I was burdened with heavy thoughts, heavy books, heavy sounds. I had become a classical-music nut who rose every morning to early mass on WQXR, ate my lunch (sliced olive and cream cheese on cracked wheat) to the sounds of Gabrieli marching around the Piazza San Marco and then tapped my foot through supper waiting for the joyous moment when I could slip into the living room and spin a precious set of Schnabel Beethoven Late Bagatelles—three voluptuously shiny black discs embossed with glorious crimson HMV labels—which I had picked that very afternoon out of the garbage piled up in a Sixth Avenue schlachthaus. Why, even my dreams were about Beethoven and Schnabel. One night I was transported magically to the Old Man's practice room. Trembling with anticipation, I said, "Mr. Schnabel, I want to ask you about the slow movement of the *Hammerklavier Sonata?*" Smiling gently, wisely, Schnabel touched the keys and replied with a luminous chord.

I wasn't expecting anything to happen that afternoon when I lowered the needle into those rasping old grooves. Yet when I heard that band barking out the opening chords of "Mission to Moscow," I got a terrific flash. This old stuff was great! It was exciting! It was music! That was the thing I could hardly believe: the crap we listened to when we were kids was really music. That day I forgave myself for my youth. I even began to think it might be fun to go out and find some more Benny Goodman records.

Evidently I wasn't the only one on that trip. A couple of months later Columbia issued the now-famous *Benny Goodman at Carnegie Hall* album and triggered a tremendous wave of nostalgia that swept down through the Fifties, gathering into its widening embrace not only old swing bands but old movies and old comic strips and old radio shows and old clothes and furniture and toys and hair styles —until by the middle of the next decade, hundreds, thousands, by now millions of people were walking around looking as if they had just stepped out of an old copy of *Photoplay*.

The cause of it all, I believe, was simply a colossal failure of sublimation. My generation had been launched like a flight of rocket-driven missiles straight up into the highest heavens of ambition and aspiration; but just as we reached our apogee, we ran out of gas and came tumbling down on the meadows of our childhood. One of the reasons for this loop-the-loop career was purely historical. We were the first generation to feel from our earliest years the powerfully seductive influences of the mass media. The year of my birth, 1927, saw not only Lindy's hop but the introduction of talkies and electric recording. Radio came of age with us. The comic-book industry, the music business, juvenile journalism, fashions, fads—the whole teen culture—rose into being as we grew up.

When the time came to put away childish things and go on to cultural maturity, we only half-shifted our gears. We did go in unprecedented numbers to college and graduate school, acquired books and records by the millions, supported unprecedented programs of cultural improvement and recreation. But these things were done with certain secret reserves. We still sneaked off to the movies like a lover going to an assignation or a junkie for a fix.

As the years wore on, we began to suffer from a mysterious loss of energy. We were afflicted with cultural anemia. Our paintings turned black, our plays absurd. Our composers took to extolling the mystic joys of silence. The high culture, the official culture, the culture we admired, extolled and revered, began to stultify in a dreary atmosphere of middle-class piety. Strong critical voices were raised in protest against the declining condition of the arts and the smugness of the middle-brow audience. Castigations and exhortations proved wholly inadequate to reverse the tide. Eventually, the fact became plain. Classic culture and art were destined to dry up and die in the middle of the twentieth century.

Then the great pop bubble began to rise from the lowest depths of our civilization. From the minds of the lumpen-puerile came the sounds of rock, the cackle of the sick joke and the lurid comic-book shapes of Pop Art. At first it seemed like a desecration. America's century-old dream of succeeding Europe as the creator and conserver of classic art was being blotted out by the nightmare of the discothèque. Slowly, though, we began to realize that this cultural revolution, this topsy-turvy substitution of the lowest for the highest elements, might have a good issue. After all, we were not living in classic times. Our whole civilization had been drastically reshaped. The arts were desperately in need of fresh energies and forms. A period of crude and violent catharsis might lay open fresh veins in the earth. Provide a rich native ore that some subsequent generation of sane and civilized men could put to good use.

My own attitude toward pop culture was radically ambivalent. I saw it as the end and the beginning. As archetypal and superficial. As apocalyptic and absurd. I wasn't impressed by the rationalizations of stylish pundits like Marshall McLuhan and Susan Sontag, but I was deeply influenced by a strange little underworld which I began to explore about the time I discovered those old Benny Goodman records.

I entered the underground one night in my own living room. I met a young man at Brooklyn College who claimed to be a jazz musician but was in fact a brilliant and instinctive comic in the style of Lenny Bruce. In those days nobody had heard of Lenny, and "sick comedy" meant nothing more morbid than *Mad* Magazine. Imagine how you would feel if in the middle of a nice student-professor chat your student suddenly turned into Lenny Bruce and began working your parlor! I was stunned, and my wife was appalled. Yet the show was too good to miss, so we invited him back. Night after night, week after week, he went on, bringing along his girl friend, his buddies, a whole Brooklyn subculture about which I knew nothing. Eventually, I realized that these crazy Jewish kids hunched in the backs of candy stores had a comic style that was the verbal equivalent of jazz. Theirs was a Jewish jazz: oral, urgent and smartassed. I loved it and I let it overwhelm me.

Then, one night I joined these hipsters. I did a bit. Appropriately, the subject was the first time I jerked off. It began when I suddenly recollected that long-forgotten event, it built upward wildly as I began to unfold the intimate details, it climaxed with a facial flash that was exactly the look I wore twenty years before at the awesome moment of release. The next thing I knew, my new friends were rolling on the floor and I had discovered another human potentiality in myself: I could be funny.

Being compulsive by nature, I had no choice but to go on being funny till I was living the life of a full-time professional comedian. Humor operates something like hysteria. Once the fit is upon you, there is no controlling it. Everything you see twists itself spontaneously into a caricature. These crazy images demand to be imparted to an audience. If you can't find an audience, you work to one or two people. If you can't find one or two, you work to the wall. It sounds absurd, but it can get pretty scary.

After a few years of playing to students and friends, people began to press me to work professionally. The thought filled me with terror. Characteristically, the terror voiced itself as guilt and shame: "How would that look—a college professor onstage saying 'motherfucker'?" Yet I dearly wanted to make it into the nightclubs because every time I opened my mouth I confirmed myself as possessing an imagination. That was really the important thing. The distinctive faculty of the artist asserted itself in me only when I was up on my feet doing my bits. After I stopped doing them, I realized something important about the whole pop scene.

Pop culture is produced by amateurs, like myself, who just get up and squawk. Unlike the old-time entertainer, who went through a whole apprenticeship on the vaudeville stage, these kids go out there and fly by the seat of their pants. If they're musicians, they're playing by ear. If they're actors, they're doing it by psychodrama. If they're comics, they're winging it. Innocent of training, they're supported by the memory of all the hundreds of professionals they've been hearing or seeing since they toddled across the living-room rug to their first radio or TV set.

Pop culture is a culture of professional amateurs on its way to becoming a culture of pure amateurs. Saturated with art and entertainment, the contemporary audience wants to get up there on the stage and prove that it's just as good as the stars. After all, this audience already has the clothes, the hair and the relaxed morals of the old *vie de bohème;* its heroes are great only by virtue of a quality called soul that anybody can cultivate; there's no very difficult technique involved in singing a pop tune or telling a funny story. Why shouldn't everybody in a democratic society have his turn on camera? True, most people won't be able to create anything interesting; but the modern world teaches us that getting one little thing out of yourself is better than getting a thousand things out of other people. There's no more self-centered creature than *Homo Ludens.*

About the time I deserted classic culture for the adolescent underground, my old obsession with Beethoven and Schnabel caught up with me in the form of an offer to become the music critic of *The New Leader.* I had never heard of this old-fashioned leftist-leaning-rightward journal till I began writing for it; but I owe it and especially its Marxist (both Karl and Groucho) back-of-the-book editor, Moshe Decter, a great debt of gratitude. Who else would have given a man who had published nothing a chance to write 750 words for nothing?

Unfortunately, the opportunity entailed reviving my lapsed enthusiasm for the classics. Serious contemporary music had never interested me; it was too esoteric and unattractive. You had to devote your life to mastering a hundred arbitrary systems of composition which were closer to three-dimensional chess than they were to Bach and Mozart. Serious interpretations of the classics interested me vitally; but the great performers of the Thirties and Forties were now declining and their epigoni had nothing new to say. As one great musician after another died, my column began to read like an obituary page.

It took me about two years to free myself of all the inherited paraphernalia of the "serious" music critic and face around to those subjects which were really mine. The first of these was Lenny Bruce, who was being hounded to death in the courts at that time.

Lenny was never a friend—I found him very hard to take at close quarters—but I wrote about him with a great deal of empathy. I am conscious of having made him somewhat more brilliant than he was by simply dropping out of my account all the dumb things he said about morality, God and the law. When he thought, Lenny was a child, or, more precisely, an adolescent; but when he freed his imagination of the clogs of intellectual pretentiousness and moral indignation, he was a dazzling surrealist with a head full of images and words that came popping out like notes from Charlie Parker's horn.

After I'd had my say about Lenny and a few of my jazz heroes, I found myself again without a subject. Drifting around for several years, all the while teaching, I edited a new magazine, *Cultural Affairs*, wrote and "hosted" a Channel 13 TV show and suffered from cultural despair. Not being one of those critics who gloat over every fresh disaster on the Broadway stage or in that perpetually dying form, the novel, I never could get my juices up to castigate the culture. God knows, I thought things were awful in the mid-Sixties, with all the serious arts going down the drain and pop culture reduced to rock 'n' roll. I was deeply grieved over the downfall of jazz and the commercialization of black humor in films like *Dr. Strangelove;* but my job as a critic has always been to locate new fields of clover and then do a dance back at the hive. I like to exclaim and enthuse and make noise. I like to ride the roller-coaster of what's happening. In fact, I'm sure something's happening tonight—if we could just find where the cats are blowing!

Sad to say, with all my eagerness to find new things, I

generally arrive on the scene as the party is ending. I was
too late for Schnabel and the Budapest. Too late for Bird.
Almost too late for the "sicks." The one exception is rock
music, which I got into when it was hitting its peak in 1967.
I had always resisted writing about rock because I thought
the music was beneath serious discussion. I still think it's
preposterous to go on solemnly about the Penguins and the
Platters as if they were something more than jukebox artifacts. The truth is that pop music today is decisively inferior
as music to the jazz bands and show tunes of the Thirties.
Rock is more advanced only in the sense that it is vastly
more embracing as a social phenomenon and much richer
as a cultural mix. Jazz is Beethoven and rock is Wagner. If
going into the Festspielhaus, turning out the lights, gazing
at the mythic figures on the stage and blowing your mind
on the exotically colored sounds of a hugely powerful orchestra is your idea of the ultimate cultural experience, then
you are a perfect Wagnerite and a hard-rocker. I am neither.

Yet I don't want to knock the rock because it got me off
at a time when I was dying for something exciting to happen. It also crystallized a thousand thoughts and images and
myths that had been floating around in my head ever since
I received an education. From the first entrancing moment
when I saw the curtains part on Jim Morrison through a
hundred nights in futuristic discothèques and recording
studios to the incredible evening in Memphis when I saw
B. B. King and Albert King battle it out with their guitars
in the Club Paradise on South Danny Thomas Boulevard,
rock has served me as a speculum in which all thirteen volumes of *The Golden Bough* have come to life.

That is the way in which I have approached pop culture
in most of the pieces printed in this book. I have recorded
the current scene as monstrous and fascinating, bizarre and
theatrical, stirring and ridiculous—as, in a word, a freakshow.
I like that word. Its ambivalent charge of affection and contempt, its forbidden frankness and disarming familiarity
make it a token of this era's queer spirit and the flaming

creatures it has hatched.

Before concluding this preface, I would like to acknowledge the help generously furnished me by so many people. Particularly, I am grateful to George DeLeon, who got me into modern jazz, comedy and rock the way you'd take a squealing, kicking kid into an ocean that later you can't get him out of. Robert Brustein is the man who inspired me to write hard, tight and courageously. Jack Kroll encouraged me through his writing and conversation to let the words follow the kooky curves of contemporary consciousness. Joel Blocker and Mike Epstein kept me at it in the early days when writing was a lonely pain. Robert Gold kept me in living touch with jazz even when I went on the nod. Ross Russell showed me by example how to write a vivid, compassionate and completely persuasive account of a jazz genius. David Carey provided me with a hundred insights and out-takes on the music business. Clay Felker got me writing again after a long lay-out by making me feel that he wanted to publish me. Dave Scherman gently jockeyed me through the unfamiliar terrain of *Life*. To all these friends and colleagues, warm thanks for what has amounted to a second education.

Contents

xvii

IV: SEX POP PSYCH SCENE

ONE

Rock

The Emergence of Rock

To EXPERIENCE the Age of Rock full-blast and to begin to grasp its weird complexities, you can't do much better than spend a Saturday night at the Electric Circus, the most elaborate discothèque in New York. Located on St. Marks Place, the main nexus of East Village otherness, the Electric Circus is up a flight of stairs from the DOM (one of the early landmarks of the rock scene which has since evolved into a "soul" club). You make your way through a gaggle of very young hippies sprawled on the porch steps, and enter a long, narrow alcove where the faithful, the tourists, and those somewhere in between wait in line for admission in a mood of quiet expectancy, like people waiting to get into one of the more exciting exhibits at the World's Fair. Once inside, the spectator moves along a corridor bathed in ultraviolet light in which every speck of white takes on a lurid glow, climbs a steep staircase and passes through a dark antecham-

From *New American Review* No. 3. Copyright © 1968 by Albert Goldman. Reprinted by permission of The Sterling Lord Agency.

ber. Here the young sit packed together on benches and, already initiated into the mysteries beyond, stare back at the newcomer with glazed, indifferent expressions as though they had been sitting there for days. Then, suddenly, there is a cleft in the wall, and the spectator follows the crowd pressing through it into a gigantic hall that suggests a huge bleached skull. Its dark hollows are pierced by beams of colored light that stain the walls with slowly pulsing patterns and pictures: glowing amoeba shapes, strips of home movies and giant mandalas filled with fluid colors. The scream of a rock singer comes at you, the beat amplified to a deafening blast of sound. Housed within this electronic cave are hundreds of dancers, a number of them in exotic, flowing garments, their faces marked with phosphorescent insignia, hands clutching sticks of incense. Some of the dancers are gyrating frantically, as if trying to screw themselves down through the floor; others hold up their fists, ducking and bobbing like sparring partners; others wrench their heads and thrust out their hands as if to ward off evil spirits. For all its futuristic magic, the dance hall brings to mind those great painted caves such as Altamira in Spain where prehistoric man practiced his religious rites by dancing before the glowing images of his animal gods.

Magnetized by the crowd, impelled by the relentless pounding beat of the music, you are drawn out on the floor. Here there is a feeling of total immersion: you are inside the mob, inside the skull, inside the music, which comes from all sides, buffeting the dancers like a powerful surf. Strangest of all, in the midst of this frantic activity, you soon feel supremely alone; and this aloneness produces a giddy sense of freedom, even of exultation. At last you are free to move and act and mime the secret motions of your mind. Everywhere about you are people focused deep within themselves, working to bring to the surfaces of their bodies deep-seated erotic fantasies. Their faces are drugged, their heads thrown back, their limbs extended, their bodies dissolving into the arcs of the dance. The erotic intensity becomes so great that you wonder what sustains the frail partition of reserve that prevents the final spilling of this endlessly incited energy.

If you withdraw from the crowd and climb to the gallery overlooking the dance floor, you soon succumb to the other spell cast by this cave of dreams. Falling into a passive trance, his perceptions heightened perhaps by exhaustion or drugs (no liquor is served here), the spectator can enjoy simultaneously the pleasures of the theater, the movies and the sidewalk café. At the Electric Circus the spectacle of the dancers alternates with the surrealistic acts of professional performers. An immaculate chef on stilts will stride to the center of the floor, where he looms high above the dancers. They gather around him like children, while he entertains them by juggling three apples. Then, taking out a knife, he slices the fruit and feeds it to his flock. High on a circular platform, a performer dressed to look like a little girl in her nightie struggles ineffectually with a yo-yo. A blinding white strobe light flashes across her body, chopping her absurd actions into the frames of an ancient flickering movie. Another girl comes sliding down a rope; someone dressed as a gorilla seizes her and carries her off with a lurching gait. Sitting in the dark gallery, you watch the crepitating spectacle below; the thumping music now sinks slowly through your mind like a narcotic; eventually you close your eyes and surrender to a longing for silence, darkness and rest.

Like those fabled cities whose walls rose to the sounds of music, the Electric Circus and other such dance halls have been drawn into being and charged with their eclectic atmosphere by the magical power of the beat. The total-environment discothèque is principally an attempt to capture and concentrate, as in a giant orgone box, the multiple energies of rock, which have evolved during the past decade into a veritable witches' brew—part aphrodisiac, part narcotic and part hallucinogen. There is no simple way of comprehending the extraordinarily rapid and complex development of the rock sound and culture. But perhaps the clearest way is to begin at the beginning and try to follow the principal trends of the music, along with their respective cultural ambiences and meanings, both in the Negro and in the white world.

Rock was born in a flashback, a celluloid loop doubled back inside a time machine. The date was 1954; the place was Cleveland, Ohio; the occasion, the first broadcast of Negro race records to an audience of white teenagers. Alan Freed, a local disc jockey, made the experiment. Almost immediately, it became apparent that he had struck a nerve that was ready to vibrate. The records he played were known in the trade as "rhythm and blues." Ground out by tiny "race" companies, they were aimed at the black ghetto. What they contained was a particularly potent strain of the urban blues that had swept over the country in the late Thirties during the vogue of the big bands. Indeed, if you can imagine an old Kansas City blues band crushed like a tin can so that nothing remains of it but top, bottom and lots of rusty ragged edges, you will have a fair idea of how the early r&b combos sounded. Concentrating on essentials, these groups used a disproportionate number of instruments (electric rhythm and bass guitars, plus piano and drums) to hammer out the beat, while the solo performers, vocal or instrumental, worked way out in front, using a primitive style compounded of honks and cries and words bawled out like curses.

It was an old and radically racial sound that Freed offered his listeners in the Midwest, and later in New York: a sound that told of dirt and fear and pain and lust. But the white kids loved it; and soon, as if to signify that the music had been adopted by a new public, Freed changed its name to "rock 'n' roll," though even this new name came from an old blues, "My baby rocks me with a steady roll." The success of rock attracted white performers: the first r&b song recorded by a white singer was "Rock Around the Clock" by Bill Haley and the Comets. Haley initiated that process of white assimilation of Negro style that for many years has been a basic feature of the movement; but the tendency of early rock was to pull away from the heavy racial sound in favor of the lighter, swifter beat of hillbilly music, which was to be one of rock's more durable elements, and a subject matter (cars, Cokes and heartaches) more suitable to white teenagers. On this new wave of country blues, Chuck Berry and then Elvis Presley rode to fame. When Presley entered the army at the end of the decade, many observers expected the fad to recede and vanish. But the culture remained firmly rock-bound.

While rock was enjoying this first surge of popularity, Negro music was undergoing a series of changes among the most profound in its history. The music of the ghetto was being revived and recharged by powerful new performers bent on outdoing their white imitators, while its basic genres —blues and gospel—were coalescing to produce a new style of enormous strength and popularity.

The greatest of these singers—indeed, the greatest basic rock performer—was Little Richard. Richard's records all sounded as if they were made in the Saturday night uproar of a turpentine logging camp. His raw, strident voice was torn from his throat in a bawling, shouting torrent that battered and scattered the words until they sounded like raving. Behind this desperately naked voice worked a boogie-woogie rhythm section tightened to vise-like rigidity. The furious energy of the singing caught in the iron cage of the rhythm produced an almost unbearable tension. Instead of illustrating the words, which often spoke of pleasure ("I'm gonna ball tonight!"), the music conveyed the agonizing effort to break through to joy. (Or just to break through: Richard usually ended his chorus with the bloodcurdling scream of a man hurling himself over a precipice.) What Little Richard was saying musically—and the Negro ghetto with him—was not that he was having a good time, but that he had the right to one and would "cut" anyone who got in his way. His note was erotic defiance. As such, Little Richard represented a new type of Negro youth. Reckless and rebellious, he gave us the first taste of the voice that was later to holler, "Burn, baby, burn!"

Oddly enough, the other great performer who emerged in this period expressed a character of precisely the opposite sort. Ray Charles was the eternal Negro, a poor blind man crying out of his darkness, singing to assuage his pain. Yet as a musician he was far from being a traditionalist; in fact, in undertaking to mix gospel and blues he violated one of the strictest taboos of Negro music. Throughout modern times, gospel and blues had almost always been rigidly segregated expressions of the sacred and the profane. Blues worked cathartically, urging that everything painful be confronted, named, lamented and exorcised in a lonely, impersonal, almost aloof style. Gospel had functioned in a completely opposite manner, by overwhelming unhappiness in a swelling evocation of the joys of life beyond the present world. Just as the blues was traditionally depressed, understated, ironic and resigned, gospel was typically ebullient, extravagant, even at times orgiastic in its affirmation. The Negro community had preserved the solace of each of these traditions by maintaining a total separation between them. The singing of blues in church was forbidden, while the blues singer steadfastly confronted his troubles without ever looking heavenward.

That is, until Ray Charles and his followers, such as James Brown, stepped boldly over the boundary and ended the prohibition. One of the first effects of this revolution was an inversion of traditional modes. Not only did these singers perform minor blues in the style of plaintive dirges, such as one might hear in church; they also added blues lyrics to the hand-clapping, foot-stamping, tambourine-banging gospel shouts. On stage they adopted many of the mannerisms, practices, and rituals of the storefront Negro church. They testified, danced ecstatically, called for witnesses, appeared to be led from above, tore off their clothes and fell and rose again like men in the grip of a religious revelation.

Charles's own manner was often that of the preacher: the voice deliberately crude, cracked, thickened with Southern

Negro pronunciations; the style figured with cantorial embellishments. The effect was that of a man seized by emotion, spilling out his feelings with absolute candor. Typical of the original gospel-blues mix was "Yes, Indeed," one of Charles's most successful early numbers. The piece opens with soft church chords played on a harmonium; next, Charles gives out the text in his deep deacon's voice, a word or two—then the gospel beat, heavy and lurching, comes crashing in with a chorus of "Amen girls" hypnotically chanting after every phrase, "Yaas, indeed!" As the piece stomps through its traditional 16-bar course, the confidently rising intervals generate an aura of optimism that reaches its climax in a moment of pure "salvation." The horns riff joyously, the chord changes signal that we are coming home, and the lead voice sings: "Well, I know when it gets ya, you get a feelin' deep down in your soul, every time you hear that good old rock 'n' roll. Yaas, indeed." The lyrics tumble here to a dreadful anticlimax, just at the point where the music becomes most transcendent, for what would have been in the original religious affirmation has been rubbed out and a pop music cliché scribbled in its place.

Once the barrier was down between gospel and blues, the distinctions between other Negro musical traditions also began to disappear. Singers, composers, instrumentalists, and arrangers began to take what they wanted from a racial ragbag of Delta blues, hillbilly strumming, gut-bucket jazz, boogie-woogie piano, pop lyricism and storefront shouting. The result—less a new genre than a mélange of musical materials—was called "soul."

The agency most responsible for this new development in Negro music is Motown, the General Motors of rock. Its founder, owner and manager is Berry Gordy, Jr., a one-time assembly-line worker, who since the early Sixties has been turning out hit tunes produced by teams of composers, arrangers and performers, all working closely to the specifications of the Motown formula.

The basic ingredient of the formula is the beat. Pushing

beyond the traditional "and *two* and *four*" style of drumming, Berry's arrangers trained the drums to bark on every
beat. Then they strengthened and enlarged the new beat by
overamplification and by doubling it with tambourine, tom-
tom, cymbals, bass and, eventually, anything that would
bounce. Today, Motown rocks with a driving, slogging
rhythm that rumbles up through the floor of a discothèque
like an earthquake.

The other active ingredient of the formula is the "shout,"
a short, arresting phrase that flashes the song's message. This
is underscored and embellished with every resource provided by Negro tradition and the Hollywood sound stage.
The most primitive types of plantation music—the sounds
of Jew's harps, tambourines, pipes and quills—have been unearthed to fill the formula's demand for a "funky" core.
Around this core have been wrapped complicated arrangements entailing the integration of strings, symphonic per-
cussion sections, choirs and soloists.

Motown's effort to concentrate all the sounds of Negro
tradition into a super-soul has often produced the opposite
of the intended effect—a typically commercial dilution of
the Negro essence. But sometimes Detroit's stylists, especially the gifted team of Eddie and Bryant Holland and La-
mont Dozier, have updated tradition so skillfully that they
succeed in adding a genuinely contemporary voice to Negro
music. Not content to paste pop lyrics over old church
tunes, this team has approached gospel in a sophisticated
spirit, seeking to exploit its ritual of salvation without sacri-
ficing the love story indispensable to the pop ballad. In their
best work they can telescope into three relentless minutes
the events of a whole evening in a storefront church without dislodging the conventional façade of the love song.

"I'll Be There," the most admired song of Motown's the
Four Tops, opens on a characteristically exotic note: pipes
and slap bass evoking a movie image of Genghis Khan and
his men trotting across the steppes of Central Asia. Then
this mirage is suddenly blown away and we are down to the

bedrock of soul: the drums pounding, the tambourines jingling and the anguished voice of Levi Stubbs exhorting his sweetheart in the manner of an evangelist preacher:

> If you feel that you can't go on,
> Because all of your hope is gone,
> And your life is filled with much confusion,
> Until happiness is just an illusion:

"Reach out!" cry the wraithlike voices that have been trailing and echoing Stubbs. "Reach out for *me!*" he adds, distending the word with a flourish of emotion. Then for one suspenseful moment all the voices cease, and we gaze into a void in which there is nothing but the nakedly writhing beat. Suddenly the emptiness is filled with the solemn sound of the "shout," "I'll be there," sung in unison by leader and chorus and accompanied by the exotic pipes of the introduction, which now assume their proper place as a kind of stained-glass window behind the singers. The final touch of religious excitement was added during the recording session: when the break in the melody opened for the last time, Levi shouted to the girl, "Look over your shoulder!" For a Negro audience this phrase summons up one of the most intense moments at a gospel service: the sight of some believer pointing wildly toward a corner of the church where he has caught a glimpse of the Holy Spirit.

Motown does a dizzying business with its exploitation of classic Negro styles, and most of this business is done in the Negro ghettos (where nobody pays any attention to the Beatles). Generally, the success of the style is attributed to Negro pride, to the joy with which Negroes respond to the basic expressions of their culture. But the regressive, almost caricatured Negritude of soul, and even more importantly, the desperately naked avowal of suffering made in the more seriously expressive songs, suggest that this music celebrates blackness less for its beauty than for its strength as a revived resource against the white terror.

Soul's revival of gospel music has been accompanied by a

return to archaic patterns of body movement which combine gestures of incantation and exorcism. In the currently popular boogaloo, for example, there is a complete pantomime of terror. The dancer's neck is twisted spasmodically as if by a lynch rope, his eyes roll up into his head, his hands shoot out past his face as if to avert blow, and his whole body tips as though he were about to collapse. The imagery of anxiety in such a performance accords perfectly with the character of the words and music which excite it, and all three qualify drastically the notion that rock is simply the revelry of orgy.

Not the least reason for the exaggeration of Negritude in soul music has been the emergence in recent years of rock groups composed of pale English boys. What the Beatles represented in their early unregenerate years was a Liverpudlian impression of Little Richard, Chuck Berry and Bo Diddley, precisely the roughest, raunchiest Negro rhythm and blues men accessible through American records. When their manager, Brian Epstein, styled the boys' hair and dressed them in chic suits, he didn't comb any of the fuzz out of their sound. The result was that English dandyism was wedded to Negro eroticism, and every teenybopper in the Western world began to dream of possessing a mod moppet with soul. Other English groups have since become so adept at mimicking Negroes that the listener (white or black) can only identify the singer's race by the record liner. In fact, one may even prefer Stevie Winwood or Joe Cocker to the ordinary Detroit sound just because the English product seems more authentic, less bedecked with the gaudy trappings of Motown. This authenticity is, of course, only skin-deep; it is a mask that the singer sustains only because his narrow expressive gambit does not oblige him to flex his features with a full range of expression. For three minutes, the length of a "45" side, he can hold this pose; but it is just as unnatural for him as the spraddling stance is for the model who is out to make a "smashing" appearance in *Queen* or *Vogue*. It takes only one record like Aretha

Franklin's virtuoso treatment of "I Can't Get No Satisfaction," written by Mick Jagger of the Rolling Stones, to remind us of the great gap that exists between those who have soul and those who merely pay it the compliment of imitation.

Once Negritude had been synthesized so that it could be manufactured anywhere in the world, rock began to cast about for fresh game. But this was less a matter of the normal development of popular music than of the cultural disorientation of the rock generation. On the face of it, there was no reason why the music that developed from white imitations of Negro styles should not have continued to evolve along the same path that swing had followed in the Forties. Starting with a basic style derived largely from Negro sources, the swing bands added more and more non-Negro elements until they had created a new pop sound. At that time, as today, there had been a dialogue between black and white, with plenty of give and take. Miles Davis, for example, borrowed the arranger of the most refined white band (Gil Evans of the Claude Thornhill band) to act as midwife at the birth of the Cool. But rock was not destined to play with counters that were only white and black.

Unlike the youth of the swing era, who thought they knew who they were, today's youth has no such illusion. Lacking any clear-cut sense of identity, however, has only made them more keenly aware of everyone else's. Rock is, in one sense, a direct reflection of their hunger for the essence of every people or period that displays a striking or exotic style. The Rock Age has assimilated everything in sight, commencing with the whole of American music: urban and country blues, gospel, hillbilly, Western, "good-time" (the ricky-tick of the Twenties) and Tin Pan Alley. It has reached across the oceans for the sounds and rhythms of Africa, the Middle East and India. It has reached back in time for the baroque trumpet, the madrigal and the Gregorian chant; and forward into the future for electronic music and the noise collages of *musique concrète.*

By virtue of its cultural alliances, the Beat has also become the pulse of pop culture. The creators of the new milieu vie with one another in proclaiming rock the inspirational force of the day. A discothèque like the Electric Circus is a votive temple to the electronic muse, crammed with offerings from all her devotees. The patterns on the walls derive from Pop and Op art; the circus acts are Dada and camp; the costumes of the dancers are mod and hippie; the technology is the most successful realization to date of the ideal of "art and engineering"; the milieu as a whole is psychedelic, and the discothèque is itself a prime example of mixed-media or total-environment art. The only elements of rock culture that are not conspicuous there are the literary ones: the underground newspapers that report the news and gossip of this world; the put-on critiques of the New Journalism; and the social and political rhetoric of the folk-rock singers, the finger-pointers, like Bob Dylan, Buffy St. Marie, and Joan Baez.

As for the audiences for rock, they are apt to manifest the same eager feeling for cultural essences that is revealed by the musicians. They like to fashion modish simulacra of cherished periods like the Twenties, Thirties or the Edwardian Age; they are strong on certain ethnic types, like the American Indian and the Slavic peasant; their holdings in the East are large and constantly increasing—and they all can do a pretty good take-off on W. C. Fields. They like to dress up in cast-off clothes purchased in thrift shops or old theatrical costume warehouses; on Saturday afternoons they make King's Road in Chelsea the scene of one of the most extraordinary pageants ever seen on the streets of a European city. To describe their dress as "masquerade" is not quite accurate because, like all true decadents, they prefer to the pure forms those piquant mixtures of unrelated things that show wit and fancy as opposed to mere mimicry. Yet their ideal costume is not obviously hybrid. It aims to achieve the integrity of familiar things. The first glance at it elicits the sense of *déjà vu;* the second, a frown of perplex-

ity. "What country do you come from?" is a query often
directed at the Beatles' costume designers, a Dutch group
known as the Apple, as they walk about London in their
enchanting peasant drag.

As this mode of dressing makes clear, the time has now
passed when it was enough to seize a single style and make it
one's own—as Bob Dylan first transformed himself into an
Okie or Monti Rock III into a Harlem Negro. Today, the
grand cultural ideal is encapsulated in the tiny word "mix."
The goal is to blend various exotic essences into mysterious
alchemical compounds.

Take for example the Beatles' "Strawberry Fields Forever," with its mixture of hippie argot, classic myth and
baroque music. Grave Elysian flutes lead the way as the
singers chant, "Let me take you *down*"; then, swooning on
the wave of an Hawaiian guitar, the voices drift into a subterranean lotus land. Gradually, the atmosphere grows
heavy and murky; the tone of the singers is stoned; their
speech is muddled and ambiguous ("No one, I think, is in
my tree; I mean, it must be high or low; that is, you can't,
you know, tune in, but it's all right; that is, I think it's not
too bad"). As the music advances in trance-like time, the
baroque bass line presses relentlessly downward, the drums
beat a tattoo, and trumpets sound like autos jamming. The
song swells into a massive affirmation of meaninglessness—a
junkie anthem. After a final crescendo, the end is signaled
by the conventional fade-out; but this is swiftly counter-
manded by an unexpected fade-in which brings delicate Indian sounds bubbling to the surface of the heavily doctored
sound track. The effect is magical—the Beatles sink into the
ground in London and pop to the surface again at Bombay!

The more farfetched and unlikely the ingredients, the
better for the mix; and likewise, the more arts and media laid
under contribution, the greater the impact. The ideal is
strongly reminiscent of surrealism, of Max Ernst's formula
of "the fortuitous meeting of distant realities." It would be a
mistake, however, to attribute any direct influence to such

doctrines, no matter how prophetic they have proved to be. Life, not theory, and, more particularly, the electronic maelstrom that has shaped the sensibility of our youth best explains the syncretism of the present moment. Our youth are accustomed to being bombarded from every side by sounds and images that have been torn loose, distorted and scrambled in a thousand ways. Nothing more is needed to suggest the frantic mix than the everyday act of twirling a radio or TV dial. It is not surprising that the archetypal image of so much Pop art is the fun house. Distorting mirrors, grotesque images, spooky vistas, traps, tricks and shocks to every sense constitute in their aggregate a very brilliant metaphor for the psychedelic experience. And, as if this were not enough, the youth have given their bizarre world one last crazy spin by turning on with anything they can get into their mouths or veins—narcotics, stimulants, hypnotics, hallucinogens.

Every contemporary medium has evolved some version of the mix, whether it be called collage, montage, assemblage or *musique concrète*. The form most often associated with rock is the light show. Two seasons ago, Bob Goldstein installed his Lightworks in a roadhouse called L'Oursin at Southampton, Long Island. To date the finest multimedia discothèque, Goldstein's club revealed a great deal about the potentialities of the mix. It was designed, like a giant Scopitone jukebox, to light up with a complete picture show every time a new record dropped on the turntable. The images that flashed upon its three towering screens (which were played contrapuntally, one against the other) were drawn from every source dear to the Pop sensibility. There were glass slides of New York's turn-of-the-century *haute monde*, film clips from Hollywood musicals of the Thirties, twist films, old newsreels, poster patterns and light paintings. The effect of this streaming phantasmagoria, which shuttled the spectator's mind back and forth along invisible tracks of association—from past to present, comic to sentimental, nostalgic to erotic—was that of a fantastic variety show, a Psychedelic Follies.

In such discothèques as L'Oursin, rock became a medium for producing a range of new sensations. Associating rock with images induces that sense of poring scrutiny, of lens-in-eye obsession, that is one of the most distinctive modes of contemporary sensibility. (Consider the excitement it generates in the central episode of *Blow-Up*.) Like the effect of LSD, that of rocking things is to spotlight them in a field of high concentration and merge them with the spectator in a union that is almost mystical. Few discothèque designers, to be sure, have Goldstein's taste and theatrical flair; most are content to break off bits and pieces of cultural imagery and imbed them in the beat to produce a haphazard rock terrazzo. But the beguiling and tranquilizing effect of spending an evening in the contemplation of Lightworks assures us—far more than all the current theorizing—that the ideal of the synesthetic art work is perfectly valid and closer to realization today than at any time since its first statement in the writings of Wagner and Baudelaire.

The concept of a psychedelic variety show is strikingly akin to the form evolved by the Beatles in the last two years. Young men of imagination who have grown up in the cultural greenhouse of show business, the Beatles have developed their own exotic blooms of parody and hallucination. Indeed, a perfect emblem for the whole concept of such a variety mix in all its ramifications—as iconography, life style and metaphysics—is furnished by the cover of the Beatles' album *Sgt. Pepper's Lonely Hearts Club Band*. (The work of the Apple in collaboration with the Beatles.)

Four stern-faced Beatles, wearing heavy mustaches and dressed in bright, satiny turn-of-the-century bandsmen's uniforms, stand with their band instruments before a shadowy crowd of pop heroes, ranged rank above rank like medieval saints. Among these sixty-odd faces (touched up to look like comic strip characters) one recognizes (with a little help from his friends) Karl Marx, Marilyn Monroe, Edgar Allan Poe, Shirley Temple, Lenny Bruce, Lawrence of Arabia,

Oscar Wilde, Aubrey Beardsley, Albert Einstein, Fred Astaire, Mae West, Lewis Carroll, Laurel and Hardy, Marlene
Dietrich, and, of course, W. C. Fields. Framing this motley
group are two full-length figures: a voluptuous white sex
goddess, Diana Dors, and a lowering black Priapus, Sonny
Liston. Standing forth from the mob, on the Beatles' right,
are four somberly dressed lads: Tussaud waxworks images
of the original Beatles. At the musicians' feet lies what appears to be a fresh grave—or is it just a flowerbed?—with
BEATLES lettered on it in red hyacinths. Out of the deep
shadows around this grave, planted with the inconsequence
of a child's rock garden, looms an unlikely assortment of
objects: a hookah, a portable TV, dolls from the orient and
the West, a football trophy and some funereal-looking
potted palms.

Despite the reassurance of cheerful colors and a naïve
style, a spooky aura emanates from the familiar faces on the
Sgt. Pepper cover. One feels himself in the disquieting presence of allegory. At least one implication is clear: the four
young men from Liverpool who seized the world by its ears
are now dead. They have passed into the heaven reserved
for pop saints. From the dead have arisen four new Beatles,
gorgeous butterflies sprung from dingy chrysalises. They
stand again at the forefront of pop: that totally eclectic culture whose cut-out-and-paste-up methods enable it to embrace playfully the serious and the trivial, the present and
the past, the orient and the occident—the ancient hookah
and the transistor radio. The other famous faces, with their
waxen expressions, suggest that promotion to the pop pantheon entails a certain demotion: the worship is rather like a
put-on, and the niches are only temporary. The Beatles are
full-bodied heroes because they are *now*. Proud psychedelic
sorcerers, they can summon up the dead and work what
tricks they will.

The history of the Beatles is pop culture's redaction of the
myth of innocence and experience. When the famous four
set out on their careers, they knew nothing of art or life. At

home only in the rough-and-tumble world of the Liverpool cellar club or the Hamburg *Lokal,* they were a shaggy and ignorant crew. They could not read music, they could barely play their instruments, and their idea of a joke was to come out on the bandstand wearing toilet seats around their necks. Since then their careers and lives have mounted upward and outward in dizzying gyres that have swept them around the whole world of twentieth-century life and culture and set them on terms of respect and familiarity with some of the most sophisticated minds in the contemporary arts. In the course of their Jet Age development, they have repeatedly changed their style and appearance, always seeming to be just one short step ahead of the going thing and therefore in the perfect position of a leader.

It was their manager, Brian Epstein, who transformed these coarse rockers into the adorable Eton boys known to fame, a change of costume that proved to be the shrewdest packaging job in the history of popular music. It would be a mistake, however, to claim, as LeRoi Jones has done, that the Beatles owe their early success entirely to the Epstein formula; for paradoxically, just as their imitations of Negro rock began to achieve universal popularity, the boys began to modify their sound in obedience to the promptings of their own souls. What emerged was a sort of ancestral reverberation, echoes of ancient English music reaching back to a time before the New World had been settled. In his recent book *Caliban Reborn,* Wilfrid Mellers, the distinguished British musicologist, provides an interesting analysis of the traditional English elements in the Beatles' music, identifying bits and pieces that once belonged to the musical vocabulary of Giles Farnaby and of Orlando Gibbons, the master of the sixteenth-century madrigalist. From this analysis, it would appear that the Beatles stand in somewhat the same relation to their culture as do the Negroes and hillbillies to ours: they, too, play by ear, and what they hear is still attuned partially to a kind of scale and tonality that has long since been forgotten by literate musicians. If Mellers is right, the tension between the "illiterate" and "literate" elements in the work of these quasi-folk artists may be what accounts for their unique effect, the resonance in their simple songs of something deep and agelessly innocent. One might add that the Beatles' feeling for baroque music is characteristically British: it is Handel that sounds the affirmative note in "Strawberry Fields Forever," as it is the Purcell of the trumpet voluntaries that wells up with such purity in "Penny Lane."

The appearance in 1966 of their album *Revolver* signaled an important transformation of the Beatles. First, the album soured the milky innocence of "I Want to Hold Your Hand" and "Michelle" with the sardonic tone of the city citizen, personified in the acrid sounds and sarcastic lyrics of "Taxman." The second change was formal: instead of singing in their one basic style, the Beatles became virtuosos and produced a pastiche of modes.

"Eleanor Rigby," one of the two most impressive songs, is couched in a nineteenth-century string idiom, suggestive alternately of a country fiddle and a Beethoven string quartet. Its old-fashioned style, urgent, chopping rhythm and lovely plangent melody provide a setting rich in sentiment for the series of genre pictures sketched in the verses. There is Eleanor Rigby, a solitary spinster picking up the rice after a wedding; and Father McKenzie darning a sock in his room late at night. They are the lonely people who live outside the modern world. The very thought of their existence wrings from the Beatles a cry of bewildered innocence: "All the lonely people! Where *do* they all come from? Where *do* they all belong?"

"Tomorrow Never Knows" is composed in an antithetical mode and provides this generation's answer to the poignant sense of human futility expressed in "Eleanor Rigby." A futuristic chant intoned by a robot voice over a hubbub of jungle noises, squiggling strings, and sore boil guitar riffs— all this underscored by the pounding of a primitive drum— the song mechanically announces its message like an electronic oracle. The message is that of the hippies:

> Turn off your mind,
> Relax and float downstream;
> It is not dying.

Revolver also contains a number of other "answers": a pioneer effort to assimilate the sound of the Indian raga ("Love You To"); a street chanty, widely interpreted as a comical drug song ("Yellow Submarine"); "For No One," which evokes the Edwardian parlor musicale, with Auntie Ellen strumming the cottage piano and Uncle Wembley winding the French horn; "Good Day Sunshine," a perky tune sweetly reminiscent of straw-hat vaudeville; and "Here, There and Everywhere," an exquisite ballad. Altogether this album offers a remarkable range of material, comprising the nostalgic, the futuristic, the hortatory, the contemplative, the Oriental and the American. It also demonstrates a great expansion of the Beatles' resources of instrumentation and recording technique. For the first time, one really feels the presence of George Martin, the so-called "Fifth Beatle," a record producer and academy-trained musician of considerable sophistication who has supervised all the Beatles' recordings.

Revolver points the way to the variety mix, but it furnishes no general context for its excellent songs, and hence they gain nothing from being on one record. *Sgt. Pepper* remedies this deficiency by assembling its tunes inside the framework of an old-time band concert. Offering itself as a record of such an occasion, it harmonizes the stylistic eclecticism of its contents by presenting each song as an individual vaudeville turn. At the same time the opportunity is created to step beyond the artificial glare of the footlights and deliver with chilling effect the final revelation of "A Day in the Life."

The effect of this last song is like that of awakening from turbulent but colorful dreams to stare at the patch of gray that signals dawn in the city. What we awake to in the song is the modern oscillation between anomie and anxiety punctuated periodically by the sound of a dynamo that has just been switched on. This sound is itself the ultimate symbol of the Beatles' world. It represents the state of being turned on, of getting high and escaping from our deadened selves; but at the same time, its alarming crescendo of speed and power suggests an acceleration to the point of explosion (an implication underscored by the Beethoven-like chords of a symphony orchestra, portending doom). The end of the song is a single tonic chord struck on the piano and then allowed to float away for half a minute, like a slowly dissolving puff of smoke.

"A Day in the Life" is a skillfully contrived microcosm of the contemporary world. Called by one critic "the Beatles' *Waste Land*," and by another "a little Antonioni movie," its brilliance lies in the exquisite adjustment of its tone, calibrated finely between apathy and terror. Reflecting meaning from every facet, the song not only evokes the chug-chug of a mechanistic society and the numbed sensibilities of its anonymous inhabitants, but also sounds with conviction the note of apocalypse.

That a song of such intellectual sophistication and artistic resourcefulness should arise out of the same tradition that only a dozen years ago was spawning ditties like "Rock Around the Clock" seems almost unbelievable. But the very swiftness of the development indicates its real nature. Unlike other popular arts, rock has not been forced to spin its substance out of itself. Instead, it has acted like a magnet, drawing into its field a host of heterogeneous materials that has fallen quickly into patterns. No other cultural force in modern times has possessed its power of synthesis. Indeed, one of the common complaints of cultural critics has been that there were no coherent movements to animate and order the vast piles of cultural detritus under which we seemed destined to smother. Evidently, the only impulse at all equal to the task has been the primitive power of the beat.

Having assumed a role of cultural authority, rock has not, as was feared, dragged us down into the mire of cultural regression. The Spenglerian anxieties have proved once again to be unfounded. Rather than either lowering or elevating us, rock has served to equalize cultural pressures and forces. It has cleared a channel from the lowest and most archaic to the highest and most recent, and through that conduit is now flowing a revitalizing current of energy and of ideas. The result has been the elevation of rock to the summit of popular culture and the accelerating expansion of its interests and resources.

Thus the Beatles have already journeyed so far from their starting point in American rock 'n' roll that their relation to the tradition has become problematic, perhaps irrelevant. In their steady drift toward the international avant-garde, however, the Beatles, and the other English groups that have followed in their wake, represent only one end of the lengthening rock spectrum. At the other end, stand the new musicians who have developed the sensuousness and violence of the original beat. Outstanding among these are the acid-rock groups of San Francisco and Los Angeles: groups with exotic names like the Grateful Dead, the Moby Grape, the Jefferson Airplane, Big Brother and the Holding Company or Country Joe and the Fish. The California sound has sublimated the basic essence of rock and mixed it with the idiom of the hippies, the motorcycle gangs and the surfers in a cultural fusion that is reminiscent of soul. Indeed, acid-rock is the closest approximation yet to an authentic white soul.

By pushing toward higher levels of imaginative excellence, rock has begun to realize one of the most cherished dreams of mass culture: to cultivate from the vigorous but crude growth of the popular arts a new serious art that would combine the strength of native roots with the beauty flowering from the highest art. In America this hope had been baffled time and time again by the failure of any of our popular arts (with minor exceptions) to achieve, after generations of development, the stature implicit in their beginnings. Like thundering geysers from underground, the geniuses of jazz, for example, have hurled themselves at their lofty goals only to fall back, spent by their unaided efforts. And this hope would have remained futile had it not been for the simultaneous emergence of two necessary conditions: first, the widespread assimilation through the mass media of the themes and technical resources of the fine arts; second, the tendency of serious artists today to exploit the myths and devices of the popular culture.

The difficulty of such a convergence of high and low modern art is well attested by recent history. On two memorable occasions in recent decades, a self-taught genius of popular music has sought unsuccessfully to study with a contemporary master. In the Twenties George Gershwin approached Maurice Ravel in Paris, only to be told that there was no way he could improve what he was already doing so perfectly. Again in the Forties, in New York, Charlie Parker implored Edgard Varèse to take him on in any capacity (even as a cook) in exchange for lessons in composition. But again the artist demurred—not because he lacked appreciation of Parker's gifts but simply because he could not imagine what two such sundered arts might have to contribute to each other. Today the situation is radically different—so much so that if John Lennon were to sit down with John Cage to discuss music, one wonders who would come away the wiser.

New American Review No. 3, 1968

ROCK THEATER

Rock Theater's Breech Birth

IN THAT LAND of the dead, that grimy necropolis, the Lower East Side, New York's moribund theater has suddenly twitched into life. All through the winter and spring, crowds like those that once promenaded through medieval graveyards and charnel houses have invaded the old ghetto seeking a new kind of theatrical spectacle, the rock concert. These human tides form an audience of a sort that would never assemble for any "legitimate" performance, on or off Broadway. Weekend hippies, one-night dropouts from suburbia's Kiddieland, they are American youth come to walk for a few hours through the neon fires of an infernal region: to rub shoulders with freaks, queens, yippies, spades, dragsters and psychos; to stare at their own reflections in the stone face of a teenage panhandler; to surmount or succumb to the temptations of these streets.

Not colorful, not ebullient, not even loud, these young people are intensely *drab*. They are dressed in brown, black and tan—the colors of the earth. They stare wide-eyed from great bushes of hair and move with loose, undulant bodies under blankets, ponchos, serapes and wide-brimmed floppy hats. What they resemble most is a mob of half-civilized Indians come to huddle and hunker inside the tribal lodge in expectation of ceremony.

The great Pandemonium where they assemble is the Fillmore East, an ancient moldering movie palace; its gloomy vaulted dome, haunted with the ghosts of a thousand old flicks and stars, makes it a veritable pop Palladium. The theater's old shell remains intact, with worn marble palace stairs, tacky carpets, Wedgewood reliefs, dirty buff walls, towering Corinthian columns and grandiose stage boxes for exiled royalty. Even the giant silver screen still hangs within the proscenium arch. But when the lights dim in the antique sconces, no symphony of Hollywood plangency fills the air, no ghostly shapes of film saga loom on the screen. Instead, the house rocks with salvos of super-amplified blues; and the screen explodes in dazzling kinetic fireworks. As steeply pitched spotlights pick out the striking figures of the Doors, the Jefferson Airplane, Big Brother and the Holding Company, or the Who, the screen offers a view out of a spaceship window. One moment you are taking off into a streaming galaxy, the next you are landing on a pulsing planet. Dozens of brightly colored fish eggs fly apart like dynamited caviar. Then they congeal into an immense fly eye laced with blood. Into desperate fibrillation goes the screen; rings of light whirl off the hot center—the stage is plunged into primal darkness.

Perhaps it is the Who that is performing. An hour of savage tribal drumming, acid-rock rave-ups and gladitorial salutes has led to the climactic moment. As the audience shouts its approbation, the celebrant prepares to sacrifice a shapely guitar. Seizing the instrument by its neck, he bashes its body against a standing microphone. Backward he lurches into a huge amplifier and topples it to the ground. The drums roar, the audience moans. Falling on all fours, the youthful rocker becomes a beast dismembering its prey. Suddenly, you cast a glance over your shoulder. The onlookers have risen from their seats and are being drawn down the aisles, as if summoned by a mighty hypnotist. Slowly they come at first, eyes fixed, faces glowing in the lights—then faster and faster, until the stage picture is obscured by vaulting silhouettes. Darkness douses the scene. As the dim, unreal house light comes up, hundreds of boys and girls are discovered standing all over the theater looking bewildered and embarrassed.

Or it is another night. Arthur Brown, king of the English hippies, is heading the bill. His band has done a lurid send-up of the Harlem Gospel Train by playing raunchy electric-organ blues for ten minutes at maniacal tempos, the organist's wildly waving hair and carelessly draped cloak suggesting some mad cavalier intent on raping the Miltonic keyboard. Then a cry from the back of the house sends a thousand heads spinning. A barbaric figure dressed in gorgeous robes, wearing a silver death mask with two flaming horns sprouting from its head, is being borne down the aisle on a peacock-feathered palanquin carried by four sturdy bearded half-naked warriors. Disdainfully tossing flowers to the faithful, King Arthur looks like a cruel Mayan chieftain, a blasphemous antipope, a great Teutonic devil arriving at the Witches' Sabbath on the Brocken.

Or it is one of those special nights dedicated to the Doors. They draw a more sophisticated audience: coolly appraising, ironically appreciative, an audience of knowing voyeurs trained to go emotionally limp but finding themselves growing taut with primordial tensions. They are watching the Doors' brief color film, *The Unknown Soldier*. To the sounds of Jim Morrison's soft, lonely crooner's voice, pictures flit across the screen. Boy and girl, bodies amorously entwined, strangely inert in the grass, alternating with glimpses of busy, ugly, self-absorbed city life. Then the Doors themselves, trekking up an empty beach bearing flowers and Oriental instruments. Are they bound for a celebration? No, they are binding big, handsome Jim to old, half-buried timbers. The camera, kneeling at his feet, catches his face from below: closed eyes, bearded chin, long clustering locks—a serene Italian Jesus. Now the sound track is picturing a firing squad: Orders are barked, rifle bolts snap, a drum roll—wham! Morrison lurches forward. His splendid head hangs like a flower from a broken stalk; his mouth vomits thick red blood.

Fiercely, the music spins a vivid kaleidoscope of war. Orange-gold napalm flashes, thatched huts burn, squat howitzers lurch—war is beautiful! Files of troopers move out grimly, prisoners stumble blindfolded, bodies lie in the sun crawling with maggots—war is hideous! "The war is over!" cries the singer; images of VJ Day spill across the screen. Sailors lift girls with upswept hairdos; an old Negro dances to the beat of a washtub; shouting throngs fill the streets, laughing and weeping for joy. At the last triumphant shout, the audience in the theater roars back at the crowds on the screen, "The Doors have ended the war!"

As these glimpses of the Fillmore East suggest, there is in rock a nascent theater that is squalling already with vigor. Securely in possession of the two halves of contemporary culture, the primitive and the futuristic, rock is wedded to myths that reach down to the lowest level of human consciousness. Its technical resources are immense and its popularity universal. Driven by an ambition to transcend the narrow ambit of the pop music business, all the best rock groups are now determined to enter the theater. As they externalize dramatically the visions that were always implicit in their nostalgic, or ironic, atavistic sounds, they are developing the materials and sensibility for several distinct types of theater.

The Beatles, in *Sgt. Pepper* and *Magical Mystery Tour*, have produced rough sketches of something that might be called the psychedelic variety show. A theater of nostalgia, distilling the poignancy of good times recollected in distress, this surrealistic vaudeville makes play with the dreamlike world of the old music hall. One promise of this theater is a delicious escapism of the kind offered by the English pantomimes, the Edwardian circus, the Victorian raree show and the children's theaters crammed into the narrow storeys of Benjamin Pollock's toyshop in London.

That enchanting singer Tiny Tim has shown us how such a toy theater would look and sound with authentic vocal cutouts from old phonograph records. Yet the same attachment to vaudeville and surrealism has opened the way into another, vastly different world—the cabaret opera of Bertolt Brecht and Kurt Weill.

Much of the peculiar intensity and irony of the Brecht-Weill collaborations is due to the genius with which they employ the tricks of the music hall as a medium for satire. In effect, they find a way to channel the culture's most harmless and irrepressible energies into a dangerous satiric current sapping the culture's very foundations.

The same pop-satiric backwash is beginning to appear in the work of the Beatles and other leading rock groups. "I Am the Walrus," the masterpiece of rock song thus far, emerges from the ambience of a television kiddies' show; its dense, ominous, abrasive texture, leaking rage at every pore, is coated with innocent, childlike nonsense verses, including such traditional rugby cheers as, "Yellow matter custard dripping from a dead dog's eye." The objects of the Beatles' rage are much harder to identify than the targets of Brecht and Weill, because the distrustfulness of contemporary youth produces a miasma of ambiguity that not only masks the attacker but obscures his enemy. Nonetheless, there is no mistaking the build-up of anger behind pop music's darkening façade.

Neither nostalgia nor irony, however, seems as suitable to rock, as fulfilling of its inmost demands, as another mode envisioned and called for thirty years ago by Antonin Artaud—the Theater of Cruelty. Essentially primitive, impersonal, ritualistic; wed to the body and the dance; so violent that the audience is exalted, stunned, or benumbed—rock is in very fact the theater of Artaud's dreams. The visionary descriptions contained in his famous "First Manifesto" read today like literal accounts of the Electric Circus or the Fillmore East.

The theater, Artaud wrote, is to be an alchemical compound of "Cries, groans, apparitions . . . theatricalities of all kinds, magic beauty of costumes taken from certain ritual models, resplendent lighting, incantational beauty of voices . . . rare notes of music, colors of objects, physical rhythm of movements . . . masks, effigies yards high, sudden changes of light. . . ."

The spectator is to be directly involved in this spectacle, just as he is in today's environments, discothèques, and mixed-media theaters. Above all, the Theater of Cruelty is designed—like the nascent rock theater—to promote a catharsis of the most basic instinctual appetites and fantasies. "The theater," he wrote, "will never find itself again except by furnishing the spectator with the truthful precipitates of his dreams, his taste for crime, his erotic obsessions, his savagery, his chimeras, his utopian sense of life and matter, even his cannibalism."

Now for the first time in the modern world, the special instruments and sensibilities demanded by Artaud's vision have been forged and are lying within easy reach, ready for employment by a master theatrician. But there are grave reasons for questioning whether this generation of performers can achieve the synthesis promised by their music. The protective environment of the recording studio and the minimal performance demands of the bandstand have left most rock musicians undeveloped as public performers.

Still struggling to throw off the idea that all they have to do is turn out onstage looking like colorful *banditi* or rubber-legged mannequins from a haberdasher's window, many of the rockers seem more involved with themselves than with their audiences. Not surprisingly, they have a profound aversion to the fanatically motivated, make-out style of American show business. Members of a new amateur-professional class, they find their models in the tradition of the singing vagabond, the country bluesman and other artists of the road.

Unfortunately, this spirit militates against their cooperation with the show-biz professionals whose skills they need in the theater. The Beatles, alone among rock groups, have consistently acknowledged their deficiencies and supplied them from the stores of an army of professional collaborators. That is why the Beatles are the best costumed, best produced, most various and technically resourceful of rock bands.

More typical of the plight of today's rock musicians—talented, successful, ambitious but maladroit in the pursuit of their vision—is the Doors, one of the leading American groups. When the Doors appeared about 1967, everyone remarked on their obvious theatrical flair. Standing at the focus of a powerful music, as fiercely inflected as jazz, Jim Morrison glowed with the slowly shifting shapes of a light show. Like those pictures under plastic that tease the eye by changing with every move of the viewer's head, Morrison offered an astonishing range of personal images. He was a virile young man, a shy maiden, a vulgar hustler, a fluffy toy animal, a crazed maenad, an angel by Michelangelo. A polymorphous personality, created, I suspect, in the way that photographs of stars are made—through prolonged exposure to sharp but distant images—Jim Morrison was a human theatricon.

After one had seen the group a number of times, however, the magic began to wear off; one looked over and around them, searching for a more comprehensive theatrical image that would not be so tightly focused on the psychodrama of the star. What one got were tantalizing glimpses of Brechtian drama, of rock ceremonial, of the aesthetic of cruelty. One tried to picture the musicians in archetypal settings: on Easter Island, for instance, with giant totems looming behind them, a garish red and purple sunset lighting the sky, while at their feet the tribe huddles, eyes fixed on the weird figure at the center of the magic circle. Statements appeared in the press promising a theatrical instauration of the Doors

—but nothing changed.

Finally, I met the boys and discovered why they were unable to take the next step in their natural evolution. The reason is one with their true identity, which has been grossly distorted by journalists and fans who continually confuse these musicians' life style with their stage presence. Far from being a grim squad of sadistic, self-destructive "heads," swinging naked from college belfries, the four young men with whom I spent a day recently were models of healthy, normal, intelligent, well-educated, idealistic American manhood.

Walking into an upstairs room at a country inn on Long Island, I was struck by their appearance at table. With their road managers, camera crew and other guests, they were almost a dozen. Sitting in long rows, bread and wine before them, Jim Morrison presiding comfortably at the head of the table, his long hair resting on his shoulders, they recalled automatically a hundred cheap lithos of the Last Supper. But why laugh? Appearances are revealing. There *is* a kind of unconscious sanctity in certain of the youth today; heaven knows how it came there, but it's real and it's beautiful.

Morrison was born a star; a certain amount of attitudinizing is inherent in his disposition. Considering that he travels with a *cinéma vérité* crew that crouches at his feet in the back of a limousine like a pair of faithful baronial mastiffs, his degree of self-consciousness is remarkably slight. The personality that emerges is reflective, modest, casually humorous and quietly authoritative.

The other members are all very different types. The guitarist, Robby Krieger, and the drummer, John Densmore, pal together; both are disciples of the Maharishi Mahesh Yogi, quietly committed to his discipline of mind and body. Yoga explains perhaps how a man built as slightly as Densmore can cut into a drum with the stunning power he displays in the quiet passages of "The End." Krieger is physically even less imposing, wandering around the stage under a mass of ruffled hair that makes him look like a slightly dazed child. Yet when he opens up his guitar in long liquid lines of electronic song, he conjures up visions of an artificial bird singing in the gardens of a Byzantine emperor.

Ray Manzarek, who plays a hard, linear organ in a style of pop toccata, looks and talks like a refined bespectacled young professor in a Midwestern college. Everything he says reveals his cool, incisive, tartly sincere intelligence. He is an unswerving idealist, who insistently demands that his generation grow up, assume responsibility, take power and transform this world into something closer to their hearts. Manzarek's credo is affirmed when Jim Morrison cries, "We want the world and we want it *now!*"

When asked about their early days at Venice West, the Lower East Side of Los Angeles, when they all lived in one house and made the hippie scene, Manzarek replies that as a developmental stage the period of high acidity had a certain value; today, however, he is obviously delighted to be married, to have his own house (with a swimming pool) and to be up and doing. He is grateful to success for the first chance he's ever had to live a thoroughly comfortable life.

The Doors' composite image was reassuring; but it was also disquieting. Much as one enjoyed their healthy calm and workmanlike approach to the job of entertaining thousands of fanatically dedicated fans, there was something lacking in the way of creative devotion and professional drive. They seemed suspended on a golden hook of success, unable to shake free.

Manzarek spoke of hiring a theater, engaging actors, performing an interesting piece called *Celebration of the Lizard*, which is a kind of exodus in the course of which the people sometimes stop to ask, "Where has the light gone?" A sort of pop *Moses und Aron*, the piece suggested the dimensions of epic theater—but all pretty vague.

Much sharper was the first association of a practiced theatrician like Robert Goldstein, the inventor of the Lightworks and other "total-environment" entertainment. I asked him whether he thought the music of the Doors had theat-

rical possibilities. He answered that he had imagined a
theater piece as soon as he heard "Moonlight Drive"; it was
to be a rock version of the Brecht-Weill *The Rise and Fall
of the City of Mahagonny*, with Haight-Ashbury as the setting. Though he did not fill in the details, the scenario practically wrote itself.

First would come the influx of hordes of kids eager to
indulge themselves in the joys of absolute freedom flowing
from the reversal of commandments from "Thou shalt not"
to "Thou shalt." Then, after a brief period of joy, the bick-
ering and the apathy begins; everyone is on drugs and the
descent into petty crime, hustling, disease and madness is
headlong.

The plunge into squalor ends with a climactic outrage, the
murder of Linda Fitzpatrick and Groovy. Suddenly, the
hippie community is shocked into a new awareness: the need
for social action. The murders compel them to abandon
their lotus eating for political militance, signalling the exodus
from the urban Eden. Swarming back to their hometowns,
the new revolutionaries undertake to overthrow the world
they once fled.

The myth exists. The theater exists. The musicians and
actors are ready. We hear the strains of a new Dionysian
music, see the arena filling with familiar shapes of flying
hair, clapping hands, twitching bodies. The ancient goat
song is being danced by a rout of heroes and satyrs. Still
lacking, however, is the impresario, the *régisseur*, the latter-
day Diaghilev, Reinhardt or Orson Welles, who will bring
forth from this rock dithyramb an authentic theater of mass
man.

Vogue, 1968

Radio City, Art Deco and Rock

LAID ON our doorstep like a squalling Gargantua, rock music has become the *enfant terrible* of contemporary culture. No small part of the problem it creates is the insoluble difficulty of finding a theater big enough and grand enough to accommodate its vast and protean energies. Too big now for those black cribs beneath the city streets where it used to rock, too splendid for sock hop balls in sweaty gyms, too pacific, too mature for a punch-throwing, can-hurling, scream-up at the Brooklyn Fox, rock has become a glamorous flying circus touring the capitals of the world like some great virtuoso.

Yet the effect of this magnificence, this Barnum and Baileying of audiences, has not been the intensification of the art or the enhancement of its performers. Too much bigness has dwarfed the rock concert and made it ridiculous. The spectacle of tens of thousands of people at Madison Square Garden poring intently over a couple of puny little stick figures going round and round on a revolving stage, like fiddling mice on the lid of a music box, is absurd.

Worse than absurd is the Caligulan idea of summoning at a whim hundreds of thousands to some improvised Circus Maximus in an isolated cow patch or drag strip. There, under conditions approximating the Johnstown Flood or the Dust Bowl wipe-out, vast numbers of popeyed adventurers undergo the artificial ordeal of the rock festival, replete with desperate calls for help, noble efforts by local Samaritans and the climactic horror of a ritual murder—beautifully photographed for you shut-ins in Linear Land by those hand-held favorites, the Maysles Brothers.

True, these mammoth festivals save the moviemakers the cost of hiring a cast of thousands. Viewed six months later in the cushioned comfort of the local cinema, they provide a voyeuristic treat for the millions who can't abide the traffic jams, the skin-drenching rains and the drug-induced *shreck* of the real thing. Yet what has all this to do with music? Many musicians who played at Altamont have renounced the whole ideal and sworn that they will never play again at a rock festival.

What rock needs at this point is simply a good home, one that will enable it to develop as an art without succumbing to the temptations of overkill. The closest it has come to this goal is that ancient moldering movie palace on Second Avenue, the Fillmore East. The Fillmore has matched the panache of the rock performer with its own seedy glamor. Well hung with battens full of perching spotlights, looped and slung with mysterious cables full of juice, the old house is a warmly commodious electric womb.

Even the approach to the Fillmore, through that Slough of Despond the Lower East Side, is a good preparation for rock music. The feeling is one of going down—going down-town, going down into the jungle, into a giant human sewer crammed with bells and brims and hips and hair. All the raunchiness of the country blues and all the sweat of the slum ghetto gospel seem to have soaked into the Fillmore's tacky carpets and fusty seats. The theater is one of the great monuments to the contemporary *esthetique de merde*.

Much as one appreciates the symbolic appropriateness of the Fillmore as a rock setting, there is no getting past the fact that the theater itself leaves much to be desired. Designed primarily for films instead of stage productions, embarrassed with a massive, low-slung balcony that is death to sound, located in a deteriorating neighborhood that is off-center for public transportation, the one-time Loew's Commodore suffers many disadvantages besides its most serious limitation—that of size. With about one-seventh of the Garden's seating capacity of 20,000, the Fillmore is losing the competition for the major attractions. There are a few great groups, like the Who, that will work a week at the Fillmore to reach the audience they could pack into the Garden in a single night, their motive being a sense of obligation toward their public and a desire to assure for their work a technically sound production. Yet as time goes on there will be few groups able to resist the temptation of the sports arenas where, as the Rolling Stones demonstrated, a group can earn in a single weekend a quarter-million dollars.

It is becoming urgent that we find a better place to stage rock concerts in New York. The irony is that we possess the finest theater in the world for this purpose—the Radio City Music Hall. Forget about your childhood impressions of a giant movie with little lights behind the seats. Forget about the "Glory of Easter" and "The Nativity." Forget about sending your out-of-town relatives to see the show while you go shopping. Instead, look at the place through contemporary eyes. You will be astonished by what you behold.

The moment you set foot in the Cunard lobby with its oriental plum walls and giant fasces of glass light tubes, you recognize with a shock that you have found it—the ideal world of contemporary sensibility. A Platonic heaven of Art Deco forms. Every chic line, every modish color and contour that the present day dotes upon has been laid up in this soaring cathedral to the fallen world. The ultimate whirl in a time machine, this intergalactic Shangri-la reverberates with a hundred beguiling echoes of America's splendid theatrical history. With one majestic gesture it brings back the old Hollywood, the old Broadway, the Thirties, the Forties, the whole nostalgic mix that stuffs the contemporary head.

When you walk into the auditorium, the effect is stunning. There is Saint Roxy's vision—brought to you direct from Capri—a theater in the shape of a giant sunrise with the rings of light coming off the stage bigger and bigger and bigger until the arc of the proscenium has grown like a drug vision to embrace 2,000, 4,000—no, 6,200—people, lying back in beautiful, soft, floating seats, dreaming their waking dreams and taking in this magnificent show on this colossal pipe organ dream stage, with the whole spectacle lapping around them in Max Reinhardt Cinerama and giving them an experience that Roxy called "theatrical" and we call a trip.

Now, what has been the problem with this super theater down through the years? Designed for stage productions, not for films, it opened ominously in 1932, as vaudeville was dying all around. After one incredible supershow, with sixteen acts ranging from Martha Graham to the Flying Wallendas, moving pictures moved in alongside the Rockettes. The world's best-equipped stage had been upstaged by a flickering, two-dimensional image. Conceived with one esthetic in view, the Music Hall had to adapt overnight to an entirely different art form. Ever since, the Hall has been haunted by the gloom of unfulfilled ideal.

Walter Lippmann put his finger on the problem many years ago when he wrote, "For such a theater it would be necessary to create some radical new kind of spectacle . . . the entrepreneurs are like men who have built a great pedestal to sustain a peanut . . . such a theater might be built because there was a great art that required such a theater. But here the theater has been built first and for years to come the question will be what in thunder to do with it."

That question seems now to have been solved by the ripeness of time. If the Music Hall is a theater in search of a spectacle, the rock concert is a spectacle in search of a theater. In a minute you can calculate the advantages of the match. Just think of midnight rock concerts every weekend, with thousands of young people pouring into the otherwise empty theater, with the energy of fresh minds and bodies stepping briskly past the ancient custodians of the Hall, the very same men who opened it forty years ago, still doing the same shows they did back in the Thirties. Think of the show the kids' costumes would make in the lobby. Think of the light show that could be mounted above that stage with its marvelous equipment, its astonishing intimacy with the spectator, its vast unbounded spaces and thrilling sight lines. And all this could be achieved while the Music Hall continued to offer its traditional fare to the general public the rest of the week.

Indeed, something had better be done soon, for the Radio City Music Hall is sinking into a more serious kind of decay than that which afflicts its tired old shows. Week after week, between holiday seasons, the greatest theater in America is half empty. The off-duty charwomen in the morning, the busloads of suburban high school kids in the afternoon, the middle-aged couples at night cannot fill the house. The traditional family offerings are no longer available for the screen. Disney is dead and Vilgot Sjoman lives.

As the wreckers tear whole blocks, like rotten teeth, out of Sixth Avenue, the cost accountancy people who decreed the demise of the beautiful Center Theater will begin to eye the Music Hall. Even now, rumors are heard that the building is marked for demolition. Nothing can save it, ultimately, but its value to the urban community. Trucking in loads of kids from the suburbs to watch the elephant dance on its front legs will not preserve the Music Hall.

What is needed now is merely an accommodation. A weekend adaptation to the modern world. Let that eroding peninsula in the sea of time begin to sustain a little contemporary life and its own tenure will be indefinitely prolonged. Let it slam its stainless steel baptistery doors against the current world and the demand for its destruction will follow apace. No one wants to corrupt the vestal purity of the Rockettes. May no pastie ever sully their sexless flesh! Nay, let them flourish in their generations, for they are the sass of the earth.

Not forty girls but one girl repeated forty times, the erstwhile Roxyettes might even lay claim to be pioneers of the psychedelic present. Dancing down through the years with the gift of eternal youth, lifting their legs with plastic precision, refracting themselves through some strange crystal that deeply waves the mind, the Rockettes are the only act ever to justify itself on the giant stage. Come to think of it, they might be just as good with rock as they were with shlock. Yes, I can see them now, bounding in leather, the favorite fetishistic image of some future light show, some piece of electric wallpaper that will loom with awesome authority over the entire generation assembled like the tribes of Israel in that great temple of the pop arts, that pop pantheon and palladium, the Radio City Music Hall.

The New York Times, 1970

in the first half hour: I was back in the early Thirties with my mother on the Steel Pier at Atlantic City, staring at the fox trotters; I was inside a glamorous speakeasy in Cleveland (the Great Lakes Exposition of 1937) watching a multi-faceted glass ball revolve in the ceiling; I was lost at some high school prom in the Forties, my ear divided between the hiss of sliding feet and the nasal sweetness of saxophones. Wow! Did I go back! But after a while the nostalgia began to wear off, and my thoughts took a different turn. Those dancers out there on the floor: what do they look like? It's the tribe readying itself for an orgy. What is an orgy? It is an alignment with force—like iron particles patterned by magnetic fields. Combine enough excitement with enough narcosis and you slip out of yourself and perform acts of public sex with no embarrassment or guilt. Is it a holy act? Yes, because it celebrates some force greater than the individual's consciousness and outside his consciousness.

That was my first impression of L'Oursin, and I am sorry it was my last. The summer was over, the crew were preparing to dismantle the electronic gear that very night; maybe they would be back next year, maybe not. As far as I was concerned, the whole extraordinary vision vanished like a mirage. A year or so later, when I was doing a TV series in New York, the producer told me that some arrangements were being made with a young lighting man named Bob Goldstein, who lived in a weird house downtown that had been furnished with thousands of dollars' worth of electronic equipment for mixed media shows. This was the author of L'Oursin, I realized; but as so often happens in TV, where much is proposed and little produced, the plan fell through and I never met Goldstein. I heard one Christmas that he had turned Bendel's into a beautiful and fascinating fairy grotto with miles of silver paper and thousands of tiny lights; but that, too, I missed. Nor did it seem to matter because I was certain that someone with Goldstein's sure-fire mixture of artistic ability and modish commercial savvy would surface soon with a new discothèque or some spectacle that would have his name all over the papers. Nothing of the sort happened, however; Helena Rubenstein borrowed (or bought) the name of his show, the Lightworks, for a new line of cosmetics, but that was all. There was no big splash and no pop explosion.

Finally, this winter, I got in touch with Goldstein and told him of my interest in what little I had seen of his work. He told me that he was making a presentation to the Parks Department for a *son et lumière* this summer at City Hall, and I was welcome to come and take a look. I went down to Christopher Street and found his number on an elegant old building about a block from the river. With a fanlight and an imposing lantern above the doorway, the house suggests the opulence of its former proprietors, robust merchants who after dickering over bales of tobacco or coils of hemp would climb the steep stairs to the top storey and feast on thick steaks and steins of beer. Goldstein is established on the second floor in a long narrow room resembling a Victorian gentleman's library cleared for amateur theatricals. In one corner there is a bit of domestic décor, book shelves and furniture with the sliced-off look of a movie set; but most of the room has been stripped to the walls and pointed toward the front. Here there is a low stage backed by all sorts of skeleton-like gear for electric projections: rolled screens, liana-like clusters of climbing electric cables and neat banks of switches and relays. Show tunes were playing when I arrived, and a score of people were sipping whiskey out of mugs when the lights began to dim and the sound swelled into the familiar bravado of a Broadway overture. Art nouveau traceries above the stage began to twinkle like marquee lights, two ghostly curtains of Christmas tree bulbs snaked together from the wings, and as moony footlights, pink-eyed down-lights and—hey there!—not one but two of those multi-faceted ceiling balls began to dazzle in every direction, the whole stage took off in kinetic fireworks. Then with all the formality of a curtain raising, the central screen rolled down and revealed some beautiful pictures of

old flying machines as fragile and graceful as tropical butterflies. The audience burst into applause like children at a
puppet theater.

Goldstein's projection arrangement is based on scientific
research on perception fields, attention spans, eye-scanning
patterns. What it comes to in effect is three large screens
canted like a looking glass and offering to the eye an endless
counterpoint of images coordinated with music. The sound
track is the basis of the whole show; with every new record
a fresh sequence of pictures begins to play on the screens.
On this night the show was divided into three parts, each
one stepping a little further out. The first act was drawn
from sources dear to camp sensibility: women in ostrich
feather hats and dripping boas entering turn-of-the-century
hotels and department stores to the strains of "Sunday
Clothes" from *Hello, Dolly!;* an ancient film about the Four
Musketeers mockingly matched with words and music from
Camelot; and a hundred musty shots of the palatial old Roxy
—ranks of ushers, rings of seats, grand staircases, even John
D.—all illustrating the catalogue aria, "Roxy Music Hall."

Act II launched jazz montages of New York from the
sound track of *West Side Story:* exhilarating take-offs from
Times Square, nightscapes in neon and a strangely affecting
moment that paused to watch pigeons fluttering down on
the head of a statue. This tourist's-eye view of the city was
followed by a flight into abstraction as dozens of colored
patterns were flashed on the screens in company with a very
effective audio mix (by Keith Lacey) that included eerily
reverberating brass and kettledrums, a jungle of jabbering
woodblocks, the Chambers Brothers chanting "Time" and a
couple of heart-hauling crescendos that terminated in cas-
cades of laughter.

When the performance was over, I had my chance to talk
with Goldstein; and after expressing appreciation for what
had been a fine slide show, I said I hadn't found this work as
exciting or mind-stretching as L'Oursin. Goldstein agreed
that the show was tame; it had been assembled hastily from
things around the house, and it was aimed at a different kind

of audience. He explained that what he really liked to do was concoct through the chemistry of light and sound the formulas for new sensations. Operating with a vast stock of artifacts from many periods, he discovers harmonies between things that have never before existed together; and these correspondences, like the boxes of Joseph Cornell, have the power to make us feel emotions for which there are no names. Everything he does is determined by the desire to achieve a certain quality that he could only describe as "psychedelic" (he apologized for the word but confessed he didn't know a better one). He sees current sensibility as reaching out hungrily to devour every fascinating sight and sound. When the world has been ransacked for its treasure of images and these have been whirled about in kaleidoscopic mixes, the culture as we have known it will be destroyed—but it will also have been reborn.

When I asked him about the powerful erotic character of his discothèque, he laughed and said that he had made the same discovery on the very first night he had shown the Lightworks. It was Christmas Eve and he decided to combine his love of entertaining with his desire to give his new equipment a trial run; so he invited to his house about seventy people, taking care that they be of all sorts, from the sophisticated to the naïve. By the end of the evening, about half the crowd had left and Goldstein was in the kitchen preparing some coffee. When he came back to the parlor, he found his guests had succumbed completely to the spell of the lights and music. They were all embracing happily, participating in a spontaneous love-in. Goldstein said he was astonished not only by the event but by the gentleness and affection everyone displayed; it was, he said, "a love feast, a pre-Christian vernal rite." At L'Oursin, however, the erotic stimulus had produced some disturbing incidents. One night Goldstein found one of the middle-aged yacht captains exhibiting himself to a group of startled ladies; on another occasion, a whole table rose at the end of "Zorba the Greek" and smashed their glasses against the wall.

Like a lot of people in the arts today, Goldstein feels he

has a redemptory mission; he has discussed with psychiatrists the therapeutic uses of lights and music, and he has
discovered the psychic dangers of the discothèque ambience. He said the flashing mechanical strobes used everywhere today could trigger an epileptic seizure. When I
commented on the difference in atmosphere between
L'Oursin and the Electric Circus, the latter full of bad vibrations with a teenage skid row strung out in the gallery, he
explained that he had no use for the hard-rock line adopted
in most discothèques. Instead of giving his audience a flog-
ging, he prefers to provide them with unlimited opportunities for dreaming. *Angst* is what spoils hard rock. Dancers
don't need this kind of stimulation; users and hippies can get
high looking at anything; the emphasis ought to be on the
values of good showmanship.

As I spoke with Goldstein and learned about his past,
which includes years of working in the theater and in the
pop music business (he wrote an early rock hit called
"Washington Square"), I began to realize that the designer
of the futuristic dance hall was really a traditional New
York type. Like Billy Rose, Florenz Ziegfeld and P. T. Barnum, he is basically a showman; but he has opened a new
avenue to the arena. Instead of hiring an army of writers,
composers, designers, singers and actors to do a show, Goldstein sits at home building fabulous production numbers
with tiny slides and bits of tape.

My meeting with Bob Goldstein ended on a troubled
note. One of those boy-men so common to our generation,
his moods fluctuate rapidly from an engaging enthusiasm
that suggests a precocious child running around in a play-
room crammed with electric toys to the embittered and
venomous tones of an aging actor who has paid some heavy
dues and never really made it. He showed me a file bulging
with projects for shows, clubs, store windows, museums; all
commissioned by someone—and all dead. This was where
most of his dreams ended. People thought buying a light
show was like hiring musicians for a Bar Mitzvah; but the
equipment was expensive and the labor of programming

costly. For a single three-minute number like "Sunday Clothes," Goldstein spent 135 hours picking through 10,000 glass slides. At L'Oursin the programming was continuous all night and there were no repeats. A crew of six was needed to run the controls, and Goldstein had worked feverishly all summer keeping abreast of the new releases. Yet the projects closest to his heart would be much more costly. Martin and Feuer, the producers, had approached him to do a new version of the Ringling Bros. Circus—"Imagine," he whispered with closed eyes, "an immaculate Edwardian circus."

Imagine a circus ballyhoo with the barker's cries piling up in widening pools of reverberation; a circus parade with the clowns strutting in a flicker of strobes and the elephants embossed with projections of eighteenth-century posters and lithos; the anarchic confusion of the three rings clarified by the shaping flow of lighting. The finale? An elaborate pageant of heraldry: banners folding into tent pavilions, knights being hoisted on chargers, a tournament with jousting and melees. Then, in a flash, the whole scene changes: the tent poles become trees, the pavilions become booths, the knights burghers—presto!—a medieval meadow covered with a fair, and the audience welcome to come down out of the stands to mill across the tanbark and shop at booths and look at the magic close-up while afar a wistful carillon plays.

What are such dreams worth? Its hard to say. With the theater in collapse and the arts in disarray, the life of our culture resides more and more in its shows. The Fashion-Rock-Film axis controls the scene, and its power arises from our longing to commune with images and become one with the bright skin of appearances. The hankering to slip from place to place, age to age, person to person is what makes the kaleidoscope spin. As we shift our shapes and change our tunes, doing a little dream work on the sly, we are fast becoming a society of private projectionists.

New York, 1968

Tommy: *Rock's First Opera*

OUT OF the murk of a dead stage, the feedback of a
wrongly turned knob, the silhouetted scuffle of grips and
grabs, into the electric blaze of Leco, Fresnel and Klieg
lights, the steely-ringing applause of an ovation and the
emotional suction of 2,000 open, gasping, gagging mouths
came the Who on the first night of their recent week-long
run of *Tommy* at the Fillmore East. Pete Townshend was,
as always, an incredibly tall, gawky, goony-looking plow
jockey in a white coverall; Roger Daltrey was, as ever, a
dazzling, prancing Golden Boy, vibrant in geary fringes;
Keith Moon was still enthroned on his drum dais, twirling
his sticks like the Black Watch and listening for the discreet
thunder of John Entwistle's bass, looming with its player
out of the stage-right shadows.

Nothing had changed with the Who—yet everything was
marvelously different. The boys who had always been
rock's toughest, truest, most brilliantly innovative talents;
the boys who had never been able to capitalize on their remarkable ideas, extraordinary energy and unique integrity;

these perennial challengers and dark horses were standing now on the rock world's ultimate stage haloed in fame, glory and gold. They had the biggest hit, the hottest property, the latest thing, the first-ever, I-thought-they'd-never, when-will-they-ever-get-it-all-together in—can you imagine such a thing?—a triumphantly successful ROCK OPERA!!!

All that was nothing, however, to the amazing break-through they had scored, the opening they had blasted out of the dreary, dying world of traditional rock into the exhilarating, intoxicating atmosphere of the future. Fresh air! That was the miracle of *Tommy*. The score was a powerful steel blade blowing all the bull out of the current atmosphere, blowing away the rancid incense of the hippies, the bells and baubles of the love children, dissipating the acrid acid fumes of San Francisco, the puddled sea spray of L.A. Exhausting these exploded bubbles, *Tommy* sucked in great draughts of clean, cool, electric-spark-smelling ozone, like a heart-expanding whiff from a giant popper.

What *Tommy* proclaims with the first blast of its Beethovenish horn is the red dawn of revolution. The love days are over, it trumpets, now come the days of wrath. War is the opera's real theme, war of generation against generation, war between the younger generation and its own leaders. A prophecy as well as a passion, *Tommy* prefigures in its score (if not in its text) the final confrontation when blood will flow in the streets and the seats of power will be dynamited. Concussionary accents, rattling bursts of drumfire, abrupt splashes of fuming cymbals make up its musical texture. Beating a tachycardiac tattoo of alarm, battle and triumph for a good half of its total length, *Tommy* reminds us that revolutions carry their colors in their drums.

The wrath of this youthful "Eroica" is directed at a society that violates and destroys its youth with cruelty and treachery. The first half of the opera is a chronicle of outrage that goes to grotesque lengths in its effort to dramatize the horrors of this world. Tommy is a deaf, dumb and blind boy who has been brainwashed by his parents (he saw his father murder his mother's lover), sadistically tortured by his kid cousin, sexually molested by his drunken uncle and sent by a gypsy on an LSD trip whose nightmarish course is grimly etched in a so-called "Underture." The first autistic hero in the history of opera, Tommy symbolizes a generation that instinctively protects itself by retreating behind inviolable barriers of psychic deadness and inertness. Like the young schizophrenics in the currently popular case histories of R. D. Laing, Tommy is terrified equally by the world's violence *and* its indifference. His *leitmotif*, the opera's recurrent refrain, is a poignant sequence that pleads: "See me, feel me, touch me, heal me!" Returning at critical moments—like the chorale of a Bach Passion or the lyric theme of a Beethoven sonata—this *planctus* sounds the current generation's most urgent demand.

In the second half of *Tommy*, which portrays the hero's recovery and triumph, the war drums are silenced and the musical atmosphere is suffused with evangelical light. Tommy is taken to a doctor who pronounces him physically sound but mentally diseased in a way he is powerless to cure. When Tommy is placed before a mirror, however, he begins to soliloquize and his song is a paean to himself! Enraged by such obvious self-worship, his mother smashes the glass and Tommy is miraculously cured.

What happens next attests to the quality of Tommy's inner life during his years of affliction. Living behind a wall of woe, amid magical visions and musical vibrations, he has become a holy fool. Like Meher Baba, the Indian god-man by whom this opera was inspired, the boy has acquired a mysterious power to make men rejoice. Cured of his imprisoning disease, Tommy floods the world with good vibrations.

Like all great saviors, Tommy comes preaching the gospel of *the way*. His religious program embodies the best elements of every faith: contemplation and charity from the Judeo-Christian tradition; divestment of soul from body, as enjoined by Oriental religion. To these familiar prescriptions, however, he adds a new practice symbolic of the modern marriage of man and machine—the cultivation and perfection of *pinball playing!*

Tommy is a pinball wizard. Standing before his dazzling machine rapt in a senseless trance, exercising with exquisite skill his only undamaged sense, the gift of touch, he has long since become the hero of a youth cult. Now free and in possession of all his faculties, he takes to the stage, enjoys the career of a rock 'n' roll star, wins the love of women and the devotion of men. Gathering his disciples about him at a summer camp, he orders them to practice pinball under the same conditions he endured by wearing dark glasses and earplugs. They rebel.

The opera concludes with a long, seamless sequence that recalls the unbroken finales of the Mozart operas. Commencing with Tommy's welcome to the campers and building through the disciples' whispered resentments to their threats of outright violence, the score mounts to a 20th Century-Fox apotheosis consisting of augmented repetitions of Tommy's soliloquy of self-discovery.

This rhapsodic updraft carries the listener out of the theater in an exalted mood: but after the spell wears off, he may begin to wonder what meaning the conclusion conveys. Have the disciples betrayed Tommy by refusing to follow his teaching and submit to his discpline? Or have they simply asserted their right to be free of authoritarian domination? The final paean to the great leader would support the first interpretation; Tommy's address to the campers (delivered in sarcastic words more suitable to a sergeant than a sage) buttresses the opposite view. Like Richard Wagner, who commenced the *Ring* as a revolutionary tract and concluded it (many years later) as a mystic celebration of cyclical destiny—without troubling to wholly obliterate the traces of his initial conception—Peter Townshend, the composer of *Tommy*, appears to have suffered from a conflict of philosophies. In any case, the alternative of submission to the guru or revolt against the master brackets rather neatly the spiritual dilemma of the present generation, who would gladly learn but not willingly be taught.

Not surprisingly for a work of such innovative power and philosophic profundity, *Tommy* has turned the rock world on its head. Not another showing of the latest musical fashions—another Sgt. Pipsqueak or Nashville Nixon—but a classic composition in a style of carborundum toughness, *Tommy* has restored to popular music its traditional ideal of art. Following the great tradition of Scott Joplin's ragtime opera, *Treemonisha*, and George Gershwin's jazz opera, *Porgy and Bess*, the first rock opera has no truck with those camp-town cuties who insist that pop music must be made with built-in obsolescence. (How can a young man mouth this specious idea when his own generation has retired more "timeless" art and revived more "dated" shows than all the previous ages combined?) *Tommy* commenced its public career as a slow roller (it took some time to get the score into our ears and minds), but it promises to go further and last longer than any other undertaking of the rock generation.

Already it has founded a new poperatic tradition. In England and America, little four- and five-man opera companies are readying works for this new repertory. The legendary English group, the Kinks, has produced *Arthur;* and Murray Head and the Trinidad Singers are about to issue (in time for Christmas) a rock opera titled *Jesus Christ*, which bears the endorsement of no less a personage than the Dean of St. Paul's at London. Meanwhile, very brisk negotiations are in progress to make *Tommy* into a Broadway musical and a Hollywood movie.

No one has suggested yet that the opera be mounted *as an opera* at the darkened Metropolitan, but the idea merits serious consideration. Even apart from the heady symbolism of such a change of guards, the avant for the derrière, think of the fabulous social opportunities such an event would afford. Can you imagine the lords and ladies of the hip establishment turning out on opening night in their frumpy finery? Flaunting their mangy furs and pasty jewels? Removing the world's longest coats from the world's shortest skirts in gravely pornographic ceremony? Raising lorgnettes with dark lenses? Rolling the programs into giant joints? (Special programs with each page a different color and the last page soaked in acid so the whole audience could come together, as the *I Ching* enjoins, during the finale.)

At curtain time, the Austrian chandeliers would be lowered so that whoever wished might view the stage spectacle through a crystal. The light show would feature the fashionably moiré steam curtain from *Das Rheingold* (with or without wallowing groupies). Mr. Bing's box would be occupied by Rosko. At intermission, the distinguished audience could surf down the banisters or space out by gazing at the Chagalls. The bar would be closed (of course), but the fountain would flow with rainbow-colored, natural-sugar fruit drinks. As a final touch, the evening's proceeds would be donated to purchase bombs for needy high school students. After all, Verdi's *Ernani* sparked a revolution in Italy —why shouldn't *Tommy* trigger the first gun of the American revolution from that citadel of uptightness, the Met?

* * *

When I wrote about Tommy *at the Met, I thought I was kidding. I should have known that one man's fantasy is another man's ball. The very next month, January 1970, the Who were launched in the Central European Opera Bowl. The group was performing at the Sadler's Wells Colosseum when one night an observer from the Danish State Opera stepped into the press box. A Nowhere Man who had never heard a rock band before, this classical talent scout was impressed primarily by the amount of noise four little men could make. Excusing himself from the after-the-show party with complaints about the ringing in his ears, he went back to Denmark to make his report. Evidently, the ringing reminded him of the sound of cash registers, because just a few days later the Who received an invitation to perform* Tommy *at the Royal Opera House at Copenhagen.*

That kicked off one of the strangest tours in musical his-

tory. It was a scenario for the Marx Brothers. Here was the flashiest, toughest, most determinedly adolescent of hard-rock groups; and there were the grand opera houses of Hamburg, Berlin and Munich lying open to the assault of these musical rapists. The results were just what you might expect. Scrambling onstage like fighter pilots during the Battle of Britain, the Who blasted their German audience with 40,000 watts of raw amplification. The mittel-European mittel-brows hardly knew what to make of the experience. They had just accustomed themselves to jazz. Now this rrrrrrock! Schweinerei!

Nobody liked the boys better than the European opera managements. Tommy *gave them just what they wanted: a guaranteed, moneymaking, plug-in, get-with-it kit. Who could accuse them of being elitists or squares or antiyouth after they had programmed a rock opera? As the tour progressed, the Who were deluged with offers to make* Tommy *into a ballet, a musical, a movie—heaven knows what! Another band would have taken the trip to the end of the line —but not the Who.*

One night on the road to Vienna, Pete Townshend had a vision. He saw himself as a fruity little Lord Fauntleroy jiggling around on a gilded stage. Awaking in a cold sweat, he ordered the opera tour canceled and a series of redemptory dates set up in the roughest, raunchiest grind houses of Yorkshire. There, in the spring of 1970, playing before their favorite public in the mill towns of Leicester and Leeds, the Who recorded the greatest of all live rock albums, the fabulous Live at Leeds.

Live at Leeds *carries to its climax the whole tradition of rock as a stage art mingling the appeals of teenage demagoguery with flash theatrics and wildly improvised playing. This is the original strain of rock that had its origin in the black vaudeville stage, in Hollywood music films (especially the rock movies of the Fifties) and in the style developed by the first English skiffle-and-beat bands. Though most English groups deserted the stage during rock's greatest period for the magical mystery of the recording studio, the Who never stopped touring at any time in their seven-year history. This commitment to the stage has played havoc with their recording schedule and contributed to their long latency period with the American public, which discovers its heroes first on records and then in the flesh. But seven years on the rock hustings has disciplined the Who into the most brilliant stage team in the history of rock music.*

The album is one half rock standards like "Summertime Blues" and "My Generation" (often misunderstood as a proud, defiant youth anthem, whereas in fact its stuttering, stammering curses are cruelly satiric, suggesting that the pill-dropping mod singer is incapable of even articulating his anger); the other half offers one of Pete Townshend's thousand-and-one improvisations on airs from Tommy. Taken as a whole, however, Live at Leeds is simply a marvelous documentary on the Who. No previous recording, for example, has so perfectly captured the sound of the Who— that rough, coarse, excoriating sound that always reminds you of Wallace Beery airplane movies with their snarling, groaning engines, rat-tat-tatting machine guns and shrilly whining nose dives. Capitalizing long before Jimi Hendrix on rock's unholy wedlock with the machine, the Who developed a whole pallette of Iron Age tone colors that produce the sadistic delight of seeing every canon of tonal beauty outrageously and triumphantly violated. What is more, the group seems to grasp intuitively modern man's empathy with the machine, the feeling of straining along with the vainly spinning snow tire or the grim satisfaction of feeling an electric drill or saw cut through wood or steel with an excruciating crescendo of noise. Half man, half machine, his lower half blurring into the image of the power-driven phallus, pop man is never more himself than when he has been completely dehumanized.

By the summer of 1970, the Who wanted nothing more to do with Tommy; yet one gig remained to be played, the biggest and most prestigious of the lot, the Metropolitan

Opera. Following months of negotiations, the Met had agreed to rent their house for one Sunday on condition that they retain control of everything from the lighting arrangements to the program notes. (*When I mentioned the Met's months-long strike in the notes, the management insisted that the reference be withdrawn. I thought it better to withdraw the notes.*) Though the Met made a great to-do about its artistic standards, the simple fact was that they wanted the money. When they learned that all 8,000 tickets had been sold at the Fillmore box office in four hours, they offered to extend the house rental to a full week.

When the great day arrived, the whole music press corps took up their stations in front of the opera house to report the anticipated freak-out. What they saw was so tame that they had to doctor up their accounts with images of bare feet padding along crimson carpets and clouds of marijuana smoke rising toward the crystal chandeliers. I had imagined the rock Four Hundred arriving in psychedelicly squiggled Rolls-Royces; instead we got the Westchester lumpenproletariat *in jeans and homemade tie-dyes.* The kids were visibly inhibited by the institutional grandeur of the Met. As they poured in under the fascinated gaze of Rudolf Bing— perched like a condor on one of the stairways—there was nothing in their behavior that even the most huffy house mother could fault.

Once inside, the crowd remained subdued until the famous chandeliers went soaring up to clear the sight lines to the stage. A roar of approval loud enough to shatter the glass followed this elegant light show, and an even greater roar hailed the Who as they stepped onstage.

From the moment the boys walked on, it was obvious they were determined to give their greatest performance. Flashing their delightfully tawdry show tricks, they worked the Met as if it were a grind house in Liverpool. Roger Daltrey, a Greek god in chamois hip-huggers, pranced and shouted ecstatically, whirling a mike around his head like an aborigine's bull-roarer. Pete Townshend pogoed across the stage *like Bugs Bunny riding an electric broom. Keith Moon, rock's greatest drummer, sat like an idiot prince bouncing a stick twenty feet into the air off a drumhead and catching it like a grandstanding center fielder. Only John Entwistle, the Who's powerful bass player, contained himself, standing stalwartly in the stage-left shadows like a barrel-chested, bare-fisted pugilist.*

Though the boys used every trick in the book to keep the crowd riveted on them, there was no gimmickry in their music. Of all rock groups, the Who have delved the deepest into the rock essence. They have reached now a level of accomplishment in their idiom directly comparable to the attainments of jazz musicians in theirs. Every song is grasped with authority, charged with energy, performed with flawless ensemble and fascinating solo work.

The instant they hit the final chord, the entire audience, thousands of freaks in fringes and tie-dyes, leaped to its feet in a stunning ovation. Townshend stammered a few words of gratitude, Moon and Entwistle engaged in a brief water battle, then the whole group jumped into a cycle of scorching encores. Whipped half dead from this two-and-a-quarter-hour performance, as well as an equally long matinee, Pete Townshend gathered his last energies to improvise an elaborate and moving coda, based on melodies from Tommy. *As the audience sat spellbound, the concert resolved itself as a huge symphonic fantasia. By the time the gold curtain came looping down and the crystal chandeliers glimmered into light, 4,000 people had become one gargantuan child, stamping and chanting, "More! More! More!"*

The New York Times, 1969 and Life, 1970

THE SOUL SIDE

Apollo Voodoo

WHEN IT'S SHOWTIME up at the Apollo in Harlem, man, you *know* it. Livid lights on the front curtain, lurid sounds from backstage, the jungle awakening behind that cloth, and then the African Queen herself: Madame Miriam Makeba snake-necking onstage in an Afro kimono with purple flowers and batwing sleeves, ears loaded with long gold earrings, arms stacked to the elbows with gold bangles, a bumper crop of beads around her neck—a sinister neck that hooks forward like the sacred asp of Egypt. Flexing her knees she lets fly with a long, arching shout, a hard polished spear of sound that comes boomeranging back from some other black woman in the wings. *Arwhoooooolie!* From Sophiatown to Harlem the message flies. *Arwhoooooooolie!* From black New York to black Johannesburg it bounces back. Call and response, I'm here and you're there, it's the oldest language in the world. And don't those people out front know it. They're digging those ancient roots, that African dignity, and they're thinking, "Now, mama, I *know* who I am."

A couple of mini-skirted, leather-booted, fuzzy-headed chicks come boogalooing out on stage—nobody at the Apollo ever *walks* on. They've got *ways* of getting out there. Screaming Jay Hawkins had himself carried on in a coffin. Little Richard used to stalk out on a red carpet laid down by his Buckingham Palace guards. Every black performer struts his signature across that stage. Once they're out there, they never stop moving. They're in *constant motion.*

Suppose you catch some rhythm and blues group up there, four boys in black shirts and banana-skin suits, they're going to shoot out on that stage like Quaker Puffed Wheat. They'll be *moving* and doing all those choreographed steps around that microphone (the one that pokes up out of the floor like a periscope). They huddle toegther. They kick apart. They lay their white gloves to their mouths, like they're whispering it to you. They roll an invisible hank of yarn on their elbows. They sock in a couple of karate chops from Harlem's new black-belt ballet. Meanwhile their leader is off on the other side of the stage, with his arms up in the air like he's being crucified. He's nailed up and taken down and tacked back up again. It looks like he'll die before he gets through the song. Then they choo-choo across to him and the whole quartet goes off in a final flurry of weave-and-bob-and-bow-and-scrape.

All this fast action gets it together for the cats who come on next. Not that this audience is hard to rouse—they're the most responsive house in New York. All pomaded and powdered, perfumed and polished, buffed, conked and manicured, they've come here ready to grooooooooove. Loaded with good things to eat, buttered popcorn and hot dogs, candy bars and soda pop, they're lobbed out in their seats as comfortably as if they were at home watching TV. A neighborhood audience, not a lot of suburban stiffs sitting uptight, this uptown crowd rolls into the Apollo just as people saunter into local movie houses all over America. Mothers bring their sons, unmarried women bring each other, and heavy men sit with their stingy-brim hats on and spread their legs out and laugh deep and slap their thighs and shove their elbows in their neighbor's ribs and whistle at the girls onstage and just plain *pleasure themselves.*

A few loose-jointed kids go tripping up to that second balcony palming those little tobacco pipes. Go up there to suck those goodies and get stoned and watch that show streeeeeeetch and shrink like the face on a rubber balloon. They'll never get busted because if a cop climbed up there to make an arrest he'd never be seen again. They'd eat him, his hat, his badge—everything. "No evidence of a crime here, lieutenant, just a lot of fat boys past their bedtime."

Some say the Apollo audience is the toughest in the world and some say it's the softest. Both are right because it's an audience that's as fickle as a prima donna. A privileged audience that often applauds itself, it feels free to indulge all its whims and humors. It will laugh at the oldest coon joke, cry at the most sentimental ballad and take to its heart the goofiest amateur on Wednesday night. It worships *audacity*, the authority of the performer who throws down the gauntlet and says, "I'm not afraid to die." But if the challenge is not convincing, the house will hurl it back with taunts and gibes. Like the night Pearl Bailey came dragging out singing, "I'm tired," and some cat leaned out of the balcony and yelled, "Well, bitch, why don't you go home, then?"

What really kills these people is *work*. Every black performer will tell you that the Apollo is a stone workhouse. The greatest performers, like James Brown, are the ones who work the hardest. Brown puts on such a draining, punishing, self-destructive performance that sometimes he falls like a pole-axed steer, flat out on the stage. They pick him up, rush him to a doctor, pump him full of saline solution, tell him he needs rest desperately. And he goes right back and does the next show. That's really the spirit of the black stage. All you know is you're going out there—about coming back you're not so sure. Coming back isn't important. Your orders are to go out there and kill 'em. You're not a singer you're a soldier, a samurai, a *kamikaze of soul.*

Although every black performer tries to be unique even the geniuses come in genuses. Take those big black chantusies, for example. Ah, there've been so many of them—Dinah Washington, Sarah Vaughan, Nina Simone, Della Reese—yet they're all the same woman. Tall, strong, muscular ladies, with their hair lifted up six feet or so in a flying bouffant whirliwig, they're the most lacquered and soignéed, shirred and tucked, draped and exposed women in America. Their gowns are made for them by couturiers who specialize in backlit bodies. Yet with all their fem-flam they look less like women than like men in drag.

Wriggling out on the floor like landlocked mermaids, they look for the spotlight and assume the *position*—one leg thrust impudently forward, outlined in ultra-high relief, the other propped behind the singer to allow her to lean backward from the waist while she holds her jeweled hand mike at the angle of a shower head and flings up her other arm as if tossing a half-empty champagne glass over her shoulder. Declaiming with this long, sinewy arm, she looks like a javelin hurler warming up for the throw. Then the great moment comes and she lofts a note up so high it almost disappears. Way up there it hovers for an infinite second, then over it tips and comes plummeting down like a dart aimed at your heart. Let her turn that trick two or three times and she'll walk off with the show.

About midway through the evening the curtain is drawn and the comic comes strolling out from the wings. He's always the same man whether his name be Dick Gregory, Bill Cosby or Sammy Stonehenge. Even more stereotyped than the fast-talking, high-strung, spritz guns of the Borscht Belt, this black standup is always a tall, thin, dapper cat who comes walking out very slow, very deliberate, with a cigarette cocked up in his jive hand. He stands there giving everyone that jive look, man, eyeing them up and down, like a John in a bar casing a B-girl. He's Calvin Cool, and he sounds like some cat standing in a barbershop, looking out that window on 125th Street, thinking out loud and giving away a lot of thoughts because this guy *has* a lot of thoughts —about people and life and *things*. You know how it is, people just don't think, so he's doing it for them, and every time he *thinks* they laugh.

What does he ruminate about? Well, he thinks a lot about Whitey. How it is with those white mothers. He takes a very dim view of the white man, a long, cool, cynical view. He doesn't have anger, he doesn't have rancor, he just has the humor of existential despair. But Whitey isn't the only thing he's got on his mind. There's also that damn fool the black man. Either he's some clown from the country who doesn't know where to get off the train, or else he's a jive cat who's trying to make people think he's better than his own kind. And that goes for those people sitting out there to-night, dig it? Like he's trying to tell this story about a guy down South who had the "haints" and some chick yells out, "You mean the *haunts!*" So he looks down on her and says with withering scorn *"Haints*, baby. You never did hear of no haunts till you come up here."

Lots of his jokes are about junkies and muggers, about black preachers and politicians—every sort of character you see on the streets or in the bars and tenements of Harlem. It's a very democratic sort of humor that reduces every one to the same level of liar, lecher and looter. Yet there are heroes, too, fantastical heroes with names like Stackolee or the Signifying Monkee. They're the ultimate badmen of the ghetto, who rob and rape and drink themselves blind. Their tales are always tall tales and their antagonists are supernatural monsters who can wipe themselves with a handful of burning coals or drink hot lead soup. The black man is obsessed with power, but being powerless he has to content himself with fantasies, with stories of giant men who stand outside the law and tell every mother to go. . . .

Song and dance, salt and sass make up the regular diet at the Apollo, but during the Easter and Christmas holidays they dish up something special, the most-prized perform-

ance of the fifty-week year, "The Harlem Gospel Train."
The setting for the Train is an old-time Baptist church, with
huge stained-glass windows and a double row of stalls filled
with women in white satin choir robes. As the curtain
parts, the choir is singing to the sound of a heavy, grunting
organ and an old colored man is shuffling in front of them,
calling out the words and admonishing the audience to heed
the message. Suddenly he spins in his tracks, extends a long,
skinny finger toward the back of the house and cries, "*Catch
it! Catch it! Look over your shoulder!*" Everyone twists his
head around trying to catch a glimpse of the Holy Spirit.
They're never fast enough, but now they're alert to the
Presence.

Onstage come four young men dressed in purple and
green with their hair teased up high. They plug into an amplifier beside the organ and start clapping and stomping and
shouting over the twanging bass line of an electric guitar.
One tall, thin Watusi-looking boy sings in a piercing falsetto
that makes the audience squeal. Breaking their clustered
stance like smartly smacked pool balls, they dazzle the spectators with sacred flash.

When the group's leader senses the moment is right, he
gives them a signal and they go into perpetual motion, dron-
ing the same phrase over and over, while he runs his voice
up and down the scale searching for a soul note, a sound that
will fracture the audience. Like a safecracker with sandpa-
pered fingertips he works over that house, trying to find
their combination, probing their ears with notes that bend
and twist and turn like a celluloid in a latch. Suddenly he
hits a nerve. Half the audience let loose with their first
screeeeeeeeeam!

The singer vaults off the stage with the mike clutched in
his hand and a long rattail wire paying out behind him.
Landing squarely in the aisle he starts working the people at
bayonet proximity. Now it's all between this hard spiky boy
and those big meaty mamas who have come here to be
seized, to be shook, to be *had* by Jesus. Crouching and run-

ning like a soldier across a battlefield, he looms up before your face, mama, and socks it to you with everything he's got—with his purple sateen jacket and his sweat-drenched head and his Crayola mustache and his bloodshot eyes and his big red chops *wide open*, baby, like the wolf ready to suck the sweet meat from your bones. Up so close he works, so tight, so hard, so *fine*, he flips those big women right out of their seats, screaming and flailing, like giant fish fighting the hook. Down the aisles run the ushers, firemen in a burning building, to grab those women and wrestle them down into their seats before they do violence to themselves or their neighbors.

But now the sacred fire has been kindled and the flames are spreading all over the theater. Up in the second balcony there's a man who's caught it, who's heard the Word and is ready to offer himself as a sacrifice. Up there in the balcony he's screaming, "I'm going to throw myself out for Jesus! I'm going to fly for Jesus! I'm coming! I'm coming now! Here I come!" Two ushers seize him from behind and pinion him against the back of his seat. Down on the main floor a woman has gone into an epileptic seizure. They have to carry her out—rigid as a coffinlid. Another one has fallen down and gashed her head. Another has torn her stocking.

The injured people are led to the left stage box where two stately black nurses in white starched uniforms and high white caps have taken their stations behind a table laden with medical instruments and bottles of recuperative salts and essences. As wave after wave of gospel boys hurl themselves off the stage, and one big woman after another rears up from her seat yelling and flailing, the nurses calmly go about their business—swabbing and corking and smelling and salting and slapping cheeks and exhorting, "Come on honey, now."

But there's no keeping hold on things. The emotional steam gauge is jiggling toward the red band marked DANGER. The whole meeting is obviously about to explode. People are falling on their knees to pray and people are shouting glory words and gospel boys are dancing on the stage like they've been bitten by a tarantula. That purple banshee is racing up and down the aisles screaming into the mike and the people are starting to scream back at him and he's throwing his heart, his lungs, his liver into every note and they're feeling that steam heat coming up their pipes, and it's coming, coming, coming—just one more push, one more wrench and *there it is . . . the apocalyptic scream.* Now, look out! The whole theater is getting to its feet, *sixteen hundred and eighty* people are standing bolt upright, raising their arms straight up in the air and waving them slowly back and forth, making a multitude of crosses, making a wave offering, making a mass gesture that has the power and authority of Moses dividing the Red Sea. And where are you, Whitey? You're drowning at the bottom of that sea. You're sitting there so scared and so lost and so little you're going to crawl out of the Apollo Theater tonight like Kafka's cockroach.

Holiday, 1969

James Brown = Black Power

TALK ABOUT your black power. Take a look at James Brown, mister. That's right, James Brown, America's Number-One Soul Brother. To whites, James is still an offbeat grunt, a scream at the end of the dial. To blacks, he's *boss*— the one man in America who can stop a race riot in its tracks and send the people home to watch television. Twice he worked that miracle in the terrible days following the murder of the Rev. Dr. Martin Luther King, Jr.

It started at Boston, where Brown was set to play the Boston Gardens. When he heard the tragic news, he canceled the show. Then it was the Mayor on the phone—asking for help. The situation was desperate. Already people were in the streets, looting and burning. Some black politician, some guy who knows where it's at, told the Mayor, "Put James Brown on television." So the announcement was made: To-night, TV, JB. Well, that got it. Everybody turned around and beat it for home. Who'd blow his chance to see the Man? That night Brown got out there—and he didn't stop. For six solid hours he held them. Out of that tube came the wildest shakin' and shoutin' ever seen. Brown sweated so hard you could almost smell him on the close-ups. When it was over, nobody had eyes for the street. The city was saved.

Next day it was the Mayor of Washington calling. The same number. "Save our city." Brown plunged right into the streets, grabbing gangs of marauding kids, talking to them like men but sending them back home like a tough uncle. When he hit the tube that night, he wasn't giving a performance in a cummerbund. He was just James Brown, standing there with a pained expression on his face yet bearing witness to America. "This is the greatest country in the world," he rasped. "If we destroy it, we're out of our heads. We've come too far to throw it away. You gotta fight with dignity." Next day, Washington was a quieter place. All of which explains why, when James Brown sat down to dinner with the President at the White House recently, his place card bore this message: "Thanks much for what you are doing for your country—Lyndon B. Johnson."

That kind of power seems way out for a rhythm and blues man, a cat with a pushed-in face, a hoarse voice, a bag of tunes that sound alike and an act that is nothing new for the black vaudeville stage. But there you have the genius of James Brown. He is the greatest demagogue in the history of Negro entertainment. His whole vast success, which is measured in millions of records, thousands of performances and the kind of popularity that had him touring the nation's ball parks with his "National Soul Festival" in the summer of 1968, is based less on talents and skills than it is on a unique faculty for sizing up the black public and making himself the embodiment of its desires. James Brown understands, better perhaps than any entertainer or politician of the present day, that the price of authority is submission. He knows that you must get down with the people to control them. Anybody who's going to stand even one step above them is not going to have them completely in his power. In fact, you must descend below the level of the audience if you desire ultimate mastery. That is why he identifies himself so emphatically as "a black man," setting himself apart from all the Negro entertainers (and all the Negro spectators) who dream of being Harry Belafonte.

That is why Brown has gotten so deep into the soul bag, dragging out the oldest Negro dances, the most basic gospel shouts, the funky, low-down rhythms of black history. He has made himself even more conservative than his audience. Nor does he ever miss a chance to talk about his humble origins in Georgia, where he was born thirty-four, thirty-six or thirty-eight years ago, and where he picked cotton, blacked boots and danced in the streets for nickels and dimes. Playing the shoeshoe genius, the poor boy who rose from polish rags to riches, he makes himself one with the lowest and youngest members of his audience.

Success in the Negro world, however, is always equated with royalty; so Brown makes a great show of his clothes (500 suits, 300 pairs of shoes), his cars (blue-black Mark III Continental, purple and silver-gray Rolls-Royce, Cadillac convertible, Eldorado, Toronado, Rambler), his twin-engine Lear jet, his two radio stations and his moated, drawbridged castle in St. Albans, Queens. Until recently, he regularly had himself crowned onstage and sat cheerfully on a throne, wearing ermine-trimmed robes.

Now he has pruned his act of such gaudy features and begun to reshape his image in accordance with the current mood of public seriousness. Offering himself proudly as an example of what the Negro can achieve in America, he has begun a tug of war with the radical black demagogues, whom he feels are leading the people astray. Whether he has political ambitions himself, or whether he would be content to lend his power to another man, is not clear; but the time comes in every great entertainer's life when he must decide whether he is going to grow old doing his act or get into something else.

Certainly no words that Brown could speak from a political platform could mean as much to his public as the thrill-

ing image of himself in action onstage. A high-voltage hala-
tion crackles around "Mr. Dynamite" from the moment he
strides jauntily on until he is dragged off, one, two or three
hours later. Once a boxer, known for his lightning-fast footwork, Brown carries himself with the taut muscular energy
of a competing athlete. He grabs the mike with a confident
right cross, ducks and bobs with the beat, lays a fist up beside his head, shuffles his feet in dazzling combinations and
winds up wringing wet, being swathed in a brightly colored,
sequin-spangled robe. A hitter hero, a scarred, bruised but
triumphant Golden Boy, he has enormous appeal for an audience that has been battered and beaten and robbed of its
confidence from childhood. Never angry or cruel, he is a
wholly admirable champion, a cocksure, carefree kid who is
always going out to conquer the world. The public gloats
over him with parental satisfaction.

Like all rhythm and blues men, Brown is a great stage
lover, a man who can take on thousands of women at a time
and reduce them to screaming jelly. In fact, he goes after the
women in the audience a lot more directly than do most
entertainers. When he does one of his slow drags, like "It's a
Man's World," the rapport between him and the girls
reaches scandalous proportions. He shouts with killing sincerity, "Just be there when I get the notion!" and the
screams come back from the house like an enormous trumpet section screeching in on cue. Those screams, incidentally,
are not from teenyboppers; they come from mature women
who enter the theater in twos and threes and at the great
moments let themselves go.

Brown is always pouring on the love, but he often
changes key or tempo. He can command and he can beg. He
can scream as loudly and with as much anguish as any
woman. And when the fit is upon him, he drives his erotic
frenzy right over the line that divides the secular from the
sacred. Like all the great soul men, his final station is in the
church, right up there on the horns of the altar, testifying in
an ecstasy. One moment he's the gladiator of the ring, taking

a lot of punishment in the final rounds but hanging in there, battling his way to victory. Then, suddenly, he's an ancient darkie from the Delta, shoulders up to his ears, arms stretched out like a ghost—and that face! Good God, the sweat is pouring down the man's face like a shower of diamonds, his eyes are rolled up wildly, his mouth is hanging dumbly open; but through all that agony there is a smile coming, a beautiful smile blooming like Easter morning.

James Brown ends in beatitude. He sacrifices himself and gives the pieces away. He wrenches himself out of his body and stands naked in the spirit. He concentrates his blackness and light comes pouring out of him. He teaches us the meaning of the phrase "black is beautiful."

The New York Times, 1968

"They Call Me Beautiful"

LITTLE RICHARD

66COME QUICKLY! It's Little Richard on television."
Rounding the living-room corner like a teenybopper in full
cry, I shot an expectant look at the screen and registered
instant disappointment. Instead of a fabulous figure stepped
out of an old movie, a sublimely vulgar creature in a dazzling
white zoot suit, standing at a glaring white piano, pounding
on it like a child having a temper tantrum while bawling,
"Tutti Frutti, Oh Rooty, Tutti Frutti, Oh Rooty"—instead
of this epitome of the original rock 'n' roll scene, there on
the screen was an elegant young man, nipped into a Nehru
jacket and white booties, a little Indian bellhop. Just as unfamiliar was his voice. Instead of a savage yawp squealing up
and up and up—like a buzz saw ripping into a raw plank—
this singer sounded like a man shouting through a glass wall.
No, said I to myself, this guy is either an impostor or a bad
Karma. What black entertainer would want to come back as
Sammy Davis Jr.?

The ensuing interview revealed beneath the Hollywood
surface a few sparks of real deviltry. When a rather shlubby

Steve Lawrence ("sitting in" for Johnny Carson) asked his guest what his friends called him, the exotic stranger with the wide Andean cheekbones, sloe black eyes and pencil-thin mustache moved closer and murmured voluptuously, "They call me Beautiful." That sounded like the "Bronze Liberace." Then he leaped to his feet to demonstrate an Indian war whoop, but the cameraman missed the move (don't they check their reflexes?), and Stevo had to ask for another take of the show's one flash of spontaneity.

Just as bad was the failure to describe the current wave of nostalgia for pre-Beatles rock 'n' roll, a wave that has already engulfed England, washing ancient doubloons like Bill Haley's "Rock Around the Clock," the first rock record, back to the top of the charts and bringing such legendary figures as Little Richard and Chuck Berry surfing in from obscurity. When the Beatles released their "Lady Madonna," Mick Jagger of the Stones quipped that it should have been done like Little Richard's "Good Golly, Miss Molly." Obviously, Little Richard wants to make such imitations unnecessary. But his return trip with Steve Lawrence and the "Tonight" crew was a bummer.

The next afternoon saw me closeted in a sumptuous suite at the Waldorf with the mysterious "Indian" prince and his manager, a jolly Buddha with a protuberant belly. Yielding to no man in my admiration for the daddy of the hard rockers, I wanted to know where he had been for the last ten years and what sort of *revanche* he was planning. Once the hottest thing in pop music, Richard had not been just another flash in the pan, like Frankie Avalon or Fabian. He was a seminal force in his world, a great innovator and reshaper of tradition. Little Richard found Negro music rhythm and blues and left it rock 'n' roll. Instead of slow, heavy, lugubrious tunes aimed at the race market, he fashioned a frenzied music that had as much appeal for white kids and Europeans as it did for Negroes. All this he accomplished in a mere year and a half, writing and recording a score of hits that sold to the tune of 32 million copies and established the basic rock esthetic.

It was Richard who taught the Beatles how to shout and go "Yeah, yeah, yeah," Richard who whispered to the Stones the secret that soul was sass, Richard who furnished Elvis Presley with Negro street chanteys and vocal gimmicks. The hillbilly lollipop was so impressed by the fireblizzard blast of Richard's voice that he demanded and obtained from his engineers an electronic prosthesis that transformed his own colorless white-trash voice into the quaking, rattling, gulp-gasp known to fame.

Soaring to the peak of the pop Olympus, Richard obtained for his part all the perquisites of royalty: his carriage was a pink Cadillac, his robes were sateen and lace, his retinue approached him in a manner both cringing and fawning. At press conferences his dressing gown would carelessly part to reveal the royal jewels. At the Apollo Theater, the ushers would struggle to prevent mass suttee from the first balcony.

Richard's magnificence, though, was bought at an unknown price in guilt. Born in Macon, Georgia, in the heart of the gospel belt thirty-three years ago, singing since he was ten in church choirs and on street corners, traveling in later years with Dr. Hudson's Medicine Show and Sugarfoot Sam from Alabam, then coming home to hear his uncles preach from the pulpit, Richard Penniman focused in himself with burning intensity the sacred-secular conflict that is pandemic to Negro culture but especially acute in its great singers.

At the height of his career, Little Richard began acting strangely. He would appear before a vast audience of screaming teenies and tell them that he had just received a message from God warning him against performing that night. Long before the Beatles withdrew to meditate with the Maharishi, Little Richard announced a retreat that soon became a movement. He enrolled at Oakwood College and studied theology. Eventually, he toured the South singing hymns and preaching a sermon titled, "Why I Left Show Business." Richard's recordings of spirituals did not sell like his rock tunes, and he ran out of capital before he could set up a functioning church. Therefore, in 1962, when the clamor for his appearance in Europe reached fantastic proportions, he succumbed to temptation and journeyed to Liverpool.

The English received him with hosannas, and he was favorably impressed by his warm-up band, a group of adoring boys called the Beatles. He established an apostolic succession by training Paul and John to sing in his celebrated high falsetto; then he took off with another unknown band of disciples called the Rolling Stones. His triumphal progress across the Continent was too good to end; so he continued it on to the Orient, winding up eventually in Australia. There again he got the call; but one of the boys in his band, Jimi Hendrix perhaps, doubted his sincerity. "I'll believe you about serving God when I see you take them diamonds off your fingers and throw them into this here river." Sparkling through the hard bright sky, the gems splashed in the water and Richard was wed again to his vocation.

Now he has decided on a full-scale show-biz comeback. As we sat in his hotel room, with its elegant Regency décor, he played over and over his latest record, "Baby Don't You Tear My Clothes" and "I Got What It Takes But It Breaks My Heart to Give It Away." The bounce and clangor of a sledge-driven spike come off the second side, Richard's black-butt piano accompanying a voice that *is* different from the old days but no less salty and authentic. The other tune, written by Eskew Reeder, opens with lime-tart country guitar, then moves on in the relaxed, stretch-and-snap rhythm of today's soul rock. Neither song registers quite the same impact as the famous records he made for Specialty of Hollywood in the Fifties. Now available again as *Little Richard's Seventeen Grooviest Hits*, these old songs constitute the single most valuable LP on the pop counters of the world.

Richard is just beginning to hit his stride again; there's no predicting how far his comeback will take him. I told him that the English fads might not be significant because they don and doff American styles like party masks; he answered that the build-up of sentiment over there for the "oldies" had been gradual but irresistible, as it was in this country, where the policy of the rock stations is now to mix the new with the old gold. Today's rock, he said, is out of touch with the kids, way over their heads. A whole generation has grown up whose music memories reach back no further than the Stones. These kids are dying for some "funky, low-down rock 'n' roll"; Richard is going to play pied piper with a run of tunes that will get "wilder and wilder."

Next time he works the *Tonight* show, he'll bring along his own rhythm—really "get down in the gut-bucket and git it." He has this new suit made entirely of mirrors. Shooting fractured lights in every direction, it makes him look like an ecstatic chandelier. He would have worn it the other night on television—but he couldn't find a pair of matching shoes.

The New York Times, 1968

She Makes Salvation Seem Erotic

ARETHA FRANKLIN

READING THROUGH a wad of recent clippings on Aretha Franklin, the new "Queen of Soul," I kept recalling an old Mel Brooks routine. The comedian, in the guise of Fabiola, the latest pop music sensation, is suffering himself to be interviewed by an eager but naïve Carl Reiner. Reiner is full of enthusiasm for the new star but perplexed by what he is doing. Fabiola takes a lunch-bucket view of his act. Hailed with journalistic hosannas—"You're dynamic! You're exciting! You're vibrant!"—the singer apathetically drawls, "I've heard that." Quizzed about the character of his music, he remains impassively silent while the interviewer exhausts himself running through a maze of categories: "It's not folk music, not rock 'n' roll, not progressive jazz, not swing—" At last with an imploring intonation Reiner gasps, "What is it?" Fabiola shifts his weight slightly, looks the reporter in the eye and replies with devastating matter-of-factness: "It's *dirty*, man."

Mel Brooks' confrontation between uptight reporter and low-down singer is re-enacted every time some journalist decides to do a piece about Aretha Franklin. Instead of concentrating on Miss Franklin's essence, her stated desire to be "deep and greasy," the critics become engrossed in tracing out her roots or sorting her style into bags marked "gospel," "blues," "jazz" and "pop." Admittedly, as an ambassador of soul, Miss Franklin bears impressive credentials: they are dated from Memphis, where she was born, and Detroit, where she grew up; they bear the seal of her father, C. L. Franklin, a well-known revivalist and gospel shouter; they are countersigned by famous Brothers and Sisters like Sam Cooke, Mahalia Jackson, Lou Rawls and Clara Ward, all of whom endorsed Aretha when she was still a girl soloist in her father's New Bethel Baptist Church.

But these ancestral influences, important as they may have been, do not define the source of Aretha Franklin's sudden and enormous success. That success is due to a quality which she discovered, or confirmed, in herself through years of professional experience. It is a quality that her audience recognized instantly and enthusiastically embraced. To put it in a word (borrowed from one of her big hits), it is the gift of being a "Natural Woman."

Establishing an identity through asserting the basic female emotions does not sound like a very original or interesting development for a pop singer—yet it is, in fact, almost without precedent in Aretha Franklin's tradition. None of the famous women of Negro song has epitomized the normal female soul or the free expression of the full range of feminine feeling. The old-timers like Bessie Smith or Ma Rainey (or Mahalia Jackson today) were massive matriarchs with the grand composure that accompanies that role. The glamorous ladies of later times, the Billie Holidays or Dinah Washingtons, loved, suffered and learned resignation before they opened their mouths. What they had to reveal was not so much an emotion as an attitude: the scar tissue of experience.

Even those female entertainers whose whole purpose seemed to lie in being alluring rarely dealt openly or comfortably with sexual emotions: there is a world of difference between Lena Horne hissing, "It's the wrong time and the wrong place" and Aretha Franklin shouting, "Reach out your arms, you're gonna get it!" The child of an age that believes in the basics, in getting down to the nitty-gritty and being "loose," Aretha Franklin embodies a whole new slant on life.

Aretha's woman may suffer, but her soul is whole and un-trammeled by depression or abuse. Delivering her feelings with astonishing power and ebullience, she releases every tightly creased irony of the blues and dispels the old stale atmosphere of patiently endured female sorrow. Lacking even a trace of self-consciousness, she cries out in ecstasy or anger, in bewilderment or terror, achieving the beauty of a perfectly realized emotion. Indeed, her naturalness is as much a matter of the spontaneity with which she lets fly every phrase as it is of the depth and solidity of her feelings. At another time, in another society, this complete freedom from emotional restraints might appear a dubious value. A Victorian would have called it hysteria. Today, it seems like a state of grace.

It seems fitting that the greatest of Aretha Franklin's re-cordings to date should be an erotic paraphrase of a tune that started life as a humorous expression of impotence. The original "I Can't Get No Satisfaction," by Mick Jagger of the Rolling Stones, was a wry, deadpan camp, a whispered confession that impressed many listeners as being a titillating put-on. A subsequent recording by Otis Redding straight-ened the tune out without freeing it from its uptight atmos-phere.

It took Aretha Franklin to make the song a jubilee: a finger-popping, hip-swinging Mardi Gras strut that is the greatest proclamation of sexual fulfillment since Molly Bloom's soliloquy. From the opening phrase, amusingly di-vided between a siren wail on the word "I" and a sudden plunge on "satisfaction"—a caricature of soul's basic pattern of tension and release—Aretha riffs and rocks and stomps behind, before and on top of the beat, until she and the band are lost in a jam session that might have gone on for hours after the final fade. (The four-minute cut-offs on her records are inexcusable in this day of LPs.) Short as the side is the distance it covers is enormous.

Although "Satisfaction" provides the finest vehicle yet found for Aretha's voice and temperament, her more characteristic number is something quite different: a slow, circling, incantatory blues set to an earthy sensuous rhythm. Stretching and swelling with anticipation, then suddenly letting go, this heavy, well-greased ball-and-sock-it beat underlies a clutch of hits, including "Respect," "Baby I Love You" and the recent "Chain of Fools."

As the pattern has evolved, the effect has grown more and more primitive, until in "Chain of Fools" the impression becomes that of a voodoo priestess concocting a love charm or mojo, while her sisters echo her chant and mimic her snaky motions in the hypnotic ceremony.

Aretha Franklin seems to be well on her way toward the goal of reuniting the sacred and profane sides of Negro music—long severed by the puritanical morality of the Southern church—at a level below the traditional division into gospel and blues. More than any other singer in the soul bag, she makes salvation seem erotic and the erotic seem like our salvation.

The New York Times, 1968

Gris-Gris Gumbo Ya-Ya

DOCTOR JOHN

ONCE, in Spanish Toledo, walking past an old church, I was accosted by a workman, cap aslouch, cigarette adroop, who asked me, with an inviting wave of his hand, if I wouldn't like to examine the interior of the building, which was closed for restoration. Reluctantly, I entered the musty vestibule, ran my eyes over some faded frescoes and unearthed paving with polite interest, thanked my guide and turned to leave when he took me confidingly by the arm and led me into the sacristy. Lighting a candle butt, he lifted a trap door and descended into the crypt, motioning for me to follow. A tiny rill of anxiety began to run across my midriff as I climbed down the precarious ladder into the stale, sweet air. Impatient to see where the man was leading me, I looked over my shoulder while descending and froze on the rungs. Looming forward out of the shadows was a grotesquely grinning company of skeletons. Alcaldes and abbots, caballeros and monsignors they were, the decaying shreds of their once-splendid robes hanging like dirty rags from their proud and fleshless ribs.

Fearful that even a single breath of that Pharaoh dust would carry some creeping disease into my lungs, I raised a leg to start crawling back up the ladder; but the grim tableau held me, and I remained suspended there for some minutes, breathing cautiously and staring intently, as the clownish workman scurried about like a jabbering huckster, testing the tooth of one cadaver, sounding another on the ribs or donning with an obscene gesture the biretta of some mummified prelate.

The same surrender to the sinister and the grotesque is fated for every listener who descends into the shadowy world of Dr. John, the Night Tripper. This record is a magic circle inscribed around one of the weirdest figures ever summoned up out of the ethnic ancestry of America. A "gris-gris" man, who slips up and down the jungle-like bayous of Louisiana, offering "medisaine to cure all yo'se ills," Dr. John is at once a witch doctor of a degenerate voodoo cult and a cunning swindler who makes his living out of the superstitious dreads and baffled dreams of his victims. The personification of Creole duality, of an acculturation that refuses to relinquish the primitive for the modern, but obstinately welds the two often incongruous elements together, Dr. John hunkers on the border between the civilized and the savage.

Wherever the Doctor finds his custom, he offers a bizarre medicine show. Commencing with the wails of a primitive cult instrument that sounds like a Haitian shofar, the performance broadens into an exotic symphony composed of little taps on skin drums, solemn crashes on oil drums, eerily sounding cane flutes and water-bug glissandos up the necks of gourd mandolins. As the Doctor langorously enumerates his prescriptions for the jealous ("controllin' hearts of get-together drops") and the overworked ("put a little of my boss-fix jam in yo' breakfast"), a trio of stoned snake girls chant, over and over, "gris-gris gumbo ya-ya." This creepy catalogue concludes with the Doctor lapsing into half-coherent mumbling, stupefied, evidently, by the sound of his own spells.

In another chant, "Walk on Gilded Splinters," he revives
to boast of his magical powers as a voodoo initiate: "I walk
through the fire; I dance through the smoke. See my ene-
mies at the end of the rope." Sometimes Dr. John will sing a
song about another character, as in "Mama Roux" (Queen
of the "Little Red, White and Blue," a Mardi Gras Indian
tribe), and in "Jump Sturdy" (a "terrible lady" who raised
electrical storms in the bayous). But always the theme is the
same: The hero of the tale possesses magical powers which
raise him above his rivals, and enable him to destroy his ene-
mies.

The atavistic energies of Dr. John's music coil about him
like an iridescent cult serpent. Yet once the listener grows
accustomed to this spectral ambience, he recognizes the
Doctor as a familiar figure. He is the comic hero of ghetto
folklore, the extravagant boaster, badman and lambaster of
language—the type of Stackolee and the Signifying Monkey. Speaking by preference elegant English ("malice"
rhyming with "chalice") or Haitian mumbo-jumbo ("corn
boonay killicon con"), he tumbles comically at times into
pure Pullman porter dialect ("some people think they jive
me"). Yet the words he employs, the crazy jambalaya of his
tongue, count for less than the fascinating *Sprechstimme* of
his musical delivery.

Rolling his tongue around the ominous hyperboles of his
spiel as if they were chocolate-covered cherries, the Doctor
offers an intriguing demonstration of the art of inflecting
words into music. Introducing himself with an impressive
vocal salaam ("They call me"—heavy pause—"Doctor
John, known as the Night Tripper"), he runs his voice up
the long "e's" of "greeee-greeez," like a boogalooing dancer
hitching his shoulders up to his ears. Boasting of his many
"clients," who "come from *miles* around," he bends the
"i" in a generous oral gesture of inclusion. The stretch-
and-snap pattern of the chant is varied further with staccato
stammers, insinuating glides, step-back fades and mumbled
phrases that sound like muttered curses. Sometimes he wails

out the name of an infamous witch doctor, like Tit Alberto, or takes a common word like *finé* and distends it into a primitive arwhoolie, "finney! finney!" At the end of "Walk on Gilded Splinters," he extends the atavistic thrust of his performance all the way down into the Ur-slime by mimicking the sounds of a jungle full of animal voices—chattering, snorting, shrieking and growling.

Perhaps the most extraordinary feature of this mysterious note from underground is its author's identity. No ancient black from the bayous, Dr. John is, in fact, the imaginary creation of a young, white studio musician currently working in California with lily-white pop singers like Sonny & Cher. Mack Rebenneck is his name; New Orleans is the city that shaped him, particularly its tightly closed society of black musicians. Slipping around the local prohibition against whites performing with blacks, Rebenneck became the disciple of "Perfesser" Longhair (last of the flamboyant rent-party piano virtuosos) and was initiated into the company of black soulmen. The final distillate of this experience was Dr. John, a character fashioned out of references in history books, and the still-surviving residue of New Orleans Creole-voodoo culture.

Like Arthur Brown, who works in blackface with two flaming horns sprouting from his head, the author of "Dr. John"—who works in Eskimo boots, fishnets, a snakeskin vest and Indian headband with a four-foot feather—seems intent upon reviving an entertainment form from the Thirties: the jungle show. Long banished from the stage because it was thought to present a defamatory racial image, this classic Cotton Club fantasia (once evoked by cunning Ellingtongues) may now revive to vie with the darktown struts and plantation sounds of the current soul scene.

Yet, one great difference separates today from the Thirties: In the age of slumming, ringside ogling of high-yaller witchcraft kindled, at most, a *frisson* of the forbidden, an illicit tingle. Today such funky field trips grow into an obsession with the occult that runs the gamut from Perfesser

Timothy Leary hawking LSD down the bayous of psyche-
delia to Yippie Abbie Hoffman trying to levitate the Penta-
gon. Neither of these practitioners, however, has succeeded
like Mack Rebenneck in combining black with magic. Perhaps his secret is his pedigree. When a musician asked him
recently where he was from, Dr. John mumbled an answer
that sounded like "Atlanta." "Atlanta, Georgia?" the musician asked. "No, man," drawled the droopy-eyed Doctor,
"not Atlanta—*Atlantis.*"

The New York Times, 1968

THE BLUES TODAY

SuperSpade Raises Atlantis

JIMI HENDRIX

LAST TIME I saw Jimi Hendrix onstage, he was playing SuperSpade. His Afro-Annie hairdo looked like it was plugged into his Sunn amp. His country duds—emerald pants, purple shirt, iridescent vest—were drawn from rainbow vats. His music—ominously circling, coiling and striking home—had the motions of a great black snake. Tossing his left-handed guitar over his shoulder, between his thighs or into fast hand spins, Hendrix came on like a flashy Western gun slinger. (Sammy Davis would have *kwelled.*) "Flash" was just the word he chose later to nail his own image: "a big flash of weaving and bobbing and groping and maiming and attacking."

Hendrix is camping as a musical mugger, but his sound identifies him as an artist—rock's most resourceful noise sculptor. Mixing fuzz and feedback at *fortissimo* levels, he rears massive acoustic constructions that loom threateningly over his audience. The sound is of a tactile solidity that makes you want to reach out and run your hand around the bend in a blue note. Some of his pieces remind you of totems of scabrous rusty iron; some move like farm machines run amok; some suggest shiny brass columns and spheres breached to reveal an interior textured like a toadstool.

Hendrix should have welded some unforgettable assemblages that night at the Fillmore East; but he didn't have his electric mojo working. Every time he'd start to fuse one sound with another, his tandem two-hundred-watt amplifiers would blow another sort of fuse. Dancing upstage to make a fast adjustment on the speaker face, then coming down again in a slow split, he got into a *pas de deux* (or was it a *paso doble?*) with his equipment. So graceful were these face-saving vamps, he almost persuaded you that all this fancy footwork was part of the act. "Jimi Hendrix, ladies and gentlemen, in *The Dance of the Dying Amp.*" Finally, he announced in a voice wry with exasperation that he couldn't last much longer. Anxiety gripped the huge house. What would happen, we all thought, if this colossal noise symphonist were left standing there with nothing but the feeble plink of an unamplified guitar? Fortunately, he quit while he was still audible, and we filed out past the mobs waiting to get in for the second show.

After the show aborted, I went home and put *The Jimi Hendrix Experience* on the turntable. Tough, abrasive, brutally iterative, the uptake suggested the ironshod tracks of a bulldozer straining against a mountain of dirt. Hendrix's program for the country blues was rural electrification. The end products were Futurist symphonies of industrial noise. I felt I was back home in Pittsburgh, walking along the old South Side with its clangorous sheet-metal plants, raucous open-hearth furnaces, whirring power stations and hissing yard engines. This new factory music brought the evolution of the blues full circle. Those famous laments had begun as labor pains: the field hand working alone in a Sahara of cotton would cry out to raise his spirits or purge his pain. When these hollers were joined to the chants of laborers and prisoners, the manacled rhythms of work were broken by wild cries of release. Now a New Negro from the North had revived the primitive form by shouting ecstatically above the blind roar of the machine. That shout was an industrial arwhoolie.

Hendrix had grown up in Seattle, and as he told me later, "there was all kinda soul there and Chinese, too." That was really the secret. He grew up in a time and place that knew nothing about the purity of tradition. Everything was mingling and mixing to produce new strains, new sounds, complex amalgams that meant many things. In the *Hendrix Experience* you could hear everything from country frailing* out of Nashville and dirty hollering from the Delta to the high-tension crackle of the Who and the surrealistic glossolalia of Bob Dylan. Yet some things were much better realized than others. Hendrix might make capital out of his image as SuperSpade, a mythical Black Man committing acts of violence before fascinated audiences of English and American teenies (his tour with the Monkees had to be terminated because the bookers were terrified of his debauching effect on the little ones). He could wink at the hipper soul brothers as he stood spotlighted between his hardworking rhythm section of pale English boys. (There's an inverted stereotype for you!) But Hendrix was the greatest living proof that today black is gray.

Apart from his lissome physical grace—a quality no white rock performer has ever displayed—Jimi Hendrix is essentially one with the white pop scene wherever it is most advanced, in London or Nashville or on the West Coast. Like the last generation of jazzmen, who transcended their Negro origins to become figures in the international music avant-garde, playing to almost exclusively white audiences, working with white sidemen, studying with white masters and consorting with white women, Hendrix's blackness is only skin deep. Nor is he simply American or English. Every time he starts to jam, he bends instinctively toward the East. His guitar becomes a sitar; his soundscape is enveloped in

* Frailing: [dialectal for "flailing"] primitive American guitar technique antedating the blues.

purple moire. Listening to track after track in the cushioned cool of my living room, I began to sink into a familiar trance. There was, I realized drowsily, a glittering psychedelic thread running through even the coarsest burlap spun by Hendrix's infernal mills.

Having stepped over the threshold of appreciation, I entered a new zone of awareness of Jimi Hendrix. I recognized belatedly that he was the only thing live and moving on the current rock scene. Judging from what I had seen and heard at the Fillmore, he was in that ardent phase of the creative cycle that transfigures a man and his work. Now was the time to get with Hendrix, to hear his story, to learn where he was going. I called his agent and she told me that I could see him at the Drake Hotel after he awoke (at 7 P.M.) and got his head together (round about midnight). At that hour the lobby of the Drake, all velvet panels and crystal sconces, with the antique furniture pushed to the walls, is practically deserted. Yet the music makers grind on in the hotel's sideshows. In the Drake Room, a brown leather retreat like the inside of a lady's handbag, Cy Walters is still driveling at the keyboard. In Shepheard's—El Cairo by Al Capp—young teams from the best colleges compete in a taut-muscled discathalon.

On the seventeenth floor, where Mr. Hendrix had his suite, the mood was Oriental pleasure dome. When I arrived, services were being held. Candles were burning in red glasses, incense was curling heavenward and mini-skirted cup-bearers were charging chalices with sparkling Lancer wine. Hendrix was flitting about like an emperor moth. Dressed in blue velvet bellbottoms, an open island shirt and no shoes, his famous fright wig at half-mast, he looked about half as big and as old as he did in his pictures. Far from being a cross between Genghis Khan and Anthony Quinn, Hendrix's offstage appearance is almost girlish. He's flirty, jivey, archly insinuating; he giggles, casts looks out of the corners of his eyes, and murmurs demure "Thank yous" after every compliment. Taxing questions he brushes aside with verbal shrugs: "I can't remember now"; "I don't know, man, it's really strange"; "I don't know too much about it." To familiar queries he responds with deft jabs. Question: What is the difference between the old blues and the new. Answer: Electricity. Question: What is your opinion of jazz? Answer: Jazz is "Blue Moon." Question: Did you receive an education in music? Answer: I tried to sign up for violin and harp, but they was always filled.

His family was not especially musical, though his father tapped and played the spoons. His first guitar he bought for $5 from a friend of his father's, sounding out the cat when he was drunk, and next day "walking all the way 'cross town to git it." (He's always walking " 'cross town" in his songs.) He tried to copy B.B. King, but he couldn't make the changes; so he started playing "honky-tonk." At the age of sixteen, he short-circuited his youth, enlisted in the army and began to haunt the servicemen's clubs looking for left-handed guitars (strung in reverse order). After doing fourteen months in the 101st Airborne, he landed in Nashville and there he learned his trade.

Joining a little group of "blues addicts," he played songs by Booker T. (Jones), Ted Taylor and Elmore James—all funky blues men. His little Silvertone amp with its two twelve-inch speakers was always feeding back; so he wove the noise into the texture of his music, and thus was born the blitzy sound that is today his hallmark. Moving around the soul circuit, he played behind many headliners and spent an unforgettable year with rock's greatest prima donna, Little Richard. Once he and another boy in the band bought fancy shirts; Richard reprimanded them severely, hissing: "I'm the King of rock 'n' roll. I'm the only one that's allowed to be pretty."

Eventually the trail led to Greenwich Village and the Cafe Wha?, where he met Chas Chandler, a veteran rock bass player who urged Hendrix to make his bid in England. Picking up his now famous sideman, Noel Redding (bass), and Mitch Mitchell (drums), at a try-out jam session in London, Hendrix broke through in a burst of notoriety, burning his guitar on the stage and making with the mayhem.

Having suffered the interviewer gladly for half an hour, Hendrix rose now to proffer enthusiastically a musician's finest hospitality: a taste of his new music. Settling me in a deep chair, he filled my glass, offered me a giant joint, clapped a pair of elephantine headphones on my ears and began to spin the tapes from which his next LP will be cut.

In the tight little world of the earphones, I heard thunderous sounds like salvos of howitzers. Hendrix leaned over and purred: "It's the gods making love." Then I began to cringe as the roar of a jet engine mounted in my ears—but something magical happened. The intimidating sound became an esthetic object; impulsively I thought, "How beautiful are our noises!" The tunes that followed spanned a wide spectrum of pop music. I recall a shouting, talking blues, backed with a heavy, raunchy beat; a long exotically instrumented jam session, reminiscent of Roland Kirk (a blind jazz musician who plays simultaneously three weird instruments—manzello, stritch and flexaphone—and blows a whistle worn on a string around his neck). There was even an Anglican Chinese—call it Chinese Chippendale—rock number that was designed as a send-up of the square-toed Handelian anthems affected by the British groups.

All these songs I recall as one does the other pictures in a gallery that houses a masterpiece. For near the end of our séance, Hendrix unwound a tape which even in the rough cast stood forth as one of the two or three extended compositions that justify our hopes for art rock. I'll call the piece "Atlantis" because it raised a sunken continent in my mind; yet I know that this rock "La Mer" must have been composed by Hendrix out of recollections of his youth spent in a seaport near the Pacific.*

"Atlantis" is an impressionistic evocation of the sea and all its sounds. Its dominant theme is one of those plangent psychedelic melodies that sing of sensuous surrender, of up-

* The piece was later released as "1983" in *Electric Ladyland*.

turned eyes and outspread limbs and head humming with cosmic vibrations. Around this unforgettable melody (played mellifluously on a backless guitar), Hendrix has composed a remarkable assemblage of oceanic motifs: lonely ship buoys (whose notes bend blue) are blended with exquisite wind chimes; throbbing ship motors become basso ostinatos for clusters of sonar pings. The sea collage is enriched with musical pastiche: a bolero rhythm shading into a military polonaise, a Krupa drum break dissolving into a flamenco bass solo. Toward the end, Hendrix sings in the entrancing voice of a siren, "Down and down and down and down and down and down we go"; and as he disappears into the vortex, the theme comes wailing up from the sea bottom. The final impression is of an empty sky pierced only by gull cries and the whine of a distant jet.

Hearing all these sounds under such conditions was an overwhelming experience. As I struggled to express my pleasure and admiration for his new music, one of Hendrix's female friends, who had been sketching him through the evening, turned to me and said firmly in words that sounded like a manifesto: "First we had a music that was all body; then we had a music that was all mind; now we have a music that is mind and body." Hendrix giggled and, flitting to the phonograph, dropped the needle on a record that almost blew me out of my seat. A brass chord, sustained, distended, thrusting into the room like the end of a girder, was snapped off savagely by a funky bass which in turn was transfixed by the most piercing, astringent, nerve-thrilling guitar sound I had ever heard. Instinctively, I looked up at Jimi Hendrix. He laughed and said, "No, man, that's not me. That's the guitar player I learned from. That's the King. That's right, Albert King." At 4 A.M., I just blinked. Man, I was zonked.

New York, 1968

Hey, Joe! Where You Goin' with That Gun in Your Hand? I'm Goin' Down to the Laundromat to Shoot My Old Lady

ALBERT KING

Country-blues singers had been mainly, though not exclusively, male, and their art had grown from the ritual of work. Those men who raised blues-singing to professional status tended to be social outcasts, whether through temperamental malaise like Robert Johnson, or through physical affliction (usually blindness), like Blind Lemon Jefferson. They had no home, but wandered from city to city, seeking a livelihood from song. The [blues-singing] city dwellers . . . were, however, for the most part, female. This was because the band-trained, town-dwelling male Negro had learned to speak through his "horn": but also because the deep resonance of the female Negro voice came to represent the mother-image which semed so significant to the rootless inhabitants of the big cities.

Wilfrid Mellers
Music in a New Found Land

Looking at Albert King, the new boss of rhythm 'n' blues, you don't see a lonely, wasted, low-living cat, who's spent his life drifting from town to town with some raggedy woman in tow. King looks like the owner of the local Carvel franchise. A big, prosperous man of forty-five (6-foot-4, 250 pounds—his mother weighed 210), with heavy jowls and double chin, he dresses in tailor-made maroon mohair suits, with diamond solitaires in his pinky rings, an inch-wide diamond stick pin in his tie and a shiny gold tooth in his grin. A country bluesman of the space age, he does his roaming (from a suburban house in Love Joy, Illinois) in a Fleetwood Cadillac and his "gitar" picking on a specially rigged Gibson "Flying V," built like a jet.

Down in Memphis, at Stax-Volt Records (Motown with dirt in the line), they'll tell you that "plain Albert" is "psychedelic," pointing out all the imitations of his lime-tart guitar sound in recent recordings by the Cream, the Butterfield Blues Band and the Jefferson Airplane. They must be right because out on the West Coast—where safaris of brown-skinned teenagers undulate to the beach every morning bearing surfboards on their heads—the little shoreside bars at Venice, Santa Monica and Malibu ring all night long with that same piercing, quivering, Assagai sound. Still an "underground hit," King's day is fast dawning west to east.

Unlike the popularity that has come late in life to a number of other old-time bluesmen, Albert King's success has not been gained by standing still while the rest of the world turns. Convinced of the eternal timeliness of the blues, determined to save the music's soul, he has labored nonetheless to connect the old blues with the new. Heating and drawing the metals of these different musics, he has forged a formidable link between rural past and urban present. Unlike a Lightnin' Hopkins or a Howlin' Wolf, King drops a little acid on his guitar strings; yet he does not, like Jimi Hendrix, blow the mind of the blues. Preserving the old song, story and ritual, he revitalizes these traditional elements with the powerful new rhythms and sonorities developed for today's soul music. The final product is doubly authentic. It is also a very high concentrate of "nasty."

King's art celebrates the contemporary marriage of the primitive with the futuristic. Derived from the ancient practice of the Mississippi Delta, boasting dirt-gripping roots that reach down into the soul of the Negro, King's music is equally impressive as a highly successful realization of the bizarre esthetic of pop America. Its vast forms, of monumental simplicity and monochromatic insistence, parallel the compositions of the minimal structuralists. Its excruciating intensity of effect, a constant goading, jabbing and needling of the listener's nerve centers, is a triumphant assertion of the art of pain, so feebly exemplified by the so-called "theater of cruelty."

King's transmutation of country blues into city surrealism was accomplished through a drastic discipline of abstraction. While still a boy twanging a wire stretched from the barnyard fence, King formed a mental image of a sound that would be the quintessence of all the whining, howling, wailing voices of the Mississippi bottleneck guitar. He crossed this virulent strain of blues with the sighing, dying fall of the Hawaiian steel guitar, and then electrified the combination, like Dr. Frankenstein plugging in his monster.

The resulting sound is a blue note of such intoxicating power that just one whiff of it is enough to make a man break a bottle and start cutting his neighbor's face. Instead of bending or warping a note here and there for special effect, King skirls *every* note, sending vicious waves along his strings like the ripples on a cobra's back. Every passage couched in this blue rhetoric concludes with a "soul" note, a sound so cunningly aimed and so cruelly struck that it pierces the listener's brain like a silver nail.

Like all great blues shouters, "plain Albert" is not without his glamor as a person. His fascination lies in the archetypal character of his life and experiences. Born in 1923 in the heart of the Delta at Indianola, Mississippi, he is the son of an itinerant preacher who left the family when the boy was five. Reared on his mother's farm at Forest City, Arkansas, he never knew his father. But like a character in a Faulkner novel, he was being prepared by destiny for a stunning recognition scene. When he was about thirty, he paid a visit to his famous friend B.B. King, boss bluesman of Chicago's South Side at the latter's home in West Memphis, Arkansas. Sitting at the dinner table, he found himself being questioned closely by B.B.'s mother, Ada. The woman kept pressing him for details of his birthplace, age and parents. Finally, she gave him a strange look and said: "You know something? You is B.B.'s brother. You see that man up there at the head of the table? That's your pappy." King still tells the story in tones of awe.

Like most Negro musicians, Albert King taught himself to play. Never dreaming of becoming a musician, he worked for years on giant motor vehicles, moving from the high seat of a bulldozer to the cab of a trailer truck to a garage where he "went to doin' mechanic work." On weekends he played an "old holler box" with a group he called the "In the Groove Band." Only at thirty-three did he go all the way into the music groove.

In those years blues business was bad business. Country people were so poor that they expected the world for their dimes and quarters. Playing sometimes from sundown to sunup, King would sit up on the stand and watch the crowds as they ate Bar B-Q, drank beer, danced in the dirt, got drunk, fell asleep, woke up and did it all over again. Assuming the promoter didn't make off with the cigar box full of change, the bluesman would end up with four or five dollars and a long ride home. Sometimes he had to borrow money for gas. Almost as bad was the abuse he took from those country crowds, the men calling him nasty names and the women putting him on to his face. Those women were dangerous customers. You had to play along with them or they would get angry and call you "hincty" (uppity). Yet you couldn't get too tight with them because some man—with plenty of liquor in him—would be standing back in the shadows catching the whole act. "You had to know," as King says, "where to get on and get off."

One night in East Chicago, a woman came up to the bandstand and started cursing King as the cause of all her troubles. Her husband had been listening to the singer's "Laundromat Blues" (Early every mornin', you grab your old blouse or two, and you go right down to the laundry where your man is waitin' on you."). Catching the woman "doing her dirt" behind the laundromat, the husband had given her a terrible "whuppin'." Now she wanted to hear the song that had been her undoing. Pulling a snub-nosed .38 out of her purse, she commanded King to play. He just sat there and sang the blues.

King's first efforts at recording were not successful; mixing up a big batch of blues for Bobbin Records in St. Louis in 1956, he dished out a stack of forgotten originals with titles like, "Let's Have a Natural Ball," "I Get Evil," "I've Made Nights by Myself," "Don't Throw Your Love on Me So Strong" and a catchy little sequel to "Last Night" called "This Morning." It was not until the mid-Sixties, when he signed with the Stax-Volt organization, that Albert King got the lift he needed to move out of the country tonks and into the psychedelic barrel houses.

What the writers and arrangers at Memphis did for King was primarily a packaging job. Aiming squarely at the youth market, black and white, Booker T. (Jones) and the M.G.'s (Stax's house band) laid on the new beats and sounds while King hollered in his hoarse plaintive voice and etched in the guitar fills. The result sounds like the last word in racial integrity, a true country sound undefiled by commercialism. The funky effect is actually the product of some very re-

Love Lucy," which is now up on the charts. Apart from its
powerful instrumental introduction—as deeply arousing as
anything on Aretha Franklin's albums—the song seems at
first listening not much better than the novelty numbers
that once were ground out by the white Tin Pan Alley: a
love song about a girl who turns out to be a guitar. But
listening more reflectively to King's paean to Lucy, who
"made me a star," you begin to penetrate his real secret.
Instead of using the instrument in the traditional manner as
an extension or echo of his own voice, solid, husky, plaintive
—really undistinguished—King throws into his guitar another voice, utterly unlike his own, a voice that is needling,
excoriating, shrill—the voice of a woman. And what a
woman that Lucy is! Her cry is as strident and wounding as
the scream of a Puerto Rican street whore. No wonder King
kept their relationship secret for so many years. It's really a
scandal. Here's this big, genial, hardworking man in love
with this jivey, bitchy, evil chick. You can almost see her
standing there, hands on hips, head awry, nose wrinkled up,
scolding, cursing and frying good brother King's glad fat.
But she can't put his nose out of joint. He looks at her with
love eyes, nodding, laughing, sometimes whooping with delight when Lucy has a great line. Ah, that "plain Albert"
. . . is he really a Tony Perkins schiz? or is he history's first
blues ventriloquist, a man who has gathered into the embrace
of his art both the male and female strains of blues tradition?

When Albert King takes his stand soon at the Scene and
then at the Fillmore East, he will comport himself like a
king. The monarch of the blues, he is accustomed to treating
his audiences and his entourage with regal authority. One
night this past summer at Memphis, I sat in his dressing
room behind the bandstand, at the Club Paradise (a nightclub, formerly a bowling alley, where as many as 4,000 black
patrons drink gin straight—or qualified with Coke—out of
bottles imbedded in paper buckets filled with ice cubes) and
watched him invest himself with his working robes. The
ambiance was less that of the levee than of the *levee*. As he

donned a purple pin-stripe mod suit and a clutch of diamonds, he received petitioners and well-wishers, exchanged volleys of jesting proverbs ("He'll cut you quicker than a country man pick a banjo." "I'll hold him tighter than a hip pocket on a teenage girl"), and slapped the palms or pants seats of a succession of skinny, stringy, rusty-jointed old jackanapes. When an ancient minstrel, now a disc jockey, came in to complain with popping eyes that Memphis, the home of the blues, could not afford fifteen minutes of blues in a whole day of broadcasting, the King surveyed him *de haut en bas,* and then launched into a tirade, the gist of which was that he, Albert King, could not be concerned with what transpired in the piddling little country town of Memphis, Tennessee, because he was now a lord of the road, roaring across America in an orchid-colored Cadillac, whose lofty, swaying aerial pulled in blue notes from hundreds of miles away—even the fabulous coyote howls of the Wolf Man from distant Los Angeles. It was an epic retort and it was delivered in stentorian tones, like Achilles shouting down the walls of Troy.

New York, 1968, and *The New York Times,* 1968

You Never Did Hear No Blues About Whitey

B.B. KING

CRUNCHING ONTO the tarmac of the Lorraine Motel in Memphis, I began to feel like Whitey the Intruder. Evidently, the feeling was shared by a few other people. As I crawled out of a local musician's car, all the black family groups stood there silently, their coat hangers in their hands, giving me those big small-town stares. My friend Don Porter, the songwriter, helped ease matters by pumping the hand of the motel owner (who asked the newcomer what he was "carryin'" and then hit him for five). Still, the place was a setup for self-consciousness. Up there on the gallery, behind the door embossed with the big purple Easter cross, was the shrine of the latest black martyr. Down here in the yard were his people, alive and angry. The burnt and boarded vestiges of their rage were strewn all across town. Times were bad, said every white man you met. They would get worse, echoed the Negro. In Memphis, everybody was cryin' the blues.

The man I had come to see was Memphis' most famous

blues singer, B.B. (Beale Street Blues Boy) King. Rarely a visitor to his own home town, King had flown in the night before to do a benefit with his half-brother, Albert, for the Southern Christian Leadership Conference. As the motel owner unlocked the door and steered me into the room, my feeling of intrusiveness rose in a cresendo of embarrassment. Stepping over the ruins of a half-eaten meal and skirting a suitcase that had spilt its contents across the floor, I stared down at the famous blues-man, big, black, bleary-eyed, lying naked beneath the sheet. He raised his curiously old-fashioned head off the pillow, smiled vaguely and mumbled some words of welcome.

As I began to explain my visit, the door opened again and in sauntered Albert King, his massive chest exposed through a wide-open red shirt, his head covered with a neatly knotted process rag. Smoking a pipe and surveying the room with a proprietorial air, Albert walked over to the TV, which was rolling up its pictures like a baby-doll's eyes, and after fiddling with the knobs for a moment, gave the set a thunderous rap and then strolled out, a diamond solitaire flashing from his undershirt.

B.B. King, meanwhile, had gotten his head together and motioned me to sit down and listen to his words. As it turned out, he likes to talk with journalists and prides himself on his ability to tell his story in correct English, pausing only occasionally to "call it." As I discovered later, he tells every reporter the same story in substantially the same words. (Any writer who wants to fake an interview can get a neatly typed transcript of the whole narrative simply by writing to the publicity department of ABC-Paramount.)

Actually, B.B.'s story is a pretty good yarn, picked out with threads that are both sad and gay, woven in and out of the buckram of Mississippi rural life. Deserted by his father at an early age, he grew up on a plantation working for the whites, chopping and picking cotton for 75 cents a day. He first heard an electric guitar in a "sanctified" church: "I loved it so, I asked my boss if he would get me a guitar and take it out of my wages. I'll never forget that red guitar with a round hole in it." Picking up the three blues chords by watching the preacher, he managed to teach himself to play. When World War II reached the South, he was inducted into the army, but the plantation owners controlled the local draft boards in Mississippi: "So after I did my basic training, they brought me back to the farm to drive a tractor. I wasn't allowed to leave that plantation until after the war was over. Sometimes I wish they had let me serve, because then I would have been able to study music."

Weekends, he used to sneak off the plantation, take the train to the nearest little town and stand on street corners playing for nickels and dimes. When the war ended, he slipped his shackles and journeyed up to Memphis, where he got two jobs: one playing for ladies in the front room of a gambling hall (while the men went for broke in the back); the other on a radio medicine show, plugging an alcoholic tonic called Pepticon.

Memphis marked the turning point in his career. Up until then he knew nothing but Delta Blues. He had watched his cousin, Bukka White, put a steel bar on his finger and get that cruel, hard bottleneck sound. He had slipped into a country tonk to hear Sonny Boy Williamson holler his mean dirty blues. Now at "Headquarters," he began to taste music from other parts of the country, especially the new "clean blues" from the "Territories" (Texas and Oklahoma). Down in the Southwest a fresh generation of bluesmen were working to slick down the blues and make them presentable to modern city audiences. Focusing the old twang and fuzz into clear, smooth tones and modifying the traditional delivery in the direction of lightness and relaxation, they were pushing blues in the direction of the pop ballad, creating a new form called the "blues ballad."

The basic impulse behind the "clean blues" was the altered attitude of the Negro in postwar America. In those days the cry of the ghetto was, "Are you ready?," a phrase that encapsulated the mixture of ambition and anxiety aroused in the Negro by the prospect of going out and competing with Mr. Charley. The new Negro was eager to shuck the last vestiges of his rustic past; he had no use for country blues or city blues or urban blues. All those old black sounds smelled of slavery. What he wanted was a sophisticated modern style that would be cool and confident and full of throw-away lines. That longing was to be fulfilled, as the Forties turned into the Fifties, by the onetime "Pepticon Boy," known later by his hipster hieroglyph, "B.B."

Becoming a black star in a black sky, King never had a reputation outside the ghetto until recently; but the black masses bought his records and attended his concerts at Chicago's Regal Theater in unprecedented numbers. Musically undistinguished, stylistically diluted, his songs packed their punches not in blue notes but in verbal imprecations. He developed a formula—maybe it was an obsession. All his good songs are written in the accusative, all of them voice the indignation of the honest man against the cheating woman. Invariably they come to their climaxes in stinging waves of anger that break with King shouting a line like, "I gave you seven children and now you want to give them back." Twanging on the raw nerves of sexual rage and guilt, King delivers a series of blue shocks to his audience, shocks of appalled recognition that set them screaming in their seats.

His old theatrical performance is available on a record titled *B.B. King Live at the Regal.* You hear a clench-throated singer—like Jim Ameche in blackface—working in front of a sloppy jump band that plays old-fashioned arrangements with boogie basses and bouncy traveling beats. As this pack of winded jazz hounds runs through its routine of excitement, the star empties his bag of show tricks: one moment he screams in falsetto; the next he pauses to preach a sermonette. Playing shrilly on his guitar, he goes into his medley of big hits, coyly introducing each number: "Perhaps some of you may remember—*It's four o'clock in the morning baby!*—thank you, thank you." The greatest talent evinced by the record is not for music but for salesmanship. When hip B.B. has to put a song across, he goes right back to being the "Pepticon Boy."

Today, B.B. King is out of the black vaudeville houses and into the white rock big time. Ever since his triumphant appearance at the 1967 Monterey Jazz Festival, he has been stoning the Generation, who regard him as the boss of the real, funky, low-down dirty blues. The experience has revitalized B.B. King as one can see from the hugely successful *Alive and Well*, especially the great "Why I Sing the Blues."

To answer the key question of his life, B.B. assumes the role of the Universal Nigger, witness and victim of the entire tragedy of black life in America. Ranging like another Juvenal in another Rome from slave ship to ghetto tenement, from slum school to welfare office, he builds relentlessly his indictment of a society that denies food to the poor, education to the ignorant and charity to the blind. This woeful spectacle he surveys not as a preacher or a politician but as a *bluesman* with an instinct for the life born from suffering, the pride wrung from humiliation. Passing from grim humor to heart-bracing indignation, he rises finally on a bass that rolls like destiny to a furious exultancy in suffering that is almost joy. "I just *love* to sing my blues," he shouts—and you know that B.B. King has found the answer to his question, an answer as honest, as paradoxical and profound as the life and art he celebrates.

In His Own Dream

PAUL BUTTERFIELD

"**I** MUST HAVE been in a fantasy," mused Paul Butterfield, as he laid a half-eaten sandwich on Albert Grossman's polished marble table. Looking very different from the Tennessee Williams Silenus he is onstage, Butterfield gazes at you limply with small, wide-spaced eyes set in a soft, pale face shaded by heavy hair combed back straight with just a suggestion of an old-fashioned center part. It's the classic face of the apple-cheeked Midwestern boy turned sallow and sleepy by late hours and the life of the road. At five in the afternoon, Paul is just getting himself together, complaining about his leaking sinuses and the problems of having no home but a band bus. When the questions begin to bend him back to his early years, he turns his head, as if to get a better view of that far-off time, and repeating dreamily, "I must have been in a fantasy," he tells his story in the softly falling phrases of the blues.

Growing up in Hyde Park, the University of Chicago's stockade on the edge of the Black Belt, Paul led a quietly schizzy life. By day he was a nice Catholic boy who wore white shirts, practiced the flute and sang in the church choir. By night he was an urban Tom Sawyer, slipping over the back fence to explore some of the raunchiest bars in the ghetto. It was not black women or white pills he was seeking but blues, the music that is now the obsession of a whole generation of city and suburban kids. These are the lads who would like to step through an album cover and come out the other side as ancient blacks from the Delta. For reasons best known to themselves (and their group therapists), they want to be magical minstrels with white on their skins and black on their souls. Paul Butterfield is their hero, but he doesn't share their fantasy. Paul never wanted to be black— just blue. "I never thought about Negroes' lives," he recalls. "I just thought about the feeling they made me feel."

That blue feeling was as familiar to Paul as his bedside radio. Just by turning the knobs, he could tune in all the basic blues frequencies; for even as late as the Fifties, Chicago was still the northern terminus of the Underground Railroad. From the Brazos Bottoms of Texas, the Cajun country of Louisiana and the sharecroppers' shacks of Alabama, the bluesmen came, following the Mississippi north through the Delta to West Memphis, where they worked the tonk strip until they were ready to start on the second leg of their journey through East St. Louis, Kansas City and Indianapolis to the streets of Chicago's South Side. Here some of them earned a scratch living in neon-smeared blues bars; some froze to death in the streets. None of them could live for long in the city without changing his tune: the lonely, timeless hollers of the country being too easily drowned out in the uproar of the metropolis.

The metamorphosis of the relaxed country blues into the aggressive, hard-driving urban blues was accomplished in Chicago. This was the city where Jimmy Yancey and Meade Lux Lewis drove the barrel-house boogie-woogie to the limits of percussive frenzy; where Muddy Waters "went to puttin' time [a heavy, slogging rhythm section] to lowdown Mississippi blues"; and where Little Walter took up his harmonica in one hand, cupped a microphone in the other and blew his soul into them, transforming the delicate, melancholic "harp" into an excoriating Pan pipe wailing an electric goat song.

There were legendary bluesmen in Chicago when Paul Butterfield was growing up, but it took him a while to realize that they were only a streetcar ride away. When he got the address straight, he didn't hesitate to make his move. With an emotion like awe, he remembers the first night he walked into Smitty's Corner, on Thirty-ninth and Indiana, to hear the great Muddy Waters. No white man had ever had the nerve to go in that place, unless it were in the line of duty. Paul walked in bearing his passport on his face. It took a while for Muddy Waters and Howlin' Wolf and Magic Sam and Little Walter to get used to this white kid hanging around; but once they realized how sincere he was, coming back night after night with his Hohner harmonica in his pocket, they displayed the unaffected generosity that Negroes often show white men who are genuinely dedicated to the black arts. They taught the boy blues in the traditional way it has been taught to generation after generation of black kids—the way Blind Lemon Jefferson taught Lightnin' Hopkins or Charlie Patton taught Roebuck Staple—not by demonstrating or explaining, but by letting the boy sit with them, hip by haunch, listening and imitating, feeling his way into the body heat of the older men.

Not surprisingly, Paul Butterfield turned out to be the one white musician of his generation who could really play the blues. Unlike his less assured contemporaries, who betray their ignorance or insensibility by playing too much and too fast, who riddle off a dozen clichés in as many bars and disclose to a discerning ear a dubious sense of time, Butterfield has had always a true sense of the real thing, even when he was too young or too inexperienced to bring it off like the masters. When he put together his own band (a white group with a black rhythm section) and cut his first LPs, he showed rare good taste in his selection of traditional material and even rarer modesty in his simple, unpretentious phrasing and restrained singing.

Lacking a traditional blues voice, one of those voices that are as tough and gnarled as an old tree on a windy hill, Paul hollered through his harmonica, tagging himself with his first phrases as the man to watch. Now the whole country is watching him, and his decision to ripen naturally has paid off. A couple of weeks ago, at that sweet-cider barrelhouse, the Café au Go Go, Butterfield touched an audience of blues devotees with a voice that is now yearning and doleful, pleading, "Baby, baby, baby," with a tender urgency that very few of our female singers can muster. Stronger too is his harp, shivering and shaking in a slow drag or cresting triumphantly on the roller-coaster ride of an up-tempo jam.

Like Jimi Hendrix, whose palimpsest of factory noises, surf mysticism and King's Row geariness has refreshed and enriched the blues, Butterfield is seeking a contemporary fusion of highly colored sounds. His blues collage is pasted together out of black New York jazz of the early Sixties, blue Memphis soul of the late Sixties, and moire-screen orientalisms from Frisco '67. The base remains unmistakably blues: "I'll always be playing the blues," Butterfield promises, "because that's what I hear in my head."

The new Butterfield Blues Band is suffused with casual joy. They loaf all over the stage like a bunch of Okies at the general store. Butterfield, a recessed soloist no more, leads them powerfully with his own singing and playing and with his physical presence, swaying before the drummer, doing a haunchy strut during a rhythmic solo or jiving with a musician who is struggling to get into a new bag. At the climactic moments, the band—rocking with the ebullience and confidence of youth at the throttle—bounces its chords off the ceiling and up from the floor with a ringing peal that recalls the great Kansas City blues bands of twenty years ago.

A permissive presence who never plans a set and gives the "go" sign to any man who feels like taking a solo excursion,

Paul Butterfield runs one real risk as a leader: that of allowing his band's powerful centrifugal energies to overwhelm the centripetal. The real beauty of a blues band arises from the fact that it is a *band* and not just a revolving stage from which a series of performers can deliver Pirandello monologues. What is worse, most of Butterfield's players—unlike their leader—have an irresistible urge to swim out beyond their depth. Several of them—notably Buzzy Feiten, a girlishly beautiful nineteen-year-old guitarist, and Gene Dinwiddie, a mature tenor man who wields his axe and wears his hat like an old-time jazzbo—are proficient blues soloists; but when they attempt the highly sophisticated jazz styles developed in this city by Ornette Coleman and John Coltrane, they reveal an immaturity and, one might as well say, *chutzpah*, that is hard for an experienced listener to take. (Jazz fans will reflect bitterly on the fact that when the masters of these styles were at the height of their powers, their collegiate audiences were so intimidated by black power that they drifted away, allowing the musicians to fade into oblivion or die in poverty; but now when this same vein is worked crudely by a predominantly white blues band, the boys and girls applaud and cheer.) Blues leads to jazz, most naturally into the kind of jump-band jamming at which Paul Butterfield or Albert King excel; and even the most surrealistic jazz sustains affinities with basic blues—a fact demonstrated dramatically six years ago when Ornette Coleman jammed with a Harlem rhythm and blues band at Town Hall; but today blues and jazz are two different games, and the men who can play one to perfection may sound when they try the other like amateurs.

A more promising use of the Butterfield Band's resources on behalf of the blues is suggested by the richly atmospheric "Last Hope's Gone," a blues fantasia reminiscent of both "jungle music" and *Pierrot Lunaire*. The dusky, sinuous opening, with its swaying bass and low gong-like piano chords, leads into a dirge for horns that recalls Ornette Coleman's "Lonely Woman." There are the same hard dissonant voices, the same broken blue notes, cutting like shards of splintered glass; but all these sounds are used to frame a free-form blues which Butterfield sings in anguished vocal patterns that rise and fall, clench and let go, like the silhouette of a black woman sobbing behind a window blind. Though the arty lyrics sometimes spoil the effect, the composition as a whole vindicates the band's adoption of the avant-garde jazz idiom—*not* as the new language of the blues but as a clamorously tragic antiphon.

Ten years ago when Paul Butterfield was floating lonely as a cloud across Chicago's black ghetto, the Generation was huddled around jukeboxes digging Fabian and Frankie Avalon and rocking maniacally in white ducks and bucks. Today, the Generation, clad in sad rags, shuffles off to sit in some old coal cellar and soak its soul in bad-mouth, bad-luck, bad-time blues. The contagion of Butterfield's dream has spread, but America's foremost Blue Boy has refused to surrender to the big sleep of fame. Packing his bags with sounds from all over America, herding his boys into their beat-up buses, Hyde Park Paul goes out to blaze a new trail through the still fecund wilderness of the blues.

New York, 1968

Why Do Whites Sing Black?

LONG, LONG AGO, when America was still a land of brutal innocence, there stood upon the banks of the Mississippi a city of carnal delight. Bearing an Egyptian name and luxuriating in Nilotic heat, Memphis was a country boy's Cairo. Every Saturday night, plow jockeys and parlor belles, mule skinners and factory frills poured into the city, making its streets roil with the tumultuous human tides of a Mardi Gras. Swarming along that famous midway, Beale Avenue, white and black, rich and poor, were beckoned on by dozens of gingerbread palaces and clapboard cribs. Whether the visitor craved a lavish sporting house boasting twenty Creoles from New Orleans or a plain hog-nosed restaurant, a gambling hell crowded with fancy men playing cooncan rummy or a cheap stag poolroom, he was sure to find it along the ten bawdy blocks of Black America's Main Street.

No less proverbial than the pleasures of Beale were its plangent sounds. The jumbling of electric pianos with wind-up Victrolas, of shouting congregations with howling bluesmen, of strolling guitar pickers with scrounging jug bands, constituted the South's most celebrated symphony. Rising in a dense, pungent cloud over Memphis, these sounds of a jubilant humanity soared high into the ionosphere, lingering there for decades, while the Avenue below crumbled into silence. Then, just when the last saloon had been boarded over, the last theater darkened, the once-flamboyant population reduced to a single survivor—"the Cat on Beale" (an ancient pimp in porkpie hat, balloon pants and toothpick shoes still seen occasionally limping along the desolate street, lined now with shabby pawnshops crammed with discarded horns and fiddles)—that invisible cloud began to descend, pulled back to earth by electronic magic and by this generation's longing for the good-time years. Spun out of the grooves of a hundred million records and spread across the country by a hundred million speakers, the Memphis Soul Sound enfolds the nation now like an evangelical tent, rocking with hymns to the newly proclaimed brotherhood of black man and white man in modern America.

The roots of soul music—a fusion of gospel, blues and jazz—are black, but its most extensive audience is white. "Audience" is not really the right word to suggest the relation of the white public, particularly the youth, to this music. The word implies a passive spectator relationship; whereas, in fact, no music public in history has ever made a style so completely a part of its life. The kids who were once content merely to listen and dance to the sounds of Ray Charles and Little Richard have moved on to adopt a whole new identity of black gesture and language—of black shouts and black lips, black steps and black hips. When they are not holed up in their rooms soaking their souls in blues, they are jammed into a rock theater, sitting hip by haunch, clapping, stomping and shouting like the congregation of a storefront church. Or they are wriggling and writhing in a stroboscopic snake pit, doing barrel-house rent party steps that were first cut half a century ago.

There is something providential about the occurrence of this musical miscegenation just at the moment when the races seem most dangerously sundered. Driven apart in every other area of national life by goads of hate and fear, black and white are attaining within the hot embrace of soul music a harmony never dreamed of in earlier days. Yet one wonders if this identification is more than skin deep. What are the kids doing? Are they trying to pass? Are they color blind? Do they expect to attain a state of black grace? Let's put it bluntly: how can a pampered, milk-faced, middle-class kid who has never had a hole in his shoe sing the blues that belong to some beat-up old black who lived his life in poverty and misery?

Recently, I popped these questions to Janis Joplin, this generation's campy little Sophie Tucker, born and reared on the right side of the tracks at Port Arthur, Texas. An auburn-haired Whitey who belts the blues like some big fat mama throwing her meat in a gilly show, Janis is this generation's favorite culture creole. "Why do you work in vocal black face?" I asked. Her answer surprised me by its frankness and self-awareness. She conceded that her style was derived from Bessie Smith, Big Mae Bell, Mama Mae Thornton and Mavis Staple. It all went back to her youth when she imitated Bessie Smith records at parties. She discovered then that when she put on her black voice (as opposed to her choir voice or her white pop voice), she experienced a thrilling sense of release. Convinced that anything that felt so good couldn't be bad, she went on to develop her own music working behind this protective façade. Today, she says, she sounds less black than she did at first because she is beginning to discover her own identity. In any case, she concludes, "being black for a while will make me a better white."

As I pondered her answer, it struck me that she had articulated this generation's great secret. They are *not* trying to pass. They are trying to save their souls. Adopting as a tentative identity the firmly set, powerfully expressive mask of the black man, the confused, conflicted and frequently self-doubting and self-loathing offspring of Mr. and Mrs. America are released into an emotional and spiritual freedom denied them by their own inherited culture. Now that they have sprung the locks clamped on the youth of previous generations, anything may happen—which is why everyone is so uptight about the youth, showering them with unmerited praise and blame. What is most likely to happen, however, is just what Mama Joplin prophesies: the white kids will swing back into their own tradition, fortified and enlightened by the adventure of transvestism. Already some of our leading culture chameleons are casting their black skins, and while their brethren labor along in the Delta mud, these quick-change artists are turning out in startling new shades of white. Super-Whitey No. 1 is Stevie Winwood, formerly the lead in Blind Faith, now the boss of Traffic.

When Stevie Winwood became famous some years ago, working with the Spencer Davis blues band, his vocal style was black on black. A fey little pixie, who looks as if he was reared under a mushroom in the Midlands, Stevie was a racial changeling. Night and day he sat in his dank basement apartment listening to his black and blue records, pretending that he was Ray Charles crying in an illiterate voice out of the heart of darkness. When he got the chance to cut "I'm a Man," "Can't Get Enough of It," and "Gimme Some Lovin'," he piled every black sound he loved on each tiny 45. Combining the lurid organ of the Harlem show bar with the clanking cowbell of the Afro-Cuban band, he threw in the slogging, wet-skin drums of Motown and the gospel's chorus of hypnotic Amen girls, capping the whole mix with his own shouts and hollers, delivered around a plug of soggy, juicy Mail Pouch. Attaining a deeper shade of black than any dyed by Negro hands, Stevie Winwood became the Pied Piper of Soul.

Then he began to undergo a metamorphosis not to be found in Ovid. Recording with his own band, Traffic, he produced astonishing records, like "Shanghai Noodle Factory," spotlighting a voice that was high, keen, clean and out of its mind. Picking up steam from his years under the cork,

Stevie had obviously developed the confidence and freedom of soul that allowed him to go soaring off into a new style that owed nothing, save intensity, to black tradition. On his recent records with Blind Faith, he has worked that high, white wail around to a weird warlock sound that sends the listener's mind tripping off the paths of space and time to fasten on remote targets like Marrakesh. The moral would appear to be that once a man has slipped his original moorings, he can go where he pleases and be what he pleases to the uttermost limits of the human imagination.

The New York Times, 1969

NOSTALGIA

And He Keeps His Ukelele in a Shopping Bag

TINY TIM

Tiny Tim is a lost lithograph by Toulouse-Lautrec. Blowing kisses like a flustered diva to the rowdy, laughing crowd at a midtown discothèque, performing like a trained marmoset before the tough, tattooed girls in a downtown lesbian bar, shrilling high like Amelita Galli-Curci on the Johnny Carson *Tonight* show, he and his vocal vaudeville always conjure up the year 1910, the Moulin Rouge and the gay, innocently coquettish world of the Chocolate Man and Jane Avril.

But what am I saying? Tiny Tim belongs not to an age but to an ancient tradition that stretches back from the gaslit stages of the Victorian period through the Commedia dell' Arte and the privileged jesters of Shakespeare—Feste and Touchstone—to the Breton minstrels, the medieval jongleurs and on back to the Roman circus, where a special class of performers portrayed with a single voice and body the romance of patrician boy and slave girl. What lifts Tiny Tim miles above the nostalgia, the rickey-tick, the pop archeology of even the finest rock groups, the Beatles, the

Stones, the Lovin' Spoonful, is that where they are doing an "impression" of something they hardly know, he is directly in touch with a musical and theatrical past that speaks from his mouth with the frightening authority of a dybbuk.

Born Herbert Kauhry and answering all queries about his age with the absolutely accurate answer "ageless," Tiny Tim has performed since he was five the old songs that constitute his current repertory. The "glorious voice" of Henry Burr singing "Beautiful Ohio" on an old Columbia Bluebird was the first music, he recalls, that "struck an impression on me." Wound up by his mother on an ancient Victrola, this record and others of the same vintage by Arthur Fields (the first crooner), Eddie Morton and Irving Kaufman (still doing commercials for Chateau Martin wines) played over and over in his old-fashioned home, until they fused with his deepest feelings and household pieties. Later they blended with the songs of Rudy Vallee, Gene Austin, Ruth Etting and Annette Hanshawe in a world of song that possesses him still in this age of electronic wizardry and futuristic funkiness.

Yet only today could Tiny Tim have become a famous entertainer. Even a few years ago, as he made the rounds of Tin Pan Alley, from the Brill Building to 1650 Broadway, ducking that zany head with the long hair into the offices of old cigar-chompers and trilling, "Hello, my dear friends, I have a demo in my hand of the next big hit," growls of impatience and scorn were all he received. Dreary little clubs in the Village, like the Fat Black Pussy Cat, Page Three and The Third Side, were the only places he could work; and what difference did it make if people like the Stones and Bob Dylan came in to dig him? Times were hard for Tiny Tim.

The new innocence saved him from obscurity; for the first time in generations, young people began to long for something pure and sweet and gay—a creature devoid of conventional beauty and glamour but possessed of an irresistible ugly-duckling charm. Such innocence was half the appeal of the early Beatles; Ringo was their duckling. Nor was the longing lost when the boys soured their style with the cynical sounds of "Tax Man." Even as acid rock reached its weird apocalypse, fuzz and feedback, Angst and shreck roaring in an appalling Witches' Sabbath, the yearning for all the opposite qualities, the giddy childish joys of the nursery, the fun and make-believe of the toy theater and the puppet show, grew apace.

Today, when Tiny Tim walks out on the stage, he still gets lots of laughs, lots of tittering and elbow-in-the-ribs condescension; but it's just the flotsam on a great, rolling wave of love that breaks over his head with his first kisses and curtsies. Even those who can't stand him have to concede that he really gets under their cuticle. He has the most fascinating face in show business—a Janus face that flickers with the allegory of evil and innocence that underlies all his art, all those confrontations between melodramatic villains and helpless, quivering maidens.

Sometimes he looks like Fagin, with his long kinky hair, enormous hooked beak and long white witch's teeth; then he reaches into his paper shopping bag, removes his ukelele, wrapped carefully in an old cardigan, and suddenly he's everybody's Jewish grandmother. Tiny Tim is a light show: everyone has a different vision of him. St. Theresa in drag is the way he appears on the cover of his recent album *God Bless Tiny Tim,* a smiling ecstatic, standing stiffly on a mound of Easter-basket grass and rolling his eyes up to a heaven that beams sunshine through the clouds.

Tiny Tim is really a holy freak: how splendid that today the word should be a term of endearment and unabashed admiration. For bizarreness is an essential part of his tradition: that exaggeration of style that borders on the grotesque and demands an answering contortion of personality that is the performer's equivalent of the submissive self-abnegation of the saint. Like all holy men, Tiny Tim is inviolable. Even in the mocking arena of the *Tonight* show, he behaved with the perfect freedom from inhibition, with the absolute imperviousness to ridicule that must have been the style of the ancient Christians in the Roman amphitheater. He reduced Johnny Carson to his straight man with a few childlike answers; Carson, his radar scanning the house, realized immediately that Tiny Tim's obvious vulnerability made him an untouchable. Asked to do an encore, Tiny Tim didn't even bother to rise from the guest's chair; he cocked up his uke, lifted his mad face in the air and went into a soprano fantasia on "The birds are coming" that was as finely focused, as technically flawless as the carefully insulated products of the recording studio. If you watch him carefully, you will see that Tiny Tim has always that inviolable space around him; he stands tall and bony, his elbows into his sides, his feet touching, as if he learned to play in a niche on a cathedral wall.

What people got to see for the first time on the Carson show was the totality of Tiny Tim's absorption in his role. Far from playing a part onstage, he is always the same raree bird, whether he is jabbering in his room at his parents' house in New York or talking before the millions on TV. When he stepped up on the platform to meet "Mr." Carson (he even says "Mr. Rudy Vallee"), he simply continued what he began at stage center. Gleefully, he told how every day he bathes with Packer's Pine Tar Soap; how he brushes his teeth with papaya powder (never rinsing his mouth); how he concocts his magic diet of wheat germ, honey, pumpkin and sunflower seeds; and how he loves the Dodgers and the Leafs and "all those beautiful girls." It was as vivid as a personal revelation as are any of the songs as distillations of his art.

Tiny Tim has never sounded better than he does on *God Bless*. Richard Perry, the record producer, did a remarkable job of contextualizing the artist's essence within the ambiance of psychedelically inspired rock music. The album is a dream theater that echoes beguilingly with all Tiny Tim's voices: the cackling twenties tone of Lee Morse, going "do-do-dee-do"; the straw-hat bel canto of George M. Cohan;

and the drollery of Billy Murray and Ada Jones, he with his lolling minstrel's voice and she with the tremolo-ridden sound of Lydia Pinkham femininity lining out Sonny Bono's 1912 hit, "I've Got You, Babe." To say that these are the most perfect impersonations of old singers ever heard would hardly do justice to the art that has re-embodied these entertainers in electronic avatars, summoning them up out of the past to caper again before a strobe-lit oleo. After an enchanting hour filled with the mysterious delight of recognizing what you never remember hearing, you will say with Tiny Tim, "these voices really live within me."

The New York Times, 1968

Elvis? Ah, the Good Old Days!

NOVOCAINE LIP. Hormone hair. Pale, poached face dripping onto black leather. Yes, it's that snarling darling, Elvis Presley, coming up on the home screen for the first time in eight years and in his first special, Tuesday night at nine on NBC. Colonel Parker, Elvis's canny manager, has mastered his maternal anxieties and resigned himself to the dangers of "overexposure." To an unimpeachably dignified American corporation, the Singer Sewing Machine Company, he has accorded the privilege of dishing up his carefully embalmed Roaring Boy as a Christmas turkey, stuffed with old chestnuts and recently rendered soul suet. Whatever one thinks of the singer's current style—a tortuous passage between the Scylla of incipient obesity and the Charybdis of tachycardia —the show is a triumph for the Colonel, the final vindication of his old carny man's philosophy.

For the maintenance of the classic Presley image in these troubled times has been an arduous task. Thank God, Elvis himself has been a wonderful boy, retreating after every movie to his ante-bellum mansion at Memphis, there to re-create himself with wholesome sports like touch football and wholesome foods like peanut butter, while he communes with his circle of handsome young companions, so grossly dubbed "the Memphis Mafia." No, the Colonel has had no trouble with Private Presley. The problems have been created by the vulgarians of the music business, who have applied formidable pressures to make Presley conform with the corruptions of contemporary civilization. It has been said that the Hillybilly Lollipop's monastic existence behind Graceland's fence of wrought-iron eighth notes has distanced him from the pop scene and threatened his currency as a culture hero.

What balderdash! There is no finer currency than the American dollar. Measured in dollars, Elvis Presley has greater currency today than at any other time in his career. For the past ten years the Colonel has paced Elvis through a course of moviemaking that would break the wind of a derby winner. Three times a year Elvis Presley has gone to the sound stages of Hollywood to make multimillion-dollar feature-length films, with holiday titles like *Blue Hawaii, Fun in Acapulco, Viva Las Vegas, Tickle Me, Easy Come, Easy Go, Live a Little, Love a Little* and, the latest in the series, *Chautauqua*. For each film Elvis receives a million dollars in wages and 50 per cent of the profits. The money doesn't stop there, however; every film yields an LP soundtrack record which may sell as many as two million copies.

With the Colonel exploiting the merchandising gimmicks suggested by each new role (everything from mannish sweatshirts to girlish pink teddy bears), with the royalties pouring in from Elvis's thirty gold records, and with residuals and replays and remakes and reissues from all the golden years, when Elvis and the Colonel grossed as much as $35 million in a single year, why should anyone ridicule the old Colonel and his cigar? Is Elvis not the highest-paid star in Hollywood? Has Elvis not sold 200 million records in this country alone? Is Elvis's baby daughter not cute? What manager has ever managed better? And shouldn't we all be grateful? For an enormous percentage of everything Elvis earns goes back to the people in taxes, making the Colonel the best de facto treasurer this country has seen since the days of Andy Mellon.

The Colonel's success as pop music's greatest tax collector rests, of course, on this country's willingness to work hard to support its habits. More precisely, the Presley success story may be traced to a very important and hitherto neglected cultural factor in ourselves: IPA, Indefinitely Prolonged Adolescence.

The way IPA works is that when people reach the years between eighteen and twenty, when they put away childish things and go on to college, they suffer cultural arrest. They stop reading *Mad*. They stop putting quarters in jukeboxes. They let dust accumulate on their 45's. Presumably, they're going on to better things, higher things; actually, they're leaving a knot in their lifeline which at some later date they will slide back to.

Then as they get into their twenties, into their marriages, homes and responsibilities, they get a hankering for the good old junk. They're rooting around in the basement one day and they uncover a stack of long-ignored records. Hey! here's "Rip It Up," "Hound Dog," "Heartbreak Hotel." Let's bring them upstairs and slip them on the phonograph. Woops! It's Elvis, out-of-breath, rattling to pieces, echoing like doomsday and shouting, "Baybeh!" Next thing you know you're up on your feet and you're doing the hucklebuck and your wife comes in, and it's a whole thing, and the kid is crying, and what the hell! . . . Whew, I can't breathe, but wasn't that fun? Picture generation after generation going through that experience, every five-year block in the population pyramid, and after a while you get a pretty strange image of contemporary society. A giant layer cake or, better, a plane stack over Kennedy, with every generation going round and round, doing their thing, beautifully indifferent to the people next door. And then imagine whole generations relapsing together, suddenly waking up to find the current pop sound too thin, too anemic or sentimental or pretentious and then hankering for the good old days, for the shlocky Fifties when the whole rock thing worked so much better—and, well, there you have the current pop scene.

Today all those English groups that spent years whoring after strange gods are making pilgrimages to the pop mecca in Memphis. The Beatles have revived their original Presley-laden style and the Stones are into the baby-blanket thing too and so are a lot of kids who weren't even around in 1956. So the Elvis special becomes a very, well, special kind of program, a marker, a reminder, a coarsely pious Christmas card which demands some appropriate response. Might we suggest a solemn "Yeah!" and a single exquisitely positioned finger-pop?

ELVIS PRESLEY AT LAS VEGAS

Gorgeous!—*or some equally effusive effeminate word—is the only way to describe Elvis Presley's epiphany at Las Vegas in March 1970. Not since Marlene Dietrich stunned the ringsiders with the sight of those legs encased from hip to ankle in a transparent gown has any performer so electrified this jaded town with a personal appearance. Without twanging a string, burbling a note or offering a hint of hip, Elvis transfixed a tough opening-night audience of flacks and entertainers simply by striding onstage in the Costume of the Year.*

What was he wearing? Nothing lavish, my dear, just a smashing white jump suit, slashed to the sternum and lovingly fitted around his broad shoulders, flat belly, narrow hips and . . . well, it's a nice fit. And then there are his pearls—loads of lustrous pearls, not sewn on his costume but worn unabashedly as body ornaments. Pearls coiling in thick bunches around his neck, pearls girdling his tapered waist in a fabulous karate belt: rope of pearl alternating with rope of gold, the whole sash tied over one hip with the ends brushing his left knee. With his massive diamonds flashing pinks and purples from his fingers and his boyish smile flashing sheepishly through his huge shag of shiny black hair, Elvis looks like a heaping portion of male cheesecake ripe for the eyeteeth of the hundreds of women ogling him through opera glasses.

So dazzling is the superstar, so compelling is his immaculate narcissism, that you hardly notice the massive forces he has mustered for his support: the thirty-eight-piece orchestra stacked up like the Las Vegas Philharmonic, the front rank of black-clad Memphis Mafiosi, armed with guitars and drums, and the side-show chorus of eight integrated voices (the Sweet Inspirations and the Imperials). Elvis kicks off his show James Brown style by collaring the mike and shaking it to the beat of "I'm All Shook Up," the kettledrumming orchestra shaking its elephantine body behind him. Coming to the guitar break, he strums the acoustic instrument slung white around his neck with the carelessness of a practiced faker. The number ends abruptly with Presley snapping into profile and thrusting his guitar bayonet-wise at the chorus.

The rest of the evening passes smoothly as the star glides through medleys of old tunes or lounges in elaborately upholstered arrangements of his new anthems. Every number ends with a classically struck profile—Elvis as the Discus Hurler, Elvis as Sagittarius, Elvis as the Dying Gaul. Between poses, he offers glimpses of his wry humor: "My mouth's so dry, feels like Bob Dylan slept in it all night." Not quite the erotic politician that Jim Morrison proved to be when he let it all hang out, Elvis manages very well with his constituency by occasionally grabbing a blue-haired lady at ringside and kissing her firmly on the mouth. Watching the women in the audience lunge toward the stage like salmon leaping up a falls becomes the show's real comic relief.

The climax of Presley's monodrama is a tremendous Cecil B. DeMille tableau. The orchestra is silhouetted against a cerulean-blue cyclorama while its members are transfigured by rich gold light pouring in from the wings. As the massed musicians sustain a mighty cathedral chord, the Great White Hope falls on one knee in the classic Jolson-gladiator pose, saluting the thousands in the house—saluting, perhaps, the house, with its three-dimensional putti *stringing yards of swagging chiffon between plastic classic columns.*

Grander than the "Fountainblue," grosser than Grossinger's, the International Hotel, the ultimate motel, 1,500 rooms redolent more of Howard Johnson than Howard Hughes, has found itself an "attraction" magnetic enough to pull the shut-in generation over thirty out of their ranch houses onto nonstop jets and down into the Valley of Loose Gold where the King of the Oldy-Moldy-Goldys presides over his people with eternal youth and joy and jamboree.

The New York Times, 1968, and *Life,* 1970

Purity, Not Parody, in a Real Rock Revival

CREEDENCE CLEARWATER REVIVAL

WITH THE SWOOPING jet sound of the Beatles' "Back in the U.S.S.R.," rock 'n' roll has come home again. The music whose future seemed once to lie among the distant stars of the international crowd with Karlheinz Stockhausen and Ravi Shankar has come back to roost with those tough old yardbirds Chuck Berry and Little Richard. In London, John Lennon, a twenty-eight-year-old millionaire and member of the Order of the British Empire, sits on the floor of his teen dream pad, wiggles his bare toes and listens to "Angel Baby" and "Give Me Love" by Rosie and the Originals, favorites of the early Fifties. High above Manhattan in the plastic-happy Hotel Hilton, the four sturdy lumbermen who constitute the Creedence Clearwater Revival, this year's top American rock band, drink beer out of a Styrofoam cooler and enthusiastically recall the Crows and the Meadowlarks, favorites of the middle Fifties.

What threw this loop into the time machine? Lots of things. Like any pop art, rock could only be sophisticated so far. Beyond this, the rock essence began to bleach out and evaporate. The kids and the blacks wouldn't listen to the music; the musicians themselves did not know how to carry it forward. Then the crash: the creeds of modern youth, the theosophies that had inspired the rapid-fire innovations of recent years—the hippie scene, the acid scene, the Maharishi, Zen—began to crumble. Left with nothing but their music and their memories, the rockers decided to go back home. (Actually, the decision was a delight; it was a chance to spin the old R&B sides and be kids again. As John Lennon said when quizzed about the stacks of ragged 45s in his flat: "These are the records I dug then, I dig them now and I'm still trying to reproduce 'Some Other Guy' or 'Be-Bop-A-Lula.'")

"Reproduce," however, means something very different on each side of the Atlantic. Reared 3,000 miles from their spiritual homeland, the Beatles view America—as did Brecht and Weill before them—as an endless movie crammed with bang-bang outlaws and kiss-kiss cuties. Parodists rather than paraphrasers, the English lads fill the gaps between their songs and their heroes with laughing gas. American rockers are too pious for the put-on; like crazy counterfeiters intent on one-upping the Treasury, their goal is to produce an R&B sound that is even more authentic to contemporary ears than the classics themselves.

Creedence Clearwater's records come over the air with the dust of the Fifties right in the grooves. A hoarse, sandpaper-throated lead singer (obviously some faceless old black who has long since drunk himself to death) is shouting in front of a grimly twanging, solemnly stomping spasm band; the theme of his song is curses, spells, apparitions—heavy, angsty stuff that points straight back to the days when Screamin' Jay Hawkins was borne onto the stage of the Apollo Theater enclosed in a black coffin. As the band pounds out its lugubrious rhythm and the guitars shake with malarial chills, the Emperor Jones drama of the primitive, superstitious Negro is enacted. The singer's voice rises in unlettered shouts and screams, the ominous beat tramps ever closer, the terrors of a simple soul—the "haunt" walking on the water, the woman walking out the door—drive his voice into a poetry of fear that cracks the numb resignation of the blues.

What comes to mind after you have reflected on these scenes is that they are being played with self-effacing skill by white boys from San Francisco, whose knowledge of the Negro soul is derived from the same source as the Beatles': those old 78s and 45s that have served this generation as sacred texts, esthetic talismans and racial/political rallying points. Amazing is the mastery of the black idiom which groups like the Creedence display; even more impressive is the modesty and artistic integrity with which they manipulate an alien tradition. Eschewing the politics of drugs, sex or race; turning their backs on theatricalism or exhibitionism; holding themselves down to the hard dense core at the heart of the rock, they burn through the trash that is being spewed from the radio today in a veritable pollution of the airwaves. Clear water is their symbol for purity, and purity is, paradoxically, what they achieve working with the stuff that is black as perfect pitch.

Life, 1969

The Beatles' Abbey Road

POP MUSIC today is being transformed by the esthetic of pop art. That sounds like tautology but it is the formula for a revolution. No longer does the pop musician go round and round in the same adolescent groove until he dies of superannuation. No longer does the pop genius go mad from imprisonment of imagination or betray his integrity by dragging his piano onto the stage of Carnegie Hall to make with the Grieg concerto in ragtime.

Now, thanks to the freaky contortions of contemporary sensibility, a commercial musician can grow and develop as an artist without abandoning the simple popular music that established his fame and earned him his millions. Slipping over their eyes the subtly distorting lenses of irony and nostalgia and taking ever more sophisticated sightings of their original tunes and times, groups like the Beatles are now filling the airways with sly pop facsimiles such as John Lennon's "Come Together" from the recent *Abbey Road.*

Heard out of the corner of your mind while driving the car, "Come Together" is just a catchy bit of jungle music with a mean whisk of vocal hiss, a hypnotic beat and the Lennon voice chanting on one note through a speaking tube. Endless repetition brings out the words like lemon juice on invisible writing, bit by bit. Lennon's singing about "Old Flat Top" (there's a Fifties word for you!), some great old cat who has grooved right down to the present with his "ju-ju eyeball," hair down to his knees and heavy mystic words of Rosko philosophy: "One and one and one is three!" The song hits you as a good-natured put-on of the whole funky, boogie, bluesy soul bag—pop music's big, black sacred cow. You love the line "[He] got to be good-looking 'cos he's so hard to see." Then in the third verse, the put-on switches suddenly from the soulman to the song's audience and to Lennon himself; for what are those cryptic lines—"He bag production/he got walrus gumboot/he got Ono sideboard" —if not John's private jokes with his Oriental missus (their film company is called Bag Productions) and his well-known public sass, here making millions strain to catch the meaning of nonsense?

Just as a mocking fantasia on the idea of being super-hip, the song is great, but there is more—not least the refrain, "Come together," an obvious pun with a tricky hook —"Coming Together" is a hexagram of the *I Ching,* the rock world's favorite oracle. How's them apples, Elvis?

Abbey Road is not one of the Beatles' great albums but it contains lots of good things: "Oh! Darling," a ritually perfect parody of a classic R&B ballad by Paul McCartney; "Something," a sentimental tune by George Harrison with a plangently rising guitar phrase off the 1939 shortwave from London; and "Octopus Garden," a little ditty by Ringo Starr that reminds me of "The Icecaps are Melting" by that other ugly duckling, Tiny Tim. The album's B side is devoted almost entirely to a medley of Lennon and McCartney tunes. This cornucopia of melodies and countermelodies, of brief snatches of song and bits of heavily orchestrated padding seems symbolic of the Beatles' latest phase, which might be described as the round-the-clock production of disposable music products. Some of the phrases are lovely, some of the segues stirring, but what sustains the production is a strong updraft of show-biz inflation that fills the mind with fleeting half-glimpses of Forties movie musicals, of Betty Grable, Alice Faye, thousands of marching soldiers—hold it! The Beatles were babies when those stars were born!

Life, 1969

That Angry Kid Has Gone All Over Romantic

BOB DYLAN

Nashville Skyline is Bob Dylan through rose-tinted shades. The ruddy hues of health, virility and rustic serenity fairly drench the cover photo (which looks like it was shot in a Tahitian sunset or through a Doris Day rejuvenation scrim). Instead of the old wintry image, the new Dylan is just a step ahead of spring. No more the Kid, trampling along the dusty highways of the East Village, casting a mournful, scornful glance over a shoulder bedecked with a carelessly flung waif-scarf, this beatified Dylan is handsome and bearded, a smiling Mormon-Shaker who pushes up the brim of his country hat with a thumb that practically drawls, "Howdy, neighbor!"

Inside this hearty sleeve, the atmosphere is no less warm and genial. Dylan is in love and the emotion has changed his voice. The classic nasal tone has cleared up like last winter's strep throat, and with it has gone the old anger, irony and humor. Instead of a Scotch-American Presbyterian Cove-nanter Hilly-Billy scraggle-neck chicken-skin mountain prophet man, the new rubicund Dylan is a relaxed country "bo" whose "Lay, lady, lay across my big brass bed" barrel-tone is enriched with faint echoes of Darktown sweet talk.

What is most remarkable about this metempsychotic album is not simply the change it has wrought in Dylan's image but the revolution it has made in his art. Dylan of yore was possessed of glossolalia, afflicted with logorrhea; he used more words per song than any man since W. S. Gilbert. His music and his singing were just a rough-skinned conveyer belt on which he heaped the riches of his verbal imagination. Snarling and hollering, fleering and jeering, he cranked out more symbols and myths, more allegories and apothegms than a whole Bowery of Beat poets. Now he's lost the gift of gab. Rock's greatest rhetorician has become a mouther of romantic clichés. "Love is all there is," he mindlessly croons, and you wonder what happened to the squint-eyed distrustfulness (and honesty) of: "Are you for real, baby, or are you just on the shelf?/I'm looking deep into your eyes, but all I can see is myself." Has Dylan "matured," as a good many of the early reviewers happily report —or has he just gone soft as apple butter?

The test is clearly the tunes themselves, which in this album carry the weight once borne by Dylan's poetry. The songs range from the maudlin "Girl from the North Country" (Dylan and Johnny Cash swaying beneath a lamppost at three A.M.) through the lime-tart, gittar-twanging "Country Pie" to the deftly campy "Peggy Day," all straw-hat throwaway lines and goony goofy steel-guitar glissandos. Every one of these songs is attractive, distinctive and skillfully sung (perhaps the word is "put over"), but the materials from which they have been made are paper-thin and plainly derivative. Dylan's ditty bag is patched together from Country & Western clichés and his delivery is not quite good enough to be believed. He comes on either as a semipro entertainer lightheartedly recollecting *Grand Ole Opry*, or he's a sandlot lover self-consciously revealing a newly won masculinity that somehow seems to sit on Bob Dylan like the first growth of beard on a teenage boy.

As a lark for the performer (long due for a change from his dronelike musical accompaniments) and a vacation for his hard-worked listeners (swamped with ironies and ambiguities), this collection of barroom and bedroom ballads has an obvious appeal. Take away the consciousness, however, that this strange voice is actually the legendary Bob Dylan doing the switch of the year and the music on these tracks tends to fade into insignificance.

Significance is precisely what *Nashville Skyline* is packed with for people who are apprehensive about the drooping state of American pop music. If a performer of the shrewdness of Bob Dylan can delude himself into thinking his former style—tough, complex and wholly original—was merely the product of "big city" influences operating on a basically simple and bucolic temperament, then there is every reason to believe that the whole pop music scene may soon slide inexorably back into the slough of sentimentality from which it was lifted a number of years ago when the first hard rockers began their program of rural electrification.

Life, 1969

Detroit Retools Its Rock

FROM THE shlocky early Sixties to the messianic advent of the Doors, American pop music was dominated by that great Detroit hit factory, Motown. From millions of car radios and jukeboxes rumbled the earthquake beat, shrilled the glassine strings, rasped and croaked, hollered and harmonized the voices of Diana Ross and the Supremes, Smokey Robinson and the Miracles, the Four Tops, the Temptations, Stevie Wonder and Marvin Gaye—dramatis personae of an endless ghetto psychodrama focused on the themes of rejection, persecution, isolation and all the other dementias of "love."

Then in 1967 Motown began to run out of gas. The white market was lured away by the siren song of San Francisco; the black began to divide its attentions among the great soul triumvirate of James Brown, Aretha Franklin and Otis Redding, singers whose earthy, direct appeal made the sequin-spangled Angst of Detroit seem artificial. When Detroit started to retool to meet the competition, more trouble developed: the great team of Eddie and Brian Holland and La-mont Dozier, who created the Motown formula and stamped out most of the big hits, got involved in a legal hassle with Berry Gordy, Jr., Motown's proprietor, and eventually left the company.

Nobody seriously expected Detroit could ever again exert the same influence on American music; but last winter the bottom fell out of the hippies and the Mississippies, and Motown seized and held three of the top ten slots on the charts for seven consecutive weeks. Behind this spectacular comeback was the reshuffling of the Motown sound and the emergence of a new team of words-and-music men: Norman Whitfield and Barrett Strong, composers of "I Heard It Through the Grapevine," "Cloud Nine" and "Run Away Child, Running Wild." Their new formula is the projection of R&B's traditionally harrowing material—love betrayal, drug addiction, juvenile delinquency—on a looming backdrop of hypnotically obsessive African rhythms and call notes. "Grapevine," a solid-gold standard written originally for Gladys Knight and the Pips as a shouting, belting, uppercutting gospel number, has been transmogrified for Marvin Gaye so that it comes out a mysterious tom-tom-colored caravan song. "Cloud Nine" is built on the contrast between the driving maniacal rhythms of "normal" city life and the ecstatic transcendence of the drug high. When the Temptations sing "I'm doin' fine on cloud nine," the image of junkie space floats off the hustling rhythmic base like an ancestral echo blown back from the jungle. Getting high and going back to the ancient tribal cool, the song suggests, are really one and the same thing.

The most ambitious of these songs is "Run Away Child," an Emperor Jones treatment of the flight of a delinquent kid who finds himself alone at night in the city with neither money, food, friends nor a guiltless heart. The Temptations' voices enter singly, like characters in a morality play, to mock, threaten and admonish the hapless Everyteen, and Whitfield and Strong build a rock drama which is more adventurous musically and more exciting dramatically than even the highly touted effort of the Who in their recent rock opera, *Tommy*. Nor is the drama confined to the convention of words and music: when the last voice has spoken, the song passes through a musical looking glass and emerges as a prolonged ritual of anxiety. It climbs relentlessly to a series of terrifying climaxes which impose on the racing rhythm of the boy's heart the thunderous warning of the ancestral spirits to "go back home where you belong."

What these strange sounds from Detroit indicate is that Motown has once again laid its cross hairs on the heart of the urban American Negro. Once again it has divined the condition of its public with a perception that surpasses the best efforts of James Baldwin, Eldridge Cleaver, Rap Brown and all those who merely *speak* for the black man. The soul these songs have mirrored in the past was that of a man whose natural condition is anxiety. Now that anxiety has been amplified still further and counterpointed against a mysterious ancestral sound which promises salvation: the power to mount above the troubled present to a throne of pride and power beyond the white man's ken. A jagged seam runs down the black man's soul these days. Is he still a frightened and frantic "gray" scuffling to score in the white man's world—or is he an African prince, secure in the possession of magic arts and a wisdom too deep for words?

Life, 1969

Portnoy in the Playpen

A COKE-JERKING RHYTHM, a Woody Woodpecker voice, a scoopful of clichés from a bin labeled "sweet talk" and you've got—*bubble-gum music*. This latest teen tic sounds like a tape echo of the early Beatles. It has the same innocence of appeal, the same stick-in-the-mind obsessiveness, the same white-bucked sound of boys and girls who don't give a damn about "war and poverty and broken hearts and frustration"—to quote a bubble-gum jacket that flaunts a photo of naked, silky-haired infants drooling on a white bearskin rug.

There is only this difference: Beatlemania was a spontaneous phenomenon that caught everyone off guard and raised a sunken continent of youth culture before our astonished eyes. What is going on today with the really younger generation—the kids of fourteen and below who dig the afternoon "spook operas" and freak for Sajid Khan (an Oriental that even a suburban mother could love)—is neither spontaneous nor creative, though it may be just as representative of where these kids have their little heads. Bubble-gum music, like many other current teen phenomena, is the product of shrewd commercial operators.

These Tin Pan Alley cats are constantly busy converting the gold of the rock music scene to the pure white teething plastic of prepubescent pop. The Big Bubble inflated two years ago on a label called Buddha. They recorded groups called the 1910 Fruit Gum Company and the Lemon Pipers. A third group, the Ohio Express, hit pay dirt with sticky confections called "Yummy-Yummy" and "Chewy-Chewy." Buddha claimed sales of over fourteen million. But the chief mercantile Svengali is Donnie Kirshner, a thirty-five-year-old hustler who employs teams of writers and arrangers to turn out the scores of songs which he wheels and deals onto the nation's turntables. In the past decade, Kirshner has published 500 tunes, of which 400 made the hit charts.

By using skilled professionals to concoct and record this music, Kirshner and his fellow tune snipes sidestep the problems posed by amateurish and temperamental rock groups. The Monkees were picked for their looks, paid for their success and played for originally by studio musicians who remained invisible and unknown. The Archies, whose bubble-gum albums (including the Record of the Year, "Sugar, Sugar,") stick to the top of the charts, haven't even the histrionic reality of the Monkees. They are simply cartoon drawings masking faceless musicians and factitious music.

Bubble-gum cannot, however, be dismissed simply as commercial hype—though that is the line taken by the older kids. Its creators hit upon a metaphor that may prove to be the most profound and prescient symbol of the coming generation. Every bubble-gum song proclaims the same primitive idea—love is really *eating!* "Yummy, yummy, yummy, I got love in my tummy," nasalizes a juvenile Terry Southern, and an entire generation of naked lunchers chomps back in Barbie Doll beatitude. If the music were not so relentlessly innocent, the songs would be haled into court as the ultimate evidence of youthful degeneracy. Even so, they are

masterpieces of that new Hollywood mode, the Clean Obscene. Imagine the little boy next door serenading your
twelve-year-old daughter with this tasty jingle: "Ooh-
whee Chewy—don't know what you're doin' to me, but
'cher doin' to me what I wan' chew to. . . . Baby, do it to
me, Chewy, chew me out of my mind!" Shades of Portnoy
in the playpen.

Actually, the meaning of bubble-gum's super metaphor is
by no means confined to sexual innuendo; it cuts to the core
of that buried life led by our millions of subadolescents.
Bubble-gum very aptly reduces these kids' lives to *maw*—to
that juvenile mouth, ever open, ever consuming, never satisfied; that yap that can never rap enough, eat enough or cry
enough when its inordinate demands meet a momentary ob-
stacle. A generation of galloping consumers couldn't have a
better theme song than these marshmallow melodies.

The pity of bubble-gum is simply its total lack of nutri-
tion. It comes in a whole rainbow of sugar-coated flavors,
but soon the taste wears thin and all you're left with is
chewy, chewy, chewy—plus a head full of cavities.

Life, 1970

Surf, Birds and Acoustic Overkill

NOISE IS the subject of an intense but inaudible dialogue today. While some people crusade against horn-blowing and dream of rural crickets, others are so terrified of silence that they hold their demons at bay behind roaring walls of transistorized sound. Neither tribe of noise freaks, needless to say, has the slightest conception of the other's needs. The acoustic sanitation workers who labor to cleanse the atmosphere of noise "pollution" fail to recognize modern man's anxious craving for vital signs: for easily recognized, easily ignored signals that life flows on around him while he endures his existential isolation. And the roar-your-troubles-away boys fail just as completely to realize how their anarchic hubbub has mounted year by year until now we stand on the threshold of an era of mass deafness.

The futility of the noise brigade's favorite strategy of turning up the volume was demonstrated a couple of years ago when rock musicians experimented with acoustic overkill. Lining up as many as a score of heavy amps in a discothèque of modest proportions, the rockers flattened their well-stoned audiences with the heaviest decibel barrage in the history of music. The grand effect—after the first delicious moment of masochistic surrender—was simply numbness and a relativistic somersault that puts the listener back to where he was before the knob was turned to 10. Today, there is a widespread reaction among musicians against *any* form of electric amplification—and a sales boom in acoustic guitars.

This same reaction against noise narcosis may account for the current interest in environmental sounds. One of the hottest underground records around is not a bootlegged disc of the Rolling Stones or a Dylan tape purloined from Columbia's vaults, but an easily procured album titled *Environments*, which offers on its plug side "The Psychologically Ultimate Seashore" and on the flip side "The Optimum Aviary."

The "Seashore" is just what it promises to be: a half hour of rolling, rumbling, sibilantly expiring wave sounds. Sloshing through the portholes of a good stereo system at low gain, the effect is deeply satisfying—less for what it does for the ear than for the associations with which it soaks the mind. Man's obsession with the sea is so profound there is virtually no limit to the effects it can produce at work, after work, during dinner, over candles or in bed. Gasping testimonials of the sort once associated with patent medicines— "cured my insomnia," "fantastic for making love"—cover the album with acclaim.

Shrewd psychology and sophisticated computer programming have gone into the long-playing ocean. To produce its infinitely modulatable waves (it can be played at any speed and still sound like an ocean), tapes of the Atlantic and the Pacific were laced together by a computer after having first been atomized into myriad sound grains. What emerged was a totally artificial "natural" sound that accomplishes what no natural sound could do under such unnatural conditions. Changing the ocean's speed alters the sound from hi-fi facsimile (at 45 rpm, the speed favored by sailors) to Mantovani languid (33⅓ rpm, the land lover's tempo) to surrealistic slow motion (16 rpm) and so to sleep.

Altering the speed of "The Optimum Aviary," thirty-two chirruping birds in cheery congress, has the effect of enlarging reverberant space around the happy creatures. From an ordinary room at 45, the bird range expands at 33⅓ to a 60 × 60 lecture hall and at 16 to a huge gymnasium filled with resonant birds big enough to terrify the bravest Gulliver.

Problems still crop up in these synthetic environments: a recording of rain made listeners feel like the tub was running over. On another disc the drowsy hum of insects was gently putting the listener to sleep when the crickets spoiled the effect by suddenly changing speed. Even one successful record makes it clear, however, that the cacophony of the urban environment can be cosmetically masked with natural sound. Cheaper than booze, safer than pot, less monotonous than the hum of an air conditioner, the sounds of sea, rain, wind, birds and crickets may prove to be the ultimate tranquilizers. At the very least, they afford a welcome antidote to a world that has become—to put it mildly—a pain in the ear.

Life, 1970

The Sound of Superscapegoat

JOE COCKER

THE JOE COCKER show opens with a hippie melee that looks like a cast party for *Hair*. The stage for the one-nighter is jammed with people tuning instruments, milling around mikes, laughing, talking and taking swigs out of wine bottles and beer cans. A gaggle of groupies drifts out on the stage apron, where they toss pink and white carnations to the audience as if they were feeding seals at the zoo. Another group of girls wearing Mickey Mouse T-shirts and hip-huggers plays with a toddler carrying a toy trumpet. Finally, the twin drummers encamped in the midst of this commune begin to lay down a heavy, lurching beat, picked up piece by piece until the band is rocking in a bleary, boozy soul groove.

While all these preliminary rituals are being performed, you search this careless crowd for the star. The photographers are busy shooting the more spectacular-looking males, like Leon Russell, with his pajama-striped pants and great masses of brindled hair. It takes an insistent spotlight and a vocal cue finally to focus everyone's attention on a pale, tired, unimpressive little man in a Wallace Beery undershirt. "The most beautiful person in the world—Joe Cocker!" screams a rasp-voiced M.C., flinging an arm toward the little man—who flinches comically, lays a feminine hand to his bosom, launches into some very British patter and then interrupts himself with a loud, wet Bronx cheer.

The band starts bashing out "A Little Help from My Friends" and Cocker goes into his *thing*. You had heard about his strange mannerisms, but you never expected he'd look like a bad case of muscular dystrophy exacerbated by Parkinson's disease and St. Vitus' Dance. There he is, though, Ben Gunn cast away in public, with all the shameful stigmata plastered over him like Superscapegoat. His fingers are fumbling blindly, obscenely, on invisible guitar frets; his knees are bent, his ankles splayed, his toes curled and pigeoned; his balance as precarious as a two-year-old toddler's. Looking at the face framed with the long curling Christ locks, you see the contorted mouth, the bulging eyes, the pale, drawn skin of a man struggling to assert himself against insuperable obstacles.

Assert himself he does, triumphantly, with a big, burly voice that comes off his clenched chest with hardly a syllabic bite out of it. It's the old Beethoven uppercut—"from the heart to the heart"—swung by a Sheffield steamfitter on an American stage. The kids are going crazy for it. The blonde girl next to you is up out of her seat, clapping her hands like an old mama in a storefront church. Cocker is pouring it on, staggering around the stage like Oedipus at Colonus. He's also Porgy, Ray Charles, all those blind criers and crazy beggars and maimed men who summon up a strength we'll never know to bawl out their souls in the streets. To a generation that has turned everything upside down in order to locate reality in poverty, filth, affliction and holy idiocy, Cocker is Original Man.

Girls say he's the last Real Man. Boys say he's a no-bull guy. Middle-aged women are beginning to dig him the way they once did Tom Jones. The charts indicate he has all the money in the United States except $3. This August he'll have a movie. If Cocker hangs in long enough he will inherit the earth. But how long will he?

When I got backstage after the show, I found him slumped on a wooden chair in a narrow, coffin-shaped dressing room, the door blocked by a cinéma vérité camera crew, a sound man crawling around the floor with a periscope mike that popped up between every conversation and Cocker carrying on a low-keyed dialogue with his piano man sidekick, Chris Stainton. "We better get into a recording studio, we're hot now," urged Stainton. "Aye, but we've had the best of it," mumbled Cocker. I asked him about the future, about films and TV. Cocker smiled wanly, the sweat still staining his hairline. "We've no plans. I try not to think beyond today. A pop star has got a long way up, a short time on top and then, lad—he better know the way home."

Life, 1970

THE DEATH OF ROCK

On and On Mick's Orgy Rolls

"**D**ON'T EXPECT them to scream!" That was the tight-lipped warning passed to Mick Jagger on the now-legendary night, November 8, 1969, when the Rolling Stones took the stage to bring back the good old days of rock 'n' roll to America. The place was the Los Angeles Forum, an 18,000-seat, color-coded, deep-freeze tank. The bill was black-heavy with people like B. B. King, the regnant blues belter, and Ike and Tina Turner, the belle and beau of the ball-'n'-sock-it circuit. Two hours of diathermy by these deep-fat fryers had put the packed house into a sweaty, happy mood, when suddenly the Forum's zeppelin searchlights switched off and through the murmurous hush of 18,000 craning minds, there sliced the hysterical cry, "THE ROLLING STONES!!!"

Wham! The stage explodes in blue-white incandescence. Out firks the manic form of Mick Jagger, a black forked radish, cinched with a wickedly studded belt and topped off with a towering red, white and blue Uncle Sam hat. After him chases Keith Richard, flame-colored, sequin-spangled, earringed, brandishing a plastic see-through guitar. Then the other Stones: Bill Wyman, a red-clad executioner; Charlie Watts, a T-shirted construction worker, and the new guy, Mick Taylor, with his bright cotton shirt puffed at the sleeves in enormous mutton chops.

Boomeranging the Uncle Sam with one hand while collaring the mike with the other, Jagger screams "Hello!," springs into the air and slams down in a split, as the Stones start bashing out "Jumpin' Jack Flash." The audience, recoiling in audiovisual shock, not only screeeeeeeeeeams, but starts climbing the furniture, dancing in the aisles and charging the unguarded stage. Tasting the crowd's warm, salty blood, Mick the Jagger goes mad, tears off his belt, flogs the stage floor, incites the mob to riot and offers himself as their superhuman sacrifice.

Up and up the fever chart zigzags, on and on the orgy rolls, until after two shows, eight hours, a couple of buckets of sweat and a million killing watts of electroencephalic energy, apocalypse is attained. It's 5:30 in the morning—the Woodstock hour—and Jagger is jigging on the ruins of Western Civilization. He's into his final medley, with a dozen powerful amps screaming, "I Can't Get No Satisfaction." Suddenly, the Stones turn the corner into "Street Fighting Man," and the whole audience levitates. Every man, woman and love-child mounts his chair, raises his right arm over his head and makes his biggest, blackest, hardest fist! What a climax! What a gesture! What pure Nuremberg!

> Held a general's rank, rode a tank
> When the Blitzkrieg raged and the bodies stank!
> —The Rolling Stones,
> "Sympathy for the Devil"

Ja wohl! Mein friends, dot's right! Dot good ole rock 'n' role could warm the cockles of a storm trooper's heart. O.K. They don't give you a torch and an armband, like in the *real* old days, and send you down the Rhine to swing with the summer solstice. But you can still squeeze in hip by haunch

with thousands of good *Kamerads;* still fatten eyes, ears, soul
on the Leader; still plotz out while he socks it to you in stop
time, and, best of all, boys and girls, you can get your rocks
off, no? with that good old arm action that means—well,
you know what it means.

No question about it, Der Führer would have been gassed
out of his kugel by the scene at the Forum. The ultimate
performer, Mario's Magician, the prophet who wrote in
"Mein Kampf" about the little guy's desire to step out of his
day job, where he feels he's a nothing, and become part of
"a body of thousands and thousands of people with a like
conviction." There, that shows you, Der Führer was so far
ahead of his time that only now are the kids catching up
with him and showing their fondness for the old freak by
digging him under the sneaky guises of comedy and camp.

Still, young people today don't know half enough about
Hitler. They've been brainwashed by those shrecky Hollywood movies made during the war years, when one Jewish
actor after another took off the Hit as a lunatic and a mur-
derer. (They say he even took dope! It wasn't dope, just a
few pain-killers.) Young people should only know that Der
Führer was a self-proclaimed revolutionary and youth
leader. He was the first great tribal shaman and magical minstrel. He was the first to mix the primitive with the futuristic, the first to get it all together, the lights, the sounds, the
great clothes and gladiatorial salutes. Why, the guy even
wore a maxi coat! O.K. He wasn't much to look at—though
he was a terrific dancer! Still who ever offered a beauty
prize to Peter Townshend, with that nose of his—or John
Lennon with *his* thing? Energy is beauty, baby. Great dicta-
tors are transfigured by zap!

Actually, the idea that rock is Fascism spelled Fashion is as
familiar as the fact that smoking causes cancer. The political
parallel has been exploited in films like *Privilege* and *Wild in
the Streets,* sermonized upon by Sunday journalists and,
most recently, the Rock-Berlin Axis has been explored by
the current generation's greatest masterpiece, the Who's

rock opera, *Tommy*. When the opera's deaf, dumb and blind hero, martyr of the older generation and messiah of the younger, throws off the shackles of his afflictions, he instantly becomes a teen tyrant who fetters his disciples with the same manacles of mind and sense once locked on him. True, the kids rebel finally and go hymning off into the rosy revolutionary dawn. But they leave behind them *Tommy's* minatory message: "Beware the victims and the martyrs; they shall become oppressors in their generations."

What no one has the courage to confess these days is the irresistible attractiveness of the Fascist ceremonial. Denied any real control over his political destiny, filled with hatred and rebelliousness against an old order that strikes him as cruel and corrupt, unrelieved by the satisfactions of work or religion, how else, one wonders, is modern man to right his psychic balance or satisfy the urgencies of his soul? The ethic of love, love, love, give, give, give, good, good, good is beautiful. When, however, has it justified itself as the rule of life? Everything we have learned from the masters of the modern mind testifies to the vanity of being better than you are. The current generation seems like an army of Doppelgängers, chanting love and peace as they march to the most militant strains ever blared from the horns of war.

To take the Rolling Stones—in many senses the archetypal rock group—as instance: what a record they have compiled as impersonators of the Devil! Granted there is more evil in one tuning peg of Jimi Hendrix's guitar than in a million copies of *Their Satanic Majesties;* still, the fact remains that the Stones owe much of their success to what might be called the "will to evil." Commencing with such callow misdemeanors as "Let's Spend the Night Together" and escalating through the graver sins of "She Comes in Colors," "Street Fighting Man" and "Sympathy for the Devil," the boys have sneered and fleered and ground their heels into the face of middle-class respectability. They have testified, to the tune of millions of dollars, to the great contemporary longing to be bad.

What has emerged from their triumphal progress—which includes some notable drug busts and the sorry death of Brian Jones—is a public image of sado-homosexual-junkie-diabolic-sarcastic-nigger-evil unprecedented in the annals of pop culture. If the youth public that is so into peace and beatitude were not titillated out of its tepees by this specter of Sodom and gonorrhea, how could they possibly promote the Stones to their present position as the laureates of rock 'n' riot?

The irony—perhaps the vindication—of this strange history is that in pursuing their evil courses the Stones have attained to beauty. In their early years, they were little better than facsimile stampers, xeroxing the work of their black betters, like Chuck Berry and Bo Diddley. In their naughty middle years, they achieved a not-so-fine art of caricature, becoming the musical equivalents of the cartoonist Crumb, reducing a plethora of pop images to a fistful of jeering grotesques. Commencing with their closest communion with sin, "Sympathy for the Devil," they suddenly shifted from a head music of ideas about other people's ideas to a genuine musical life flow. The rolling, roiling, *moto perpetuo* of "Sympathy" showed that the Stones had a real musical body that answered to the rhythm of Mick Jagger's body, shaking and soliciting from the stage. Now, in their forthcoming album, *Let It Bleed*, this movement toward musical and sensuous beauty reaches its culmination in a remarkable track that blazes a new trail for English rock.

The beauty part of the new record is not the expanded version of "You Can't Always Get What You Want," featuring a sixty-voice boys' choir, or the new country version of "Honky Tonk Woman"—though those are good cuts for everyday consumption. The real Thanksgiving feast is offered on the first band, titled "Gimmie Shelter." An obsessively lovely specimen of tribal rock, this richly textured chant is rainmaking music. It dissolves the hardness of the Stones and transforms them into spirit voices singing high above the mazey figures on the dancing ground. The music takes no course, assumes no shape, reaches no climax; it simply repeats over an endless drone until it has soaked its way through your soul.

Half blue grass and half green gage, "Gimmie Shelter" is music to get stoned by. Taken as a counterpoint to the ranting rave-ups the Stones staged all over America, this cool, impersonal, self-absorbed incantation suggests the schizzy split dividing every contemporary head. It suggests what is actually the fact: that the same kids who are Sieg Heiling one night at some diabolic rally in Pandemonium may be lying the next night in their tents and sleeping bags passing the peace pipe from hand to hand as they watch the tribal fires flicker and go out.

The New York Times, 1969

The Beatles Decide to
Let It Be–Apart

THE BEATLES died last week, victims of that dread condition, maturity. Paul McCartney picked up a phone, called John Lennon and said, "I've decided to leave." The pop world's greatest partnership was thereby dissolved. Explanations flew thick and fast. Some writers blamed Yoko Ono, John's wife, some Linda Eastman, Paul's bride. Allen Klein, the Beatles' current manager, came in for his share. But the real villain was time, the decade that had transformed the Beatles from four identical boys to four different and disagreeing men.

The signs of creeping maturity have long been apparent. The Beatles' music aches now with nostalgia for the good old days of rock 'n' roll. Their response to revolution is the gentle philosophy of *"Let It Be."* When asked why he quit, Paul said, "I have a better time with my family."

Actually, the Beatles had every incentive not to grow up. Their myth was wedded to youth. Yet they never stopped developing from the first day they got together as a schoolboy skiffle band in Liverpool to the last night they recorded in EMI's electronic jungle on Abbey Road. For years every album marked a new level of attainment and thrust them into wider contact with the whole world of contemporary culture. Like those fabulous musicians of ancient legend—like Amphion who raised the walls of Thebes with the sounds of his lyre—the Beatles reared with their electric guitars the inflatable, pulsile, Day-Glo walls of the Rock Age. They generated with their poetry, music and wit a whole new milieu of discothèques and light shows; of long hair, mod fashions and hippie costumes; of groupies, dopers and teenyboppers. Standing above their world like the zany sorcerers in the *Magical Mystery Tour*, they controlled its emotional climate, season by season, for the better part of a decade. By 1967, moreover, whether by accident or design, the Beatles were creating art that satisfied highbrows and at the same time were working right down there on the basic level of mass-marketing-million-sales-gold-disc-top-forty-transistor-jukebox-pop!

Their immense success never turned the Beatles' heads, but it made them swell dangerously. After the death of their manager Brian Epstein, the boys began to act as if they could do everything as easily and triumphantly as they wrote and recorded songs. They botched a movie, made a disillusioning pilgrimage to India, and then committed their most grievous error by founding Apple Corps Ltd., their pop culture cartel.

A naïve attempt to reconcile the rival claims of artistic idealism with a natural desire to make more money, the Apple was in trouble from the day it started. It was managed by Paul while John went through his marital crisis, George practiced his sitar and Ringo puttered around his Tudor mansion like a plumber called to fix a leak. Apple accomplished few of its purposes and lost huge sums. With the millions rolling in and rolling out again like bilge on a sinking ship, John persuaded Paul to hand the checkbook over to Allen Klein, the Rolling Stones' manager, a man Paul found offensive.

Chagrined, Paul retreated to a farm in Scotland, where he watched Klein prune the Apple, John pose nude with Yoko, Ringo and George take star turns in films and records. The rumors about Paul's death had symbolic truth. He was dead as a Beatle. As a man, as an artist, he was very much alive, preparing his declaration of independence: an album entitled *McCartney*, which is 100 per cent Paul. Writing, singing and playing all the songs, his wife Linda snapping the cover pictures, Paul topped off the package with a printed interview that spelled out death to the Beatles. The cruelest cut came with a question obviously designed to schmaltz over the rift. Asking Paul, "Was there a moment when you thought, 'Wish Ringo were here for this break?' " the interviewer received a curt, cold answer: "No."

Even for a dry-eyed observer, it is hard to imagine the boys going it alone. Their strength was that each member mastered his role and each role locked into the others. If Paul was pretty, John was tough. If John was way out, Ringo was down to earth. If Ringo was cute, George was almost somber. Round and round they went, like movements of a Swiss watch.

But take the watch to pieces and what is left? Not much, which is reason for sadness. Still, regrets seem out of place when you consider what these boys accomplished. Nobody who grew up with them will ever get over the Beatles.

Life, 1970

"Grab the Money and Run"

DISAFFECTION WITH "counter-culture"—the mishmash of myths, music and *mishigas* animating our youth—is beginning to manifest itself in the writings of the most observant and thoughtful of the younger rock critics. While the mass media go right on endorsing every fad and foible of a decadent pop culture, while "soul" is co-opted by Coca-Cola and "revolution" becomes a phrase in a pants commercial, the kids who have grown up on the rock scene are starting to register their disgust with its perversions and their despair of its ever attaining its ostentatiously proclamed millennium.

Recently, virtually an entire issue of *Rolling Stone*, the rock world's most authoritative journal, was devoted to an exhaustive inquest into the Rolling Stones' farewell concert at Altamont, California. The free concert—ballyhooed by Mick Jagger as "a Christmas and Hanukkah rite to American Youth"—resulted in the murder of an armed black spectator by a gang of knife-wielding Hell's Angels (hired for $500 in beer to protect the vulnerable Mick), three accidental deaths from various causes and enough bad vibrations to shake the rock establishment to its foundations. As one participant lamented, "There was no love, no joy. It wasn't just the Angels. It was everybody. In twenty-four hours we created all the problems of our society in one place: congestion, violence, dehumanization."

Hardly noticed on the East Coast, Altamont grossed out the West. The Los Angeles *Free Press* expressed its view in a page-length caricature of Jagger with flowers in his hair and an Adolf Hitler mustache, his arm flung fraternally around a ghoulish Angel, while a crowd of long-haired kids hailed the pair with the Nazi salute.

Rolling Stone, with a thoroughness rare in these days of capsule news dispatches, searched out the disastrous event in every direction. The picture that emerged of the rock establishment with its rapacious greed, its shifty, manipulative tactics, its utter unconcern for people's lives and decencies and its incredible megalomania was worthy of a muckraking masterpiece on the Robber Barons.

The new Robber Bands, make no mistake, come from England bent on crass exploitation. Anyone who has traveled with these musicians or simply sat for an afternoon in their dressing rooms can testify to the contemptuous and paranoid view they hold of this country. "Grab the money and run" is their basic philosophy. Whether, like Blind Faith, they shark together in a so-called supergroup, make a fast million in a single tour and then disband; or whether, like the Stones, they dictate outrageous terms through their pushers and then pretend to give something back to the people with a free concert (which is in fact a film-making project to coin even more money); or whether, like the Beatles, they take the attitude that only through making vast sums of (American) money will they be able to save the world, the freebooting of these rock bandits ought to end forever the idea that the counter-culture is founded on some genuine ethical ideal, or that it marks in any significant way a break with the prevailing capitalistic system.

The other side of the discontent with counter-culture,

represented by Salingerian pathos over broken dreams and busted ideals, was beautifully expressed by Ellen Willis, twenty-seven-year-old rock critic of *The New Yorker,* writing recently in *The New York Review of Books.* In a long, elegiac reflection, Miss Willis examined the myths and beliefs of the counter-culture through the lenses of two current films, *Easy Rider* and *Alice's Restaurant.* Her conclusion is that "at this point, hate and love seem to be merging into a sense of cosmic failure, a pervasive feeling that everything is disintegrating, including the counter-culture itself, and that we really have nowhere to go." Underscoring the sense of lost opportunities that haunts the current moment, Miss Willis finds the dominant mood crystallized in the phrases: "What went wrong? We blew it!"

"*It.*" Though Miss Willis forbears to mention such things, "it" includes *art,* as exemplified by albums like the Beatles' *Sgt. Pepper; ecstasy,* as induced by mind-stunning discothèques like L'Oursin and the original Electric Circus; *euphoria,* as produced by the dozen or more Afro-oriented dances that sprang up with soul music and now have died— along with *all* dancing in the white world. *Communitas* perished as an urban ideal with the decay of Haight-Ashbury. *Meditation* suffered a setback when the cult of the Maharishi was exploded. *Ritual* was abandoned along with the early hippie mystique. *Spirit voyaging* declined after the first great excitement over psychedelics died down. *Revolution* has a pretty pathetic ring to it today; *guerrilla warfare* was always a bad joke. *The streets belong to the people—* yes, the Silent Majority, which holds the power to elect a government headed by Richard Nixon. In sum, what the kids blew was a millennial moment—one of those rare opportunities when a crack appears in the mundane shell.

The question "What went wrong?" takes us back to the fall, the fall of '67, when the exodus began from the Hashbury after a summer of paradisiacal joy. Then, if ever, the Woodstock Nation should have prevailed. Instead, what prevailed was apathy and drugs, petty crime, hustling, hassling, disease and madness. By the time of the pretended "Death of the Hippie" in San Francisco, and the very real deaths of Linda and Groovy in New York, the whole ideal of counter-culture was on the ropes and sagging. Seen in this perspective, Woodstock was merely a three-day revival meeting.

What clinches the argument for the decline and fall of counter-culture is the fate of rock music, which was the catalyst that quickened this whole world into being, sustained it and guided it through its short but kinky history. The fall of rock occurred at the same time as the fall of the hippie. It was in the winter of '67–'68 that the Beatles (read John Lennon) decided to do an about-face and retreat (with hip finesse) to their earlier manner, or even further to the music of the old masters who preceded them, like Buddy Holly, Chuck Berry, Little Richard and Elvis Presley. Rocking from the failure of their tedious home movie, *The Magical Mystery Tour*, growing alarmed at the bad box office signaled by mounting prestige among intellectuals and declining popularity among teenyboppers, the Beatles decided to abandon the rich vein that had produced *Sgt. Pepper* and those fascinating compositions, "Strawberry Fields" and "I Am the Walrus." This act of creative apostasy announced the beginning of Rock Revival, the great roll back to 1957 and the joys of being once again a simpleminded teenager. Electing to scrape the old bubble-gum off the wall and munch it into mulch again, the Beatles and their millions of followers became the first generation in history to decline the great adventure of their destiny in favor of a premature return to childhood and the cloying pleasures of nostalgia.

Today, as a result of the determination of the past two years, rock culture stands at the opposite pole from where it stood in its peak period. At its peak, the input of raw creative energy was so overwhelming that the elaborate system of filters, buffers and diluters that normally stands between the public and the creative mind momentarily broke down and the masses were mainlining pure, uncut musical heroin.

Rusty old Tin Pan Alley seemed to have sunk into the hole left by the rising Atlantis.

But as the ideals and myths that had sustained rock began to crumble, into the gap rushed the banished swarm of parasite producers and wheeler-dealers. In no time rock was computerized into the stalking zombie it is today, lurching along without a thought, a purpose or a plan beyond that offered by the record rating charts and the airline timetables. By now, the music is a mass of nearly exhausted clichés that pours twenty-four hours a day from the radio like Muzak without strings.

What is even more dismaying than this industrialization of the art is the acceptance of the bubblegum mentality by even the finest rock musicians. The latest albums of rock geniuses (the Beatles, Bob Dylan) show an unhappy drift toward the purely commercial aspect of their music. Too much complacency, too many ego trips, too great a facility with the tucks and pleats of current fashion has led them toward a subtly specious music that is attractive but not compelling, enchanting but not convincing. As for the dozens of groups and performers who are not so gifted, they present the collective image of a monotonously revolving kaleidoscope, loaded with bits of hand-cut, tie-dyed, plastic gospel, blues, rock, jazz, pop, folk, pop, blues, and so on in endlessly shifting combinations of this week's, last month's, tomorrow's "sound."

No Tin Pan Alley Svengali could have molded anything more plastically perfect than the Band, lauded to the heavens recently in a *Time* cover story. Endearing, amusing, bouncy and bathetic by turns, packaged in homespun and hominy, peddled with homilies about integrity and respect for old folks, the Band, or the Bland, is a promo man's dream. They don't have to be edited, cooled, controlled or explained; they run no risks of offending anyone; they fit in perfectly with the worship of mediocrity that is beginning to take the place of the old devil cults. With their twangy, rubbery, pogo-stick beat—produced, mind you, with an au-

thentic folk instrument called the electric wah-wah pedal—
the Band is ideal for the adult bubble-gum market.

It is beginning to look as though J. Edgar Hoover, Spiro
T. Agnew, Mayor Daley, Judge Hoffman and Ronald Rea-
gan, the deans of our great universities and the police and
sanitation departments of our cities no longer have any
cause to fear an uprising from the red Maoist masses of
American youth. The generation that three years ago
seemed destined to uproot traditional moral values and revo-
lutionize our culture has now begun to drift aimlessly along
the lines of least resistance. We need no longer fear all the
lurid predictions of the pop press.

The real fear should be that a generation which rejects its
inherited culture with such facility will inevitably reject or
betray its own youth culture with the same jettisoning zeal.
Counter-culture is largely anti-culture; one step more and it
becomes non-culture.

The New York Times, 1970

Drugs and Death in the Rundown World of Rock Music

FIRST, it was Jimi Hendrix, rock's flamboyant superstar, snuffed out at twenty-seven, dead on arrival at a London hospital. The cause? Suffocation from vomiting while unconscious from sleeping pills. Accidental overdose? Suicide? The coroner could not say.

Then it was Janis Joplin, rock's greatest soul belter, also twenty-seven, found dead on the floor of a Los Angeles motel room, fresh needle marks on her left arm, a red balloon filled with a white powder stashed in her trash can. Coroner's finding: accidental overdose of drugs.

Why should a young man and woman of such energy and talent, endorsed with immense success, showered with love, raised to the glory of demi-gods, imperil their lives with dope? If you were drawn even for a moment into Jimi Hendrix's breathless quest for life, his urgent headlong pursuit not simply of pleasure but of the most elusive and exotic states of mind and soul, you would know that his death was an inevitable product of his life and of a society that on one hand idealistically proclaims every virtue from Sophocles and Jesus to Sigmund Freud, and on the other hand pushes Dow Chemicals, pushes Parke Davis, pushes Lockheed, pushes, pushes, pushes . . . Hendrix once sent someone a bag of cocaine with a high-flown note inscribed in flowery script: "Within I grace thee with wings. O lovely and true Birds of Heavenly Snow and Crystals, Fly my love as you have before. Pleasures are only steps and this . . . just one more." That was the rhetoric of his life and it swept him along heedless of dangers that made his mere existence a daily miracle. It sent him flickering among the candles and bottles and fuming incense of his nocturnal day, it moved him to sniff cocaine and drop acid and drink wine all in a row, like the chord changes in a tune on which he was improvising.

Janis Joplin was possessed by a very different demon. She doted on the image of the hard-drinking, hard-living, hard-loving soul mama. She gloried in self-destruction, tearing out her throat with every song, brandishing a bottle of Southern Comfort on the stage, turning rock-solid blues like "Ball and Chain" into screaming, wailing sado-masochistic nightmares. "Sure I could take better care of my health," she once said. "It might add a few years—but what the hell!"

Janis said she never touched drugs. But how could she avoid them? Dope was as essential to her myth as blues, booze and the frantic beat with which she tore out her heart. Whether she needed dope as a human being was beside the point. It was crucial to her act.

The reckless lives of both Jimi Hendrix, a poor black who became a superstar overnight, and Janis Joplin, a middle-class Southern white infatuated with a fantasy of black soul, are not unique within the context of our myths of art, show business, the jazz genius, the existential hero. Hendrix and Joplin had the additional pressure, as the king and queen of rock, of ruling over a crumbling kingdom. Since the peak year of 1967, when they flashed on the scene, rock has run down badly. This year of 1970 has seen the most lavish outlays ever made in the history of the pop recording business; yet hardly a star has come up with anything that could match his previous records. The rock festival has degenerated into a grotesque tragicomedy peopled by swindling promoters, gate-crashing kids, club-wielding cops and money-mad stars.

The world that once adored those innocent boys, the Beatles, which decked itself with flowers, practiced transcendental meditation, came together in the joyous Woodstock festival, danced wildly and spoke gently of love and peace—that beguiling world now lies broken. The rock culture has become the drug culture. Convinced that everything is fraud, feasting on films that feed their paranoia, feeling helpless and betrayed, huddled together, thousands of ordinary kids are a set-up for the pusher—and the "magic" drugs that promise ecstasy, stifle fear, shut out insistent demands, that provide an urgent sense of purpose in lives devoid of goals. Yet what they are addicted to ultimately is not drugs but dreams—the myths and fantasies which they have imbibed from the mass media.

What is really frightening is that so many of these kids seem indifferent to life. Where they once enhanced their looks and asserted their careless vitality through gay psychedelic plumage, they now shuffle around in drab, raggedy, dead men's clothes. Instead of exulting in the physical joys of dancing, the sensuous pleasures of love, the whole sensorium of rock music, most of the kids I see in the college classes I teach, at the rock concerts, or hanging out in the East Village seem depressed and apathetic, reckless about dropping, popping or smoking anything that promises a momentary high.

It is within the context of this New Depression that the deaths of the rock stars must be pondered. When I talked recently to friends of Jimi Hendrix and Janis Joplin, they painted almost identical pictures of the two stars during their last days. Both appeared to be groping for a new phase. Already past the frenzy of sudden fame, wise to the make-believe in their own legends, aware that both they and rock had lost the spark, both performers were trying to prepare new songs with new bands to reaffirm their status as super-stars. It seems likely that the transition proved too much for them. After a brief high ride on the hot blast of the great years, the sudden chill of change, of reality, must have been deadly.

Life, 1970

T W O

Sick Jew
Black Humor

Boy-Man Schlemiel

THE JEWISH ELEMENT IN AMERICAN HUMOR

WALK INTO any New York bookstore today and probably the first beckoning display you encounter will be the Jewish fun books. Stacked in revolving metal racks are the James Bond spoofs, *Oy Oy Seven, Loxfinger, Matzoball;* the "How-to" books, *How to Be a Jewish Mother, A Jewish President, A Jewish Madam;* and many other shrugged-shoulder versions of standard entertainment genres. There are comically matched photo and captions, *Kosher Kaptions;* straight humor, *Some of My Best Jokes Are Jewish;* and even Yiddishized parodies of "classic" comics—*Supermax, The Lone Arranger* (The Masked Marriage Broker) and *Tishman of the Apes.* Just a little less prominently displayed are the latest works of the American Jewish comic novelists. These range in style from the Pop art of Wallace Markfield's *To an Early Grave* to the show-biz fantasy of Bruce Jay Friedman's *A Mother's Kisses;* from the Aristophanic farce of Saul Bellow's *The Last Analysis* to the subtle social comedy of Philip Roth's *Letting Go.*

The popularity of Jewish humor in America today can, however, be only partially gauged standing in a bookstore. To register its full impact you should also take a look at the subway posters where Chinese and Negro faces masticate slices of rye bread above the line, "You don't have to be Jewish to love Levy's"; or catch a TV commercial in which a barber is affectionately called *bubbee* or a husband denounced as "stark raving *meshuga*." Yiddish, once a dying language, has been revived a word at a time by Madison Avenue and Broadway until it is now the lingua franca of American humor.

In one sense it is not surprising that American humor has adopted a Jewish tone. Particularly in the show business world, Jews have dominated the comedy scene for fifty years; in fact, there is no other area of American cultural life in which they have been so dominant. Among the more famous, we have Charlie Chaplin, Ben Blue, the Marx Brothers, Eddie Cantor, Danny Kaye and Jerry Lewis in films; Jack Benny, Ed Wynn, Milton Berle, Sid Caesar and Phil Silvers on radio and TV; Bert Lahr and Zero Mostel on the stage; and Joe E. Lewis, Henny Youngman, Mort Sahl, Lenny Bruce and many others in nightclubs. Then there are well-known cartoonists, Saul Steinberg, Rube Goldberg, Al Capp and Jules Feiffer; comedy writers, S. J. Perelman, A. J. Liebling, Milt Gross and Bud Schulman; and gag writers Goodman Ace, Mel Brooks and Mel Tolkin.

From this list of names, which could be extended indefinitely, it is obvious that the Jew has long provided most of the *comic talent* in the entertainment business. The big difference today is that now the Jew also provides the *comic material*. Jewish culture—its manners, folkways, values, its language and style of delivery, physical and verbal—serves as the frame of reference for much contemporary American humor. The sort of material that could once have been used only before Jewish audiences in the Catskill's "Borscht Belt," on the Lower East Side, at a fund-raising dinner for the U. J. A. or among such in-groups as the Lambs and Friars, the material that was once regarded as unintelligible to Gentiles and possibly provocative of anti-Semitic responses has now become common property.

It was in the mid-Fifties that the style of American humor began to undergo this radical transformation. At that time, as part of the license of "sick" humor, the Jewish comedian first dared to be explicitly Jewish before a Gentile audience. Unlike the traditional Jewish comic—Jack Benny, for example, who never allowed the audience to glimpse his Jewish identity and who even used as his foil a grotesque stereotype called Schlepperman—the new "sick" comics, headed by Lenny Bruce and numbering such gifted performers as Nichols and May, Shelley Berman and Mel Brooks, made their Jewish identity paramount. At the very same time, young writers like Philip Roth, whose *Goodbye, Columbus* was published in 1959, began likewise to broach the problems of Jewishness in a ruthlessly frank manner. From nightclubs to novels, it was all essentially the same: a new generation of American Jews had found a voice for their anger and self-pity in a potent new humor.

The willingness of these Jewish writers and performers to "expose" themselves was, of course, merely an intensification of feelings shared by tens of thousands of young American Jews. Security made the difference—security built up through several generations who, no longer persecuted, were progressing triumphantly toward their goals of social and cultural achievement. Furthermore, this generation had received a vital spiritual reinforcement in the establishment of the state of Israel, an influence that is hard to measure but which registered profoundly within the American Jewish community. Perhaps the generally permissive atmosphere of the postwar period should also be taken into account; in any case, the traditionally conformist tendencies of American Jewry changed. The old feeling of shame was transformed into one of pride and, in some cases, of arrogance. The American Jew, once a *nachschlepper*, now marched in the van, an acknowledged leader of contemporary culture. Because of his obvious achievements and the special tolerance he now enjoys, the Jew is more than ever free to exercise the license of comedy—to speak directly and openly.

Just as important as the Jew's willingness to talk, however, is the Gentile's willingness to listen. Perhaps "willingness" and "listen" are not the right words, because they suggest simply an attitude of passive tolerance. In fact the popularity of Jewish humor rests on a more positive basis, particularly on a need to discover some adequate metaphor for a whole complex of contemporary ideas, feelings and stigmas—a need met by the concept of Jewishness. Lenny Bruce defined this symbolic signficance of Jewishness in characteristically concrete terms:

> To me, if you live in New York or any other big city, you are Jewish. It doesn't matter even if you're Catholic; if you live in New York you're Jewish. If you live in Butte, Montana, you're going to be goyish even if you're Jewish. Evaporated milk is goyish even if the Jews invented it. Spam is goyish and rye bread is Jewish. Negroes are all Jews. Italians are all Jews. Irishmen who have rejected their religion are Jews.

Here Bruce is not only equating Jewishness with urban sophistication, knowledgeability, and "hipness"; he is also connecting it with the problem of identity faced by any alienated group. It is clear that the style and content of Jewish humor strikes a deeply responsive chord in the younger generation of highly aware, alert and urbanized Americans who are enthusiastically embracing it. Jewishness represents *their* psychological plight, too. For the Jew the plight centers around the challenge of alienation and assimilation, the humor itself spun from the tension of a very real conflict: his Jewish versus his American identity. For the non-Jew the conflict is more diffused, but powerful nonetheless: his personal versus his mass-cultural identity. Every American today is caught between the nostalgic yearning for a safe, comfortable, well-defined personal past (childhood, family, religion), and the difficult challenge of adapting to an increasingly (and frighteningly) depersonalized society.

As James Joyce divined when he made the hero of *Ulysses* Leopold Bloom, *the Jew with his "hang-ups," his self-doubt, his self-hate and his awkward, alienated stance is a twentieth-century symbol for Everyman.*

Modern American Jewish humor has a special ironic, ambivalent—both contemptuous and nostalgic—tone which is intimately associated with the confusing dilemma of assimilation. This special tone was first heard in Central Europe, in the places where the Jew was first "emancipated." It colored the Berlin cabaret performances of the Twenties, the theatrical collaborations of Brecht and Weill, and the gibes of Bemelmans, Perelman and others condemned by Goebbels in 1938 as a "Jewish infected minority" and denounced for "jokes that cease to be jokes when they touch the holiest matters of national life."

In the search for the source of this modern humor, one can go even further back: to the first great writer of the Jewish "Emancipation." The prototype of the ambivalent Jew using a comedy lens for self-scrutiny is Heinrich Heine. Heine was reared in Düsseldorf, whose population was predominantly Catholic, by parents who were observant but far from orthodox. As a boy he was drawn to Catholic teachings and was even eventually baptized. After a thorough preparatory education he worked in the family business run by his wealthy uncle, a banker. This experience intensified Heine's sense of inferiority as well as his disdain for the business Jew. In general he was emotionally drawn to Jews, but intellectually repelled by orthodox Judaism; his attitude was a mixture of admiration and antagonism.

From a young age Heine was uncomfortably aware of himself as an outsider, as a Jew among Christians. His early poetry, for which he was called "the German Byron," described the melancholy pain of unfulfilled love: it was a poetry of rejection. He tends, however, to mock his own emotions, to gaze like a cynical observer at his own pain.

Because of this inclination, Heine has been aptly described as "the poet of divided and self-alienated consciousness par excellence." Of himself, he once stated significantly, "I cannot relate my own griefs without the thing becoming comic." In his later years Heine wrote brilliant prose, and then, renouncing his early Romanticism, returned to verse in a different tone, incorporating his many unresolved conflicts in a remarkable mixture of styles, tones and varied emotions, combining "folk-lore naïveté, worldly cynicism, grotesque fantasy, poignant lyricism and earthy humor." The Jewish element in Heine's wit rests on his sense of caricature, his fusion of sentiment with irony and above all his penchant for self-satire. Along with his love of life, he communicates a profound feeling of alienation from the world—a feeling shared by all assimilated or partly assimilated Jews whose position in society is inevitably ambiguous.

Despite the gap of over a hundred and fifty years, Heinrich Heine's use of the comedy lens is relevant to the American Jew today. The long history of Jewish humor encompasses hundreds of years, countless countries, and numerous specific traditions. Its power in contemporary America, however, rests neither on the fact that humor is a form of solace for the downtrodden nor on the notion that it is used as a safe discharge of rage against oppression. Although the American Jew is now more comfortable than in any other country at any time, he nevertheless—like Heine—resists total assimilation just as firmly as he resists orthodox Judaism. His conflict is one of alienation and identity; and his attempt to conform produces discomfort and confusion. He is neither a proud alien (which the Gentiles would like), nor a devout Jew (which the Jews would like), nor, certainly, truly indistinguishable from the others (which he himself would like). Since he cannot totally surrender his identity, he views life from an isolated position—his head cocked ironically awry, his eyes and mind always alert to control his environment by total intellectual awareness and his tongue poised to mock both himself and others, Jews and

Gentiles alike. For the Jew a highly developed verbal wit serves as both shield and salvation.

The power, richness and complexity of Jewish humor in America builds on three distinct levels, each of which generates disillusionment, anger and conflict. The three levels are family, social and cultural. The three conflicts are: the child versus his parents; lower middle-class Jewish society versus upper middle-class Gentile society; and the glamorized images of the mass media versus the harsh everyday realities, i.e., fantasy versus reality.

The family relationship is particularly crucial because it establishes the basic psychodynamics of Jewish humor. The Jewish comic never completely severs his childhood connections with—and antagonisms toward—his family, particularly his mother. Even when grown, he remains a boy-man. Within the Jewish family alienation between generations is often strikingly accelerated because the parents are highly ambitious for their children. In America first-generation Jews typically reared children who made money and were professionally successful, but who did not basically abandon the cultural values of their immigrant parents. Children reared by this highly successful second generation were quite different. Very sensitive to style, taste and appearance, they were embarrassed by and contemptuous of their parents' "vulgar" goals; in turn, they reacted violently to demands for success and family loyalty. This third generation —which has produced the younger comics—is characterized by hatred for parents, prolonged adolescence, rebellious intermarriage and an inability to formulate life goals. Their extreme alienation stems from several factors common to Jewish family life: (1) the breakdown of firm order and strong values, resulting in extreme permissiveness; (2) the pattern of the parents' secret ulterior manipulation of children—demonstrative love veiling strong demands—which causes such confused resentment within the child that he often totally rejects his family; (3) the pressure for success "no matter what you do," exerted by parents whose permissiveness has robbed their children of the habits of discipline, concentration and endurance required for achievement; and (4) perhaps most important, the Jewish mother's destructive domination, her demands for love and success from her son, which are linked to her refusal to grant him the independence required for manhood.

Philip Roth depicts the antagonism between Jewish generations in a subtle but deadly style, particularly in *Letting Go*, where Jewish types are "put on" to the hilt—portrayed as shallow, vulgar, pretentious, smug, domineering, self-pitying, fatuous and affected. And yet with Roth, as often also with the less refined writers, there is an attitude of tenderness coexisting with one of rage. Similarly, Bruce Jay Friedman in *A Mother's Kisses* presents a biting—and yet warm—portrait of the struggle between a son and his mother. He has captured both the flamboyant, commanding mother with her embarrassing pushiness and lack of self-restraint, and the inhibited, troubled adolescent dragged through life on mama's apron strings. Although the mother is really amusing and well-meaning, her refusal to allow her son any independence is, for him, galling and pitifully unmanning. The boy is very attached to and yet very angry at his mother; he cannot, however, express his anger toward someone who is so "good" to him. His only outlet is farcical ambivalence—a love that pursues through mockery and an anger that disguises itself as humor. Friedman's vision is both comic and disquieting.

From these third-generation conflicts within Jewish family life and from this world which Roth and Friedman illuminate comes the boy-man, the Jewish comic (writer, performer, cartoonist, etc.), who is in turn the major force in modern American humor. (Typically, he has a juvenile-sounding name: "Woody" Allen, "Jerry" Lewis, "Soupy" Sales, "Lenny" Bruce, "Sandy" Baron, etc.) This Jewish comic is the adolescent urban funny boy—hysterically intense. The key to his comedy—and the ironic clue to his tragedy—is that he is intellectually and verbally overdeveloped at the same time that he is emotionally and sexually underdeveloped. Although on one level he is sharp and sophisticated, on another level he is merely childish and petulant. This Jewish comic, the boy-man, often comes from Brooklyn or the Bronx, the urban perimeter of New York. He lives in the street, on corners, in candy stores and "luncheonettes" and at the movies. He is nervous, restless and loud—always talking, laughing or screaming.

My own experience with this Jewish hipster is intensely personal. For seven years I lived—like the characters in *A Mother's Kisses*—in "three rooms in Bensonhurst." I learned that Bensonhurst and similar neighborhoods in Brooklyn and the Bronx have produced as many Jewish comedians as Vienna Jewish analysts or Odessa Jewish fiddlers. My introduction to this frenetic comic world grew out of a casual meeting with one of my students at Brooklyn College—and a conversation about jazz. Eventually this student introduced me to his circle of friends, young people in their mid-twenties who had always lived in the lower-middle-class neighborhoods of Brooklyn. They were an odd lot: some were in a shady home-repair business; some in television; some went to school; and some did nothing. Having known each other and shared their lives since adolescence, they enjoyed above all getting together and talking—in a "show biz," not a conversational, way. They had developed an indigenous humor, wild and fantastic, collectively inspired but individually performed. Gradually the group fell into the habit of gathering in my living room every Saturday night, with everyone having his turn onstage. The atmosphere was that of a jam session. The group's excitement released each performer, sending his fancies flying sky-high. The form for the evening was simple: generally a review of the week's events which would cue the performer into past experiences, social observations and then any and every sort of material—all produced purely spontaneously. This impromptu volleying of funny fantasies was called the *Spritz*.

I remember the excitement, the abandon of this scene,

what it felt like to be caught up in this frenzy—and especially what it felt like to generate and to control it. It gave you a tremendous sense of power to see people in front of you doubled over with the pain of laughter. Then you would work twice as hard to drive them over the edge into total hysteria. Sadistic? Absolutely. And the "bits" were wild and obscene. Sex experiences topped the list; they were treated with all possible invention, elaboration, exaggeration and surrealistic fantasy. The "What if" bits were also popular, spun off with the stabbing force of black humor. "What if the pilots in the big airlines were really juiced out of their skulls and had to ditch their plane and passengers?" "What if the junkies were to take over the U.N.?" This kind of fantasy was not merely satirical, not merely incongruous in the usual manner of humor. It was desecratory. In doing such bits myself I found that at some moments you flew out of yourself, becoming purely a channel for inspiration; there was an almost total loss of self-consciousness and of awareness of the present moment. In the personal narrative of past experience you used yourself ruthlessly, exulting in the exposure of the weaknesses and deficiencies of an earlier self. Using the former self as the butt of the present self meant indulging in an orgy of triumphant self-hatred, an exorcism of the loathed self-image.

One thing that emerged clearly from the spontaneous comic brilliance of these ritual staging sessions was the fact that anger stimulated and inspired all of us. There was just enough Jewish identity left in these young people's fairly well-assimilated families to make an issue of it—an issue which stirred them deeply; in a word, they felt contaminated by their parents. Their satire was born in the rejection of their immediately surrounding world, in the desecration of first the family, then the neighborhood and finally the whole milieu in which they had grown up. Instead of swallowing or disguising their emotions, these young Jews—consumed with self-hate or shame—came out in the open and blasted the things that hurt them.

Basic to the mentality of these Brooklyn comics was this:

they had polarized to a grotesque degree the values of intelligence, good breeding and culture on the one hand; and their own condition as crude, wild, Jewish outcasts and pariahs on the other. Even in later life their tenacity in holding to these opposing images was absolutely incredible. No amount of experience, persuasion or love could efface these convictions; they were primary images imprinted indelibly on their souls and—curiously—retained as much by a fondness for them as by an incapacity to shed them. For if they were vulgar and uneducated, yet they were also "smaht." If they lacked culture, yet they had fun. The balance psychically was such that they were as much in love with their imperfections as they were enraged by them. What they needed, and found, was a medium in which to register this confused and complex self-awareness. That this medium was comedy followed from the fact that they could not express their feelings with perfect seriousness. Like the hypochondriac who fears he is dying of a fatal disease, they knew in one part of their minds that they were not so badly off as they liked to imagine; that, in fact, their sense of inferiority was an exaggerated conceit. Comedy, therefore, provided the license and the medium for the extreme exaggeration of reality that corresponded with the intensity of their feelings.

These Brooklyn bright boys that I knew were a particular group, but they were not unique. Their obsessions and their inspirations are typical of the Jewish comic, the boy-man, who is exerting such a powerful influence on American humor today. And this humor cannot be understood without digging to its core, to its family roots: to the pain, the humiliation, the anger and the alienation imprinted early on the boy who eventually finds release in comic raving, ranting and raging. He grows up to be not a man, but a boy-man, because—no matter how bright, verbal or intellectually attuned—he is in part still a child "acting out" to gain attention, a child having a tantrum to punish his parents, a child cursing the forces of darkness which terrify and torture him.

Having derived its first surge of anger and conflict from

the family, Jewish humor builds next on the social setting: the problems of assimilation—of survival—for the Jew in a Gentile world. The American Jew, whose roots are basically lower-middle-class, is forced to adapt himself to a society whose values are set by upper-middle-class Gentiles. It seems puzzling on the surface that he should still be preoccupied with the Jew-Gentile confrontation and conflict, should still fear the *goyim*, even when he is apparently secure and well integrated; however, it may really be a sign of the Jew's growing confidence that he exposes his sense of alienation so openly rather than hiding his anxious fantasies within. Recognizing himself as an outsider, an alien among Gentiles, the Jew regards his position with characteristic ambivalence: both pride and contempt. Traditionally the Jews think of themselves as clever and knowing, scorning the *goyim* as dumb and slow-witted. In complete contrast, however, the Jews also traditionally identify weakness, suffering and disaster with themselves; in turn, they attribute health, physical strength and normality to the Gentiles. In order to deal with this confusing mixture of pride and contempt, the Jew has classically adopted the figure of the *schlemiel* as a symbol of his predicament.

Using the theme of the *schlemiel* is standard not only for the nightclub comic's routine (beginning with his ridiculing himself), but also for the comic novels written by authors such as Wallace Markfield, Bruce Jay Friedman and even the more serious Saul Bellow. The classic *schlemiel* is the "I" dramatized as inept, inadequate, foolish, exploited or self-deceiving in a situation that elicits the audience's sympathy or tears. Today's entertainers, however, have transformed the basic pattern; they have so distorted the *schlemiel's* dilemma by comic imagination that he becomes terribly funny rather than sad. The psychological dynamics underlying the pose of the *schlemiel* help explain its duration and popularity: it is safer to attack ourselves or to laugh at ourselves before others do, because in this way we gain the offensive. By controlling the re-enactment of our inadequacy imaginatively and cleverly, we also have the psychological satisfaction of enlisting sympathetic laughter. As Freud has shown, people side with us when they laugh at something with us; and this solidarity exists even when we encourage them to laugh with us *at us*. The *schlemiel*'s power rests on his daring to lay bare his own weakness and to acknowledge his own limitations. Although he may appear pathetic or absurd, the *schlemiel* conceals behind his mask a hidden strength: a shrewd sense of self-preservation.

Bruce Jay Friedman's *Stern* is the most vividly drawn, the most completely unmasked *schlemiel* created by any modern American writer. The novel which bears his name presents an exhausting and penetrating image of the Jewish fantasies underlying most modern humor. Stern, in his early thirties, is "a tall, round-shouldered man with pale, spreading hips" who lives with his wife and child in a Gentile community. His story is an emotional odyssey initiated by a small but dreadful incident. Coming home from work one day, Stern is shocked to hear from his wife that when their child had tried to play with the other children, a neighbor— a man—had pushed her down, snatched up his own child and bellowed: "No playing here for kikes." Equally horrifying, his wife reports that because she was not wearing underpants she had exposed herself to the man when she fell. Interpreting this event symbolically as a rape, Stern absorbs this news as the confirmation of one of his worst fears, building on it obsessively until he is driven almost insane. He is, and has always been, the perfect victim—unable to talk with his neighbors, afraid of everyone, fearful even of calling the police. He is not only ashamed of things that are not his fault (like his ravaged garden eaten by caterpillars), but he is also prey to dreadful anxieties and is forever imagining disaster. Paralyzed by baffled anger which he cannot express, he is plagued by paranoid fantasies: that the cold wind will freeze his penis, snapping it off; that his wife will be unfaithful to him at every opportunity; that his child will fall ill and die.

Stern's insecurities relate to his early childhood, to his being continually exploited by his mother and to his even witnessing her infidelities. His Jewish education was a farce, superficial and meaningless; for him being a Jew comes to mean nothing more than being required to suffer. Fixated on an adolescent identity and overwhelmed by repressed, hostile emotions, Stern retreats into illness, is sent to a rest home, and—not surprisingly for a victim—receives little comfort from his family. Among the very ill he feels some relief, only to become once again excessively anxious when he returns to reality. Eventually he exacts some small satisfaction from the man who insulted his wife. Nothing, however, has really changed. Fear is basic to his being and will always haunt him.

Stern is pure black humor which, if presented seriously, would be an unbearable nightmare; instead, it is all played on a note of absurdity and intense hilarity, the fears made funny and thus tolerable. Stern's playing the *schlemiel* to the ultimate degree diminishes him to quivering helplessness and yet at the same time saves him—by allowing him to escape into sickness. Reduced to the complete and captive victim in a rest home, he finds strength—not enough to triumph, surely, but enough to survive. Although Stern pays a horrifyingly high price as a *schlemiel*, he also uses this role as a means to withdraw from painful realities. It is in truth his fantasy life from which he cannot protect himself; in real life, however, being the *schlemiel* serves as a refuge and as a rationalization for him.

Similarly, it is significant that Stern continually uses his Jewishness as a rationale for his inferiority and inadequacy. It is probably true that some of his deepest fears and weaknesses originated in the Jewish family and its conflicts, his particular family; and that he has been cursed from childhood with obsessions and terrors that inevitably trail him through the years. Stern himself, however, blames Jewishness in a different sense, a social sense. He sees himself persecuted on a larger scale—by people around him, not by his past. For many years he has divided reality into two parts, seeing everything virile, attractive and acceptable as Gentile; everything ugly, cowardly and eccentric as Jewish. By acting on this conviction and moving to the Gentile hinterlands—the neighborhood he chose for his family—he was inviting trouble for himself at the same time that he readied his excuse: terrible things happened to him simply because he was Jewish. Basically Stern is grateful to have such an excuse as an available and expandable container for his frightening anxieties.

Here, one explanation for the immense popularity of Jewish humor in America should be underscored: the seductive appeal of the *schlemiel* pose—in many variations—as an excuse, an apology and a rationalization. To be a *schlemiel* is to have a stronghold for retreat. Stern's convenient use of his Jewish identity to justify his feeling of being an outsider, a victim, a man who doesn't belong—and his total inability to direct his anger at those who really provoke or exploit him —help explain the wide appeal of Jewish humor. Perhaps more than in any other way the Jew as *schlemiel* is the symbol of Everyman in America 1967, a symbol which stimulates not only sympathy but also empathy. Today there are countless Americans of Stern's generation who suffer from similar feelings of inadequate virility and masculine power, similar repressions of turbulent negative emotions and similar convictions of inferiority and alienation.

The two cornerstones of Jewish humor—family and social—are united finally by a third building block: the cultural. Of the many factors responsible for creating the problems of this generation we have been discussing, the one most relevant to comedy has been the incalculably persuasive influence of the mass media on emotional development. Growing up in the Thirties and Forties, the American child was fed on late-afternoon radio serials (usually stressing virility), in the evening he sprawled on the floor to read comics, and on Saturdays he sat in the charged darkness of the movies, entranced by seductive images and situations.

This generation, the first to have been so totally conditioned to desire and to expect a world of make-believe, was frozen into a state of imaginative and emotional retardation. Since reality could not possibly rival the glamorous illusions so deeply implanted by films, radio and newspapers, they found in comparison that their lives seemed excruciatingly drab.

The movies not only whetted the sexual appetite beyond any hope of fulfillment, they also promoted notions of masculinity and femininity that were impossible to live up to: gauze-clad harem beauties, supremely masculine men and scenes of dissolving sexual ecstasy—enticing but unattainable images. This kind of mass-cultural conditioning produced a generation seething with sexual expectations that are not only highly unrealistic but also constantly being checked by America's lingering Puritanism. Suffering from a sense of inferiority in comparison to the magnetic movie idols, and madly determined to preserve its youth and vitality, this generation is fundamentally disillusioned and angry at the farcically immense gap between the illusions they have been spoon-fed and the realities they inevitably find paltry. Ironically, the degree of disillusionment with adult life in America is more intense than elsewhere—not only because there has been an extreme exposure to illusion but also because the chances of fulfilling wild fantasies *are* in fact more real here. When it is impossible to relinquish a fantasy and equally impossible to fulfill it, the stalemate is extraordinarily painful. Here, comedy provides one kind of solution: to reactivate the fantasy, to act it out while simultaneously making fun of it; to turn it inside out in order to attack and enjoy it all over again at the same time.

The satisfaction and release obtained by reactivating those fantasies which have in reality been very frustrating explains why the favorite subjects of modern comedy are: the standard movie formulas of the Thirties and Forties, characters from the comics and adventure radio programs, and the common symbols for American ideals. Furthermore, because these images evoke a combination of hatred and nostalgia they serve as triggers for comic indignation. One of Lenny Bruce's routines illustrates how symbolic American values can be exorcised by violent desecration. He tells how when the door-to-door saleswoman pushing a well-known brand of cosmetics called at his house, he drugged her, stripped her, decked her out with galoshes and a mustache, raped her and wrote on her belly in lipstick: "You were balled!" Here, the lady is representative of The American Dream Girl, the type portrayed on film by June Allyson— sweet, innocent, pretty, healthy and voluptuous; presumably as succulently inviting as a piece of candy. Bruce's comic reduction of her is a vicious attack against an unattainable dream, an unrealizable fantasy.

In this same vein, the literary version of the sick comic's stand-up routine is presented in Terry Southern and Mason Hoffenberg's novel, *Candy*. Although the more important of these two authors, Southern, is not Jewish, his satiric strategy is identical with Bruce's. Again, an innocent girl— one who keeps earnestly proclaiming that "to give of oneself is a thrilling privilege"—is degraded and humiliated in scene after scene. To smash the tantalizing image, horribly and yet hilariously, is the purpose of the book. In *Candy*, however, it is not only the "Dream Girl" who is attacked. A whole gallery of cinema stereotypes is mocked and defiled: a bearded college professor, an ideal suburban couple, a white-coated doctor. From begining to end this novel is a rollicking revenge on mass-culture illusions.

The reactions of the current generation of Americans to the disillusionment brought on by the conflict between reality and the fantasies of the mass media are too complex to be contained within any formula; already they have found outlets in Pop Art, camp and other styles that have no Jewish affinities. This disillusionment, however, has fused with the feelings of disenchantment, anger and ambivalence that are the stuff of Jewish humor; and this fusion explains not only many of the symbols of this humor but also the source of its appeal to Americans generally.

The overwhelming impact of the Jew on American humor today has meaning that is not suggested by the surface ripples made by Jewish fun books and the fad of Yiddish phrases. Jewishness itself has become a metaphor for modern life. The individual Jew—the alien in search of identity—has become a symbolic protagonist. As he dares more and more to expose his inner turmoil to self-satire, the Jew is discovering in turn that Americans are more and more receptive to his comic consciousness: to ironic mockery of personal plights, to bittersweet retreats from painful realities and to angry thrusts at broken dreams. The Jew having become a symbolic representative for our time, his humor—his great cultural weapon and consolation—can now be appreciated in its raw form by millions of people who have no connection with the Jewish community and who are not even aware that what they are laughing at is Jewish humor.

Explorations, 1967

A Lenny Bruce Triptych

1. THE COMEDY OF
LENNY BRUCE

> *Since the shaman functions as a safety valve,*
> *and as a regulator of the psychic life of the*
> *clan, he lives under the permanent feeling of*
> *bearing a great responsibility. . . . Sometimes,*
> *if he loses control of the spirits, he must be*
> *killed.*
>
> S. M. SHEROKOGROFF

I<small>N THE WINTER</small> of 1962 in Chicago, the comedian Lenny
Bruce was convicted of obscenity and sentenced to one year
in jail and a $1,000 fine. Shortly afterward, he was also con-
victed by a Los Angeles court of narcotics possession. These
convictions, currently being appealed, are by no means the
only run-ins Bruce has had with the authorities. Since returning from his world tour in 1962, Bruce has been arrested
seven times in all: twice in Los Angeles on suspicion of narcotics possession; four times for obscenity (he was acquitted
in San Francisco and Philadelphia); and once for assault in

Van Nuys, California. Earlier, he had been twice barred from entering England; on the first occasion, he was turned back within an hour at the airport, when authorities simply denied him a work permit. The second time, entering England via Ireland, and bearing with him affidavits attesting to his probity, sobriety and general moral earnestness, Bruce was allowed to stay the night, only to become on the following day the subject of emergency intervention by the Home Secretary, who declared his presence not to be "in the public interest." On these occasions, as in previous encounters with the agencies of law enforcement, Bruce showed himself courteous, even disarmingly so, to his antagonists and a trifle bewildered, it seemed, at the havoc he could create merely by turning up. He boarded a plane and went back home.

Bruce has been called "blasphemous," "obscene" and "sick"—and not only in the expected quarters (Walter Winchell, Robert Ruark, assorted *Variety* pundits, etc.) but by critics like Benjamin DeMott and Kenneth Alcott. On the other hand, of course, there are equally sophisticated critics like Robert Brustein and Kenneth Tynan who have arrived at opposite conclusions, finding Bruce not only essentially "healthy," but the physician, as it were, for the illness from which all of us are suffering. While certain spokesmen for an American "underground" have claimed him for their own, Bruce has also earned a vast popular following, far exceeding the limits of any coterie. Long before his present notoriety, indeed, he was one of the most successful nightclub performers in the country, earning on the average $5,000 a week and with his record-album sales totaling well over 100,000. Fellow comics are among Bruce's keenest admirers and, if not always admitting their debt to him publicly, frequently reveal it by imitation. Among his most articulate disciples are the British social satirists of groups like the Establishment and *Beyond the Fringe*, who have been even more unstinting than the Americans in acknowledging both his fascination and his influence.

What, then, explains Bruce's unique effect? Certainly, his impact cannot be attributed to his material alone. By now, so completely have the so-called "sick" comics caught on—and so quickly has the authentic radical satire of a few years ago been rendered innocuous by sheer acceptance and then imitation—that it no longer requires daring, originality or courage to attack sacred cows like integration, Mother's Day, the flag. Such things are done, albeit in diluted form, virtually on every network. Yet Bruce seems immune from that permissiveness that is in the end perhaps more subversive of true protest than censorship. Uniquely among members of his profession (and matched in others perhaps only among jazz musicians), Bruce continues to shock, to infuriate, to be the subject on the one hand of a passionate and almost unprecedented advocacy, and on the other of a constant surveillance amounting to persecution, so that today, at the height of his drawing power, it is doubtful whether a club in New York would dare to book him.

Bruce slouches onstage in a crumpled black raincoat ("dressed for the bust," as he confidingly informs the audience, in anticipation of arrest), pale, unshaven, with long black sideburns—beat, raffish, satanic. Ordering the lights up, he surveys the house: "Yeah. You're good-looking. You got lotsa bread." He pauses. "Good-looking chicks always got lotsa bread. That's a hooker syllogism." Having opened on this amiable note, he abruptly switches his tone and manner to lull the audience into temporary security, then launches into an apparently off-the-cuff discourse on themes of the moment:

"You know? Liberals will buy anything a bigot writes. They really support it. George Lincoln Rockwell's probably just a very knowledgeable businessman with no political convictions whatsoever. He gets three bucks a head working mass rallies of nothing but angry Jews, shaking their fists and wondering why there are so many Jews there."

Even in this relatively minor bit, the distinctive qualities of Bruce's satire are in evidence: it is authentically shocking and nihilistic to a degree that is not altogether apparent at first. To make fun of liberals these days is an act of conventional daring; to make fun of George Lincoln Rockwell these days is an act of slightly less conventional daring; but to make fun of a "proper" moral response to George Lincoln Rockwell constitutes the violation of a taboo. What Bruce is doing by finding in George Lincoln Rockwell an ordinary businessman out for the main chance, goes far beyond the modish cliché of "the guilt we all share"—it amounts to an implication of normality itself in the monstrous. Perhaps this accounts for the slightly hysterical quality of the laughter that his performances usually elicit. It is helplessness in the face of a truly nihilistic fury that makes the parody currently fashionable in the nightclubs and the off-Broadway theaters seem safe and cautious.

Bruce's vision forbids the smallest hint of self-congratulation, allows no comfortable perch from which the audience can look complacently down on the thing satirized. Even his "conventional" routines take a bizarre and violent course, which transforms them into something quite different from mere parody. There is one, for instance, in which an "ordinary white American" tries to put a Negro he has met at a party at ease. The predictable blunders with their underlying viciousness ("That Joe Louis was a hell of a fighter. . . . Did you eat yet? I'll see if there's any watermelon left. . . .") are within the range of any gifted satirist with his heart in the right place; but Bruce gives the screw an added turn by making the protagonist, besotted with temporary virtue, a forthright and entirely ingenuous Jew-hater as well—sincerely making common cause with the Negro. This is closer to surrealism than to simple farce, a fantasy on the subject of bigotry far more startling than a merely perfect sociological rendition of the accents of race hatred would have been. And as the routine proceeds, the fantasy gets wilder and wilder, with the white man becoming more and more insinuatingly confidential in his friendliness ("What is it with you guys? Why do you always want to do it to everybody's sister? . . . You really got a big wang on you, huh? Hey, could I see it?") and the Negro becoming progressively stiffer and more bewildered.

Similarly, Bruce has a fairly conventional routine that might have been dreamed up in its general outline fifteen years ago by a stand-up comedian from the Lower East Side, but that he pushes to what would have been unthinkable lengths fifteen years ago. The performer, in the guise of himself, encounters a "typical" Jewish couple while on a Midwestern tour; they are at first shy and admiring, until the inevitable question is asked and the discovery is made— Bruce is Jewish; then their respect and timidity give way first to a slightly insulting familiarity and finally to overt, violent aggression. The routine which, again, would once have been played for folksiness, becomes bizarre and disturbing when Bruce uses it to expose within the couple depths of prurient malevolence far in excess of their apparent "human" failings. The climax is an orgy of vituperation in the familial mode that becomes a glaring and devastating comment on Jewish life in America.

Until a few years ago, this kind of humor had never been seen in a nightclub or theater. It appeared to be completely original, yet obviously it mined a rich, seemingly inexhaustible vein and was, moreover, enforced by a highly finished technique. Critics responded to Bruce at first as though he were *sui generis*, a self-created eccentric of genius without discernible origins. Yet nothing could be further from the truth. What Lenny Bruce is doing today in public had been done for years in private, not only by him but by dozens of amateurs all over New York City—at private parties, on street corners, in candy stores. His originality consists in his having been the first to use this private urban language in public, and his genius lies in his ability to express the ethos out of which he comes in unadulterated form.

He is, in other words, a genuine folk artist who stands in a

relation to the lower-middle-class adolescent Jewish life of
New York not unlike that of Charlie Parker to the Negroes
of Harlem. And like Parker, he derives his strength from
having totally available to himself—and then being able to
articulate—attitudes, ideas, images, fragments of experience
so endemic to a culture that they scarcely ever come to conscious awareness. Thus for many people the shock of watching Bruce perform is primarily the shock of recognition.

The psychological mechanism of this kind of comedy is
well enough known by now: it is a means of expressing hatred and contempt and still escaping punishment. But the
matter is complicated by the fact that the comic's sensitivity
to imperfection and ugliness is heightened by a conviction
of his own inadequacy, vulgarity, and hypocrisy, leading
him to become doubly intolerant of these faults in others.
They haunt him; they are demons that he seeks to exorcise
by comic confrontation. The psychological source of such
satire is, thus, a persistent, ineradicable hatred of the self,
and this is particularly striking in the case of Bruce, whose
sense of moral outrage is intimately connected with an
awareness of his own corruption. ("I can't get worked up
about politics. I grew up in New York, and I was hip as a kid
that I was corrupt and that the mayor was corrupt. I have
no illusions.") If the practitioner of this kind of comedy is
in any way morally superior to his audience, it is only because he is *honest*, and willing to face himself, while they,
the audience, are blind enough to think *they* are pure.

Lenny Bruce is not, as one might suppose, a product of
the New York urban ghetto. He grew up in an Andy Hardy
town on Long Island and never spoke a Yiddish word till he
was twenty-five. He served during the war on the cruiser
Brooklyn, participating in all the famous landings (Salerno,
Anzio, etc.), and only after the war did he drift into the
show-business jungle of Times Square, encouraged by the
example of his mother, Sally Marr, who had moved during
the war years from a suburban dancing school to a skimpy

career as an M.C. and comedienne.

For several years, Bruce moved around digging other comics, haunting their hangouts, trying to work out an act of his own. Finally, in 1949, he appeared on the Arthur Godfrey talent show and won. Soon he was doing a conventional "single" at the Strand and other presentation houses, but he loathed "the business" and often thought about deserting for the merchant marine or some other less meretricious profession.

The decisive moment for his career came in 1957 while Bruce was working on the West Coast as a screen writer and burlesque comic. At about this time Mort Sahl, also on the Coast, was becoming famous. ("I was just a product of my time," Sahl has said. "This license was lying around waiting for someone to pick it up.") The novelty of Sahl's act undoubtedly stimulated Bruce's breakthrough and helped establish an audience ready to respond to Bruce's first original creation: a series of satirical bits based on a potent symbol evolved in the early "home-cooking" days—the shingle man.

A type of "con" man prevalent after the war, the shingle man spent much of his time on the road, usually traveling in groups, doing comic routines, smoking marijuana, taking time off now and then to talk gullible slum residents into buying new roofing. Though strictly a small-time operator, the ruthlessly manipulating shingle man came, in Bruce's universe, to represent any and all wielders of power and authority—up to and including the most grandiose. The great world, in short—all political, social or religious activity—is nothing but a gigantic racket run by shingle men. In a Bruce routine called "Religion, Inc.," for example, organized religion was reduced to a three-way phone conversation between the Pope, Billy Graham and Oral Roberts making plans in hipster jargon ("Hey, John! What's shaking, baby?") for a world-wide religious revival complete with giveaway items (a cigarette lighter in the form of a cross and cocktail napkins bearing the imprint "Another martini for Mother Cabrini").

Similarly, in another routine of this period, Bruce portrays Hitler as the brainstorm of a couple of shrewd theatrical agents, who discover the new "star" while he is painting their office and set him up with costumes (an armband with the four "7's"), music, routines—in short, an act. Lavishly applying the metaphor of the shingle man to every social institution in the book, Bruce embarked upon a career whose underlying intention has remained constant, though his style has gone through many changes: to set up a remorselessly unqualified identification of power and respectability with corruption.

It is a mistake to regard Bruce simply as a social satirist, for he has long since transcended the limitations of that role, just as he has long since gone beyond mere irreverence in his routines. Indeed, for the most apposite metaphor describing what Bruce does, one must turn from show business to the seemingly remote domain of cultural anthropology. Géza Roheim's description of the shaman, exorciser of public demons, sharply reveals the true character of Lenny Bruce's present "act." "In every primitive tribe we find the shaman in the center of society and it is easy to show that he is either a neurotic or a psychotic, or at least that his art is based on the same mechanisms as a neurosis or psychosis. The shaman makes both visible and public the systems of symbolic fantasy that are present in the psyche of every adult member of society. They are the leaders in an infantile game and the lightning conductors of common anxiety. They fight the demons so that others can hunt the prey and in general fight reality."

Although "sick" humor appears to be a remarkably unfeeling reaction to misery, particularly to physical deformity, it actually is an oblique protest against the enforced repression of those instinctive emotions of revulsion, anxiety and guilt evoked by deformity. It represents a distorted rebellion against the piety that demands automatic sympathy for literally every form of human limitation. Though neither Mort Sahl nor Bruce can be wholly identified with "sick" comedy, the shock techniques used by both gave them something in common with the outrageous jokes that were spreading through the country during the middle and late Fifties. (With Sahl, also, Bruce shares other things: the technique of the encyclopedic monologue, the courage to deal in forbidden subjects, the use of hipster language and an obvious identification with the jazz world.) For a time Bruce's act was sprinkled with "sick" jokes, but they never constituted more than a small portion of his verbal arsenal.

Unlike Sahl, however, whose specialty is political satire, Bruce has never had much to say about politics; the abuse is too obvious. There is a further difference: Sahl is primarily a wit and a social commentator; while Bruce's imagination is a more creative one, which has enabled him to produce a remarkable variety of characters, situations, and lines of comic action. The next stage in Bruce's development saw the shingle man superseded by a richer, more personal metaphor—show business itself. Balancing his own profound self-contempt against his loathing for the "business," Bruce created his most complex parable, a routine called "The Palladium." A cocksure little nightclub comic, crude, untalented, but "on the make" for success, is disgusted with working the "toilets" (second-rate clubs) and determines to take a crack at the big-time. Booked into the London Palladium, he is slated to follow "Georgia Gibbs," a performer who knows exactly what the public wants and "puts them away" every time. His vulgar, corny gags fail to get a laugh and he "dies." Desperate to succeed, he begs for another chance, but is swamped in the wake of the singer, who caps her cunningly contrived performance with a lachrymose tribute to "the boys who died over there."

The little comic lacks the wit to change even a single line of his mechanical act, and again he is about to "die" when, confronting disaster, he blindly ad libs a line: "Hey, folks, how 'bout this one—screw the Irish!" This puerile bid for attention instantly transforms the somnolent audience into a raging mob who sweep the comic off the stage and wreck the theater.

Clearly, show business for Bruce stands for American society itself—and, indeed, in no other country have entertainers come to be more profoundly symbolic of national values than here. The anxiety to please which takes the form of tear-jerking sentimentality and fake humanitarianism in "Georgia Gibbs" is no less ruthlessly dramatized in the portrait of the brash little comedian, whom we can take as a comic degradation of Bruce himself, and whose story is a reflection of Bruce's own development. Not only does he expose the agonies that assault the performer whose very life depends on his success with the audience; he also satirizes one of the most remarkable features of his own present role as shaman—the direct, brutal onslaught on the passions and prejudices of his audience that stems from desperation in the face of failure and that sets off an appalling explosion of primitive hatred.

While he lacks the dramatic gifts of Elaine May, Sid Caesar or Jonathan Winters—with their actors' techniques of mimicry, foreign accents, and sound effects—Bruce is nevertheless at his best in personal narratives put across with just a suggestion of the dramatic. His work, in fact, is intensely personal and provides an obvious outlet for his private rage; nevertheless, there is a part of Bruce that is utterly disinterested. Like any satirist, he knows that the only effective way to attack corruption is to expose and destroy it symbolically; that the more elaborately and vividly this destruction is imagined, the greater will be his own satisfaction, and the more profound the cathartic effect on the audience. Thus, gradually moving from a wholly conventional act through a series of increasingly wild and outspoken routines, Bruce has indeed become the shaman: he has taken on himself the role of exorcising the private fears and submerged fantasies of the public by articulating in comic form the rage and nihilistic savagery hidden beneath the lid of social inhibition.

In one of his recent routines Bruce orders the house lights out and then announces: "Now, you know what's going to happen? I'm going to piss on the audience. The clapping is from those who had it before and enjoyed it." This promise of outrage is not kept, but is followed rather by Bruce's version of how the audience had reacted. "What did he say?" Bruce asks, taking the part of a male patron, "Did he say he's gonna 'S' on us?" Now he mimics a woman's voice: "Oh, shut up, Harry! He does it real cute."

This routine vividly illustrates Bruce's attitude toward his audience; he regards it as an object of sadistic lust, he hates and loves it; it is the enticing enemy, and he attacks it repeatedly. In the past his aggression was masked, but now it is naked. He may pick up a chair and menace a patron; if the audience laughs, he will observe soberly that he might have killed the man and that if he had, everyone would have accepted the murder as part of the act. Here he demonstrates, almost in the manner of a classroom exercise, the repressed violence of modern society. By making the audience *laugh* at incipient murder, he has tricked them into exposing their own savage instincts. The implication is that given the slightest excuse for condoning a killing, even the absurd rationale of its being part of a nightclub act, society would join eagerly in the violence it so conscientiously deplores.

This public display of the ugly, the twisted, the perverse —offensive though it is at times—nevertheless serves a vital function, for it gives the audience a profound sense, not only of release, but of self-acceptance. Again and again, Bruce violates social taboos—and he does not die! Like the witch doctor or the analyst, he brings the unconscious to light and thereby lightens the burden of shame and guilt. By its very nature his material cannot come out clear, decorous and beautifully detached; it must be, and is, charged with self-pity, self-hatred, fear, horror, crudity, grotesquerie.

What is unsatisfactory in Bruce's work is his frequent failure to transmute his rage into real comedy. Sometimes he has nothing more to offer than an attitude ("Everything is rotten. Mother is rotten. The flag is rotten. God is rotten."). At other times, what starts with a promise of rounded development will flatten out into a direct and insulting statement. A sophisticated listener forgives the comic these lapses, understanding that the ad lib approach and the often intractable material are apt to betray the performer into mere obscenity; but people with no natural sympathy for this approach are shocked and offended—there has never been a lack of people in the audience to walk out during Bruce's act.

The reason for these occasional lapses into crudity is the almost total lack of "art" in Bruce's present act; he deliberately destroys the aesthetic distance that is a convention of the theater, established by tacit agreement between audience and performer that what is happening on the stage is an illusion of life rather than life itself. Like other performers who deal in direct communication, Bruce has always tried to *reduce* the barrier between the stage and reality. He has never wanted to appear as an entertainer doing an act, but rather as himself, no different onstage from off, not really a performer, but a man who performs in order to share with others his most secret thoughts and imaginings. The desire, however, to eradicate the distinction between art and reality has at this stage almost completely destroyed the artistry with which Bruce formerly presented his material. Gone, now, are the metaphors of the shingle man and the show business manipulator; gone, too, are the storytelling devices of the personal narrative and the dramatic impersonations. All that remains are sketchy, often underdeveloped, sometimes incoherent scraps of former routines.

The new material consists of deep, psychologically primitive fantasies, hurled at a defenseless audience without the mitigating intervention of art. Frequently, Bruce assaults his listeners with scatological outbursts consisting of the crudest and most obvious anal and oral sadistic fantasies, undisguised.

Much of his current material is in fact unquotable—not so much because of the language but because its comic effect depends on nonverbal associations and is thereby scarcely intelligible in the reading. In one long and complicated routine, which changes from one performance to another, he explains that the Lone Ranger's bullets are really pellets of Ehrlich's 606 ("That's why he keeps his mouth tightly shut") and that the Lone Ranger is a homosexual ("Bring Tonto here. I wish to commit an unnatural act. Wait a minute! Bring the horse too!"). (This deliberate perpetration of outrage on the persons of the most innocuous figures of American folklore—the Lone Ranger, the Avon representative—is, of course, one of the leitmotifs of the recent "sick" humor. The same thing was once done in a grimier way in those pornographic comic books that showed the heroes of the comic strip—familiar to every American child—in complicated sexual situations.)

As his material has become more direct, Bruce has tended more and more to *be* the act. Because the imaginative impulse is naked, unsublimated, Bruce's intention is less and less communicated by what he says, and depends now, to a great extent, on affective devices—his manner, his tone, especially his physical appearance. Whereas in the past Bruce would walk briskly out on the floor, good-looking, impeccably groomed, wearing a chic Italian suit, now he comes on stiff-legged and stooped, wearing shabby clothes, his face a pale mask of dissipation. Having discarded the civilized mask that people wear in public to protect themselves, Bruce comes before his audience as a mythic figure—beat, accused junkie, "underground" man—who has suffered in acting out their own forbidden desires. Where they are cautious, he is self-destructive, alternately terrifying the audience (the very fact that *he doesn't care* is awesome) and arousing their sympathy and concern. (He now regularly opens his act by enacting and commenting on his recent arrests.) Merely looking at Bruce these days is a disturbing experience.

Finally, Bruce is dramatizing his role as shaman by embellishing his act for the first time with consciously contrived bits of hocus-pocus. He turns the lights on and off, strikes drums and cymbals, swings into crude chants. He prowls about the stage, sometimes exposing himself to the audience, at other times crouching in the darkness and hiding from it. He opens and closes doors and climbs onto furniture to symbolize his power over the bewildered spectators.

In the darkened, cavelike club, charged with tension, the audience sits hunched over, tense, breathless, their eyes fastened on the weird figure in the center of the magic circle. While the tribe looks on with fearful absorption, the medicine man puts himself into a trance in preparation for the terrible struggle with the tribal demons (anxieties). And then—when the performance is over and the "unspeakable" has been shouted forth—there is mingled with the thunderous applause a sigh of release. Purged of their demons by the shaman, the tribe has been freed, for the moment, to "hunt the prey and in general fight reality."

Commentary, 1963

2. ONE LAW FOR THE LION AND OX

On December 21, 1964, the comedian Lenny Bruce was sentenced in a New York court to four months in the workhouse for giving "obscene, indecent, immoral and impure" performances in violation of Section 1140-a of the Penal Law. Thus ended the longest, costliest, most vigorously contested and widely publicized trial of an American artist or entertainer in recent years—and perhaps the most exhaustive judicial investigation ever undertaken of allegedly obscene performances. In bringing together all the parties affected by censorship—the performer himself, the avant-garde who rushed to his rescue, the liberal intelligentsia who provided his defense, and the offended middle class represented by the magistrates—the Bruce trial dramatically demonstrated the inadequacy of the current legal code to deal with the complex and conflict-laden issues of the sexual content of modern art and entertainment. After nine months of legal maneuvers, thousands of pages of expert testimony and the lengthy deliberations of the bench, this trial left everyone who has been associated with it profoundly dissatisfied. The three-judge panel split its decision, with the dissenting magistrate, J. Randall Creel, writing, "the judicial process revealed itself as a most limited and inadequate, if not improper tool [for determining what is obscene.]" The defendant broke openly with his distinguished liberal attorney (who promptly sued him) and assumed his own defense, stating that he believed in censorship and did not wish to be exonerated at the cost of weakening the law. The sophisticated public opinion that had championed Bruce in the early course of the trial changed during the muddled final phase to disgust. By the time sentence was passed, it was impossible to say which was more resented—the decision or the defendant.

What had gone wrong? How had all the care and work and expertise produced such a frustrating result? The first and most obvious culprit was the law itself. Or perhaps one should say the laws, for though Bruce was indicted under a New York City ordinance—an archaic statute whose anxiously overlapping adjectives had never been clarified because the law had been so rarely invoked—the character of his trial was really determined by state laws that have frequently been tested and refined through appeals to the Supreme Court.

Every American state except New Mexico has now adopted the definition of "obscenity" promulgated by the Supreme Court in 1957:

> "Obscene" means that to the average person, applying contemporary standards, the predominant appeal of the matter, taken as a whole, is to prurient interest, i.e.,

a shameful or morbid interest in nudity, sex or excre-
tion, which goes substantially beyond customary limits
of candor in description or representation of such matters and is matter which is utterly without redeeming
social importance.

Clear as this carefully worded statement may appear, it has
given rise to endless legal arguments. Thus it has been said
that what constitutes "shameful" or "morbid" interest (except in the most extreme cases) is likely to be decided not as
a matter of law but as the highly subjective reaction of the
individual judge. "Prurience," the key term, has been defined by high authorities in two distinctly different formulas: as "inciting lustful thoughts" or as "filthy and disgust-
ing." Lenny Bruce has always operated according to the
former notion; but his judges condemned him under the
latter interpretation, ruling that though the comedian's
monologues were not erotic, "they insulted sex and debased
it."

Just as crucial as the problem presented by relative interpretations of the statute's wording is the objection that the
yardstick of the "average person" is utterly inappropriate to
a complex society and particularly to such a heterogeneous
community as New York City. As if to destroy whatever
semblance of reality this legal fiction might still possess, the
Supreme Court ruled during the course of the Bruce trial
that the "average" was to be understood as a national, not a
local standard—as the average of 180 million people!

Yet despite the extreme permissiveness with which the
Supreme Court has applied the law of obscenity in recent
years (and many have been the complaints that the Court
has virtually wiped out the law), a performer like Lenny
Bruce still stands in jeopardy. For Bruce's work is the expression of an underground society of Jewish hipsters whose
very identity consists of parodying and therefore defying
conventional American values and whose language and
humor reeks of "filth" because obscenity is this society's

basic gesture of defiance and liberation. After habituation to this hipster underworld, its verbal violence and coarse manners cease to offend; but for people like Bruce's judges, Roman Catholic or Protestant, middle-class and well-bred, such a style must appear an intolerable violation of public decorum.

But it is the last clause in the definition of obscenity ("redeeming social importance") that generated the most intense controversy during the Bruce trial. Because this single clause affords blanket coverage to art, Bruce's defenders concentrated on presenting him as a brilliant, mordant satirist of modern society. The judges, on the other hand, saw the "satire"—which was in fact primitive and incoherent—as "a device for exploiting the use of obscene language." Accusers and defenders alike failed to perceive the true character of Bruce's performances, which are in a manner of speaking magical and therefore outside the customary area of relations between art and the law.

Bruce's "art," like that of the shaman in primitive society, depends primarily on his ability to locate and expose the fears and resentments—the "demons"—that beset and torment his audience. Lacking the elaborate artifices of a Genet, Bruce goes about his exorcism in an intuitively direct manner by violating verbal taboos or offering threats of violence or outrage. Then, having laid bare through these shock tactics the elementary emotions and fantasies of his hearers, Bruce applies his extraordinary gift for humor to literally laugh away all this perilous stuff.

It will be evident from even so simple an explanation as this that Lenny Bruce must be "offensive" to be effective, and that the test for whether his work possesses "redeeming social value" lies in a judgment of his success in utilizing obscenity for cathartic effect. Such a judgment could be just only if it were based on actual observation of the comedian's performance, for his words are often only a kind of commentary on what he *does;* but all the evidence available to the court was half-audible tape recordings and transcripts disfigured by mistakes of every description. Faced with this difficult situation, the Bruce defense tried to simplify the performer's highly problematic relation to society by applying to his work as it appeared in the transcripts a thick coat of whitewash. A parade was organized of critics, columnists, editors, professors and clergymen who testified that they found nothing offensive in the comedian's language, gestures and fantasies, though these form one of the densest scatological textures ever exposed on an American stage. It must be said in justification of the intelligence and taste of at least some of these witnesses that they were deliberately overstating their position to protect the defendant from what they regarded as a prejudiced and ill-informed tribunal. But even allowing for strategy, it was quite apparent that most of these liberal intellectual witnesses were not properly responsive to the effective energies of Bruce's performances. (Regrettably, none of them had actually witnessed the performances.)

A crucial irony, therefore, began to emerge at quite an early point in the trial: Bruce's defenders were in one sense less firmly in contact with his work than were his judges, who felt at least the shock of outrage. This basic failure of rapport erupted finally in disagreements between Bruce and his attorneys on the question of his defense strategy. The lawyers, who had never seen Bruce perform, and were less interested in defending his art than in simply getting their client off, wanted to challenge the constitutionality of the law under which he had been indicted. Bruce, convinced that he had not violated the law, wished to have his case tried exclusively on its merits. Though he did not say so publicly, the comedian probably recognized that he and his defenders were not really at one in their attitudes toward his work and that the whole tendency of the defense was toward destroying the very restrictions on which he had spent years carefully structuring his performances. At last Bruce went into court and informed the startled judges that he could no longer "communicate" with his counsel (a felicitous choice of words). Later, he was quoted in a newspaper as saying, "I believe in censorship. I believe in the watchdog."

Bruce's break with the liberal–avant-garde coalition that had so vigorously and efficiently defended him provided the most ironic and revealing moment in the entire legal drama. It demonstrated anew the performer's integrity and courage. Before this act he was sure of eventual acquittal merely by playing the role assigned him by his supporters—that of the blameless artist persecuted by an uncomprehending world. After the break, Bruce became a totally isolated figure, struggling singlehanded with the overwhelming complexities of the law and scorned most by those whose help he had rejected. As a man dedicated to honesty, however, Lenny Bruce could not lend himself to a philosophy that his own experience contradicted in every detail. Instinctively, he knew that by contributing to the attrition of the law he would be weakening the social taboos which the law protects, and that once these taboos were wiped out the valuable cathartic effects of symbolically violating them would also be lost—that, in short, the possibility of his magic would be destroyed. And as a veteran performer, Bruce knew only too well the evil effects of constantly giving way before the irresponsible demands of the audience for greater license; he had felt, as no critic or lawyer had ever felt, that self-defiling compulsion to please by complying with the crowd's cowardly craving for vicarious violence. Indeed, it had been the ennui of sophisticated nightclub audiences, accustomed to hearing everything and therefore responsive to nothing, that had first goaded Bruce into employing his dangerous shock tactics. Clearly, then, he less than anyone could go along with the liberal cant of "removing barriers to freedom of expression." Faced with the possibility of having to plunge into provocative *acts* through the loss of affective content in words and fantasies, he found himself siding with his judges and advocating the values of censorship.

If the application of the law to the satirist is fraught with problems and paradoxes, it is equally so with respect to the avant-garde, which was also on trial in New York at the same time. Jonas Mekas, the founder of the Film-Makers' Cooperative and the prophet of the underground movie world, was tried under the same law as Bruce, convicted but given a suspended sentence. *Flaming Creatures* by Jack Smith and *Un Chant d'Amour* by Jean Genet, the former portraying orgy, the latter masturbation and homosexual rape, were the films for which Mekas was arrested—and it is films, traditionally the most oppressively censored of the arts, on which today's avant-garde and the law collide.

The philosophy activating the new American avant-garde is vastly different from that of a Lenny Bruce; for, like many satirists, Bruce is essentially an inverted Puritan who sees art as a means for symbolically revenging frustrated innocence and idealism. The avant-garde, on the other hand, are genuine radicals who reject alike the alternatives of art or conformity and insist on the right to act out the life-affirming impulses which they are convinced will establish the earthly paradise. Unlike the old Bohemia (how quaint that word sounds today!) which existed primarily to provide the artist with a stimulating, nonrepressive milieu in which he could freely work, this generation's Bohemia—a cool camp staked out in the heart of a swarming slum on the Lower East Side of New York—uses creative activity as a rationale for a way of life that is an inversion of conventional middle-class patterns. Rejecting marriage, eschewing work for money, overturning social taboos and seizing on every means for heightening the impact of experience, such as "consciousness-expanding" drugs and sexual experimentation, these beat "saints" constitute a social class, and their clash with American society is a class war fought under the banners of art.

The potential influence of the avant-garde is far greater than is generally believed, for contrary to what most people think and what the avant-garde itself proclaims, its relation to American society is more an echo than a defiant challenge. It is characteristic of the cultural life of America at this time that every phenomenon of art and manners should reveal the twin features of antagonism to authority and the failure of sublimation. The whole tendency of the avant-garde "revolution" is toward an ever greater degree of infantilism and regression, an acting out of ever more rudimentary fantasies of sex, anger and narcissism. As these are precisely the same tendencies that are slowly coming to the surface of middle-class conformity, the avant-garde is merely a projection of the mass unconscious. Surely it is no accident that in its latest and best publicized phase, called "camp," the avant-garde has embraced with the nostalgia of unrelinquished childhood all the most blatant and banal aspects of American popular culture from the comic strips to the horror films, from the cut-outs on the backs of cereal boxes to the flaring poster of the unattainable movie queen. The values of innocence—spontaneity, candor, "luv"—and the emblems of American childhood make a very appealing demagogy for the cultural regressionary.

Confronted with the sudden collapse of legal barriers that have stood for hundreds of years as safeguards of public decency and morality and constantly provoked by a militant avant-garde who ape the tactics of civil disobedience developed in the civil rights struggle, it is natural that the conservative elements in the community should seek to reestablish the institution of censorship through legal or social instrumentalities. But it seems equally clear that censorship is an institution that has failed by the test of experience. Every recent attempt to apply it through legal action has resulted in the sort of confused and frustrating litigation that characterized the trial of Lenny Bruce. Ideally, there could be a censorship law elastic enough to permit the private showing of such films as *Un Chant d'Amour* while at the same time protecting the general public from what it regards as objectionable and corrupting. Ideally, there could be a law that would be so clear in its stipulations as to what is "obscene" that a social satirist could gauge precisely that split-fraction where he appears to be beyond the fringe but is actually just within the protection of the law. But such ideals cannot be realized in practice, and the attempt to attain them through the elaboration of an explicit and exhaustive code would undoubtedly create a whole set of problems hitherto unglimpsed. Obviously, censorship rests on conditions of social homogeneity and respect for authority that are waning in a country like the United States. Blake's proverb, "one law for the lion & ox is oppression," has for us a meaning that becomes more poignant every day.

Censorship No. 2, 1965

3. THE ELECTRIC RESURRECTION OF SAINT LENNY BRUCE

Death always loved Lenny Bruce. But Lenny was coy and wouldn't surrender. He clung to life with the tenacity of a dying comic. Even after he lost his audience, alienated his friends and became a symbol of foul-mouthed madness, he struggled on through court after court, obsessed with his dream of self-vindication. Finally, he got so tired and sick, he had to lie down. Death was gratified. She lifted her lover into show-biz heaven and restored to him everything he had lost—plus much more. The public bought his act as never before, the courts reversed his conviction for obscenity and the dirty comic became a bearded saint of the pop pantheon. So now let us celebrate Saint Lenny and his miraculous Electric Resurrection. Repeat after me. *Lenny is dead. Lenny lives. Long live Lenny dead!*

The week before he died, Lenny Bruce was so broke and so short of friends that he had to hustle his parole officer for ten bucks. Last year he earned—guess!—*$100,000.* Heavy, right? But *bupkas* compared with what he'll gross next year. Lenny is really moving now. Has his mind on business all the time. Look at the deals he's lined up. Let's see, there's the Columbia Pictures contract: a three-million-dollar *Lenny Bruce Story*, to be written by Bruce Jay Friedman. Then, there's *The Essential Lenny Bruce*, the paperback *shtick*-book, selling at 5,000 per week with 300,000 copies in readers' hands. Soon it'll be time for a sequel: how does *The Private Lenny Bruce* hit you?

The future? Got it covered, baby. There will be a series of records based on the book, one record for each chapter till the act dies. By that time the full-length biography will be out with all the insane tales from Lenny's secret life. In the planning stage are the really far-out things, like the multimedia mix with actors, film, tapes, still photos projected on six screens and white vinyl weather balloons—the whole psychedelic apparatus focused on a *Theater of Lenny Bruce*.

What really happened? The answer is as simple as a deposit slip. Live, Lenny was a problem. Dead, Lenny is a property. Live, Lenny was worse than obscene—he was *boring*, always ranting about dumb things like the First Amendment. I mean, really! Dead, Lenny is this beautiful myth. He's got Esthetic Distance now, and the wild thing about E.D. is that once you've got it, the more whacked-out your behavior, the better for the legend. People will dig anything, providing it's no threat to them. They thrill to the war on TV. They can't read enough about the horrors of the ghetto. They never commit themselves to a hero until he's been assassinated. Well, mister, Lenny Bruce qualifies.

What is more, Lenny dead is Lenny docile. A dead comic can be sorted, sifted, filtered and distilled. You can pick out the good parts and throw the rest away. In the trade it's called "packaging," and Bruce's packager is one of the best, Alan Douglas of Douglas International. Alan is the part of show business that most people never discover; which is a shame, because in this period of minimal talents and major promotions, some of the most polished performers are the guys whose heads are permanently tipped into telephones.

Sitting high above the city in his suite at the Plaza re-

cently, Alan leaned across his carved Florentine table, and
with occasional interruptions to answer his phone, enshrined
before a Hieronymus Bosch facsimile, he explained to me
the secret of the Lenny Bruce comeback. As he spoke, I
tried packaging him. Face: elongated, refined, sardonic; figure: lean, elegant, dressed in Edwardian clothes; hair: Afro-
Jewish bushman; speech: New York Forties hipster with
cultural overlay. Alan was saying that when Lenny died, he
arranged with Lenny's mother, Sally Marr, to become estate
representative. The estate didn't amount to much: a couple
of boxes of carelessly labeled tapes, a mountain of legal documents and some private papers. In the hands of a less expert
merchandiser, the stuff would have barely sufficed for a
hack-written biography. Alan had other plans, however; he
studied the Bruce property like a Sephardic diamond cutter
with a rough rock from Capetown. When he split Lenny
into pieces, he knew exactly where to put them. Into one
package he bundled the life-story rights, research materials
for a biography, a well-known director (Stewart Rosen-
berg) and producer (Marvin Worth). Columbia bought it.
Then, he renegotiated the Ballantine book deal (one of
Lenny's fast-buck promotions) so that it would entail copy-
ing and editing all the remaining tapes. Ballantine bought it.
Meanwhile, to protect his product, he had to buy off some
schlocky operators who would have stunk up the market.
His work isn't finished yet, but Alan figures he's sold all the
gems, why push with the baguettes?

As we sat talking in his elegant office in New York's most
luxurious hotel, my mind began to back-pedal to that other
room, downtown in the Marlton Hotel on Eighth Street,
where I used to visit Lenny during 1964, the year of his
great legal battle in New York. What a dump it was! I
would sit uneasily on one corner of the bed, waiting for the
wrecker's ball to come through the wall. Green was the
color of the room and the carpet looked like it had been
dyed with old bottles of India ink. There was so much un-
strung, twisted magnetic tape over everything, the furniture

appeared to be floating in the Sargasso Sea. Lenny lived looped in tape. He was that character Beckett put on the stage. Krapp, the man whose every act and word came back to him eerily echoing out of a machine. We would be talking, when suddenly—without a word of preparation—Lenny would touch a button and his voice would emerge from a tape recorder. Then, he'd get that look on his face that a ventriloquist wears when he's listening to his dummy, that unnaturally fixed, attentive yet abstracted look that masks the secret working of his throat.

Lenny liked to look at himself in the vocal mirror, but he was outraged when the reflection was falsified, which was a common occurrence during his trials because the evidence and testimony often involved garbled transcripts of his performances or police officers doing his material—to the best of their recollections—and lousing it up. "They bomb and I serve their time," was Lenny's view of the situation. Even more infuriating were the mistakes the court stenographer would make in the record: Lenny would say "Loew's Pitcairn" and the dumb, prejudiced clerk would hear it as "Loew's tit can." To expose this distortion, Lenny decided to smuggle into the courtroom a tape recorder secreted in an attaché case. I recall picking up the case one day and being astonished by its weight. "*Zug gornisht!*" (Don't say a word!), he warned, whispering the secret in my ear; then he strode jauntily down the aisle to the lawyer's table, where the forbidden spools quietly revolved all during the trial, catching every remark—even those the judge ordered stricken from the record.

Lenny loved the idea of turning against the police the same devices they used to entrap him. Plainclothesmen were always coming into the clubs with recorders strapped to their bodies and mikes in their tie pins; they taught Lenny a lot. Once, he decided to extract a confession from a Los Angeles coffeehouse proprietor who would not admit in court that he had refused to hire Lenny because of pressure from the DA's office. Lenny had his mother, Sally Marr—a top banana when they all worked in burlesque—fitted out with a recorder whose microphone was hidden under a couple of Band-Aids. She went to the club and heard the owner admit that he was being pressured from "downtown." But Sally was so anxious about the apparatus secreted on her body that when she idly dipped a fork in water she imagined an electric current was running up her arm. Wildly she jumped up and ran out of the club, knocking over chairs, waiters, patrons. When she got home, Lenny discovered that the tapes had been installed the wrong way.

After the tape recorder, Lenny Bruce's favorite instrument was the telephone. I used to sit in his room and watch him handle his calls. When the phone rang, he would screen the call with his fake-out voice, a low indistinct sound like someone just waked from sleep or speaking through a black veil at a funeral. When he had placed the caller, he would abruptly modulate to the appropriate key. If it was a lawyer, he would sound brisk, technical, obsessed with detail; numbers, Latin jargon, exotic names like Jacobellis (an important precedent) would fly through the air. The next call might be a show-biz buddy. "Sweetie, bubbee, baby, what's with mother's little rapist? No, man, I'm booked to play the Village Theater—dig, the show is called 'Lenny Bruce Speaks for Profit, Tiny Tim Sings for Love.' Beautiful?" Or it might be a woman, which called for very low tones and the most extreme obscurity of language, really no language, just a series of "Hi. No. That's sweet. Later. Mmmm. O.K. Tonight."

Lenny Bruce lived in a closed oral circuit that ran from mind to mouth to ear and back to mind again. He was virtually illiterate. When he had to write a letter, he always looked for an amanuensis. Or if the situation was an especially urgent one, he could scratch out a few words, using a combination of fourth-grade block lettering and a handwriting that wandered psychedelically all over the page in drooping sentences that looked like Dali watches. I remember receiving one of these rare epistles after the appearance of my first review of Lenny. He had gone to England hoping to profit from the liberal attitude toward narcotics addicts, and also, I suspect, hoping that the English would treat him with more dignity than his American audience. His reception soon cured these delusions; no one met him at the plane except some officials, who subjected him to a brutal examination for drugs and then packed him off on the next plane to America. In mid-air he decided to write to his soul mate, who had published a review hailing him as a show-biz shaman. Laboriously he addressed a postcard "To my love friend, Goldie"; then he printed, "Best review I ever received." But what was really on his mind was the horrible indignity to which he had been subjected; on the nightclub floor, he would have done twenty minutes on the whole scene, really gotten it out of his system—but here in the cabin of this dumb Air India plane, what the hell could you do? He would try: "Deported! How sad!" No, it was impossible. But here's an idea: take this dopey magazine with the pictures of these *goyische punims*, cut out the faces, paste them around the lip of an envelope and caption them. Now this is getting to be fun. Hmmm, here's a square-faced Irishman; write, "For no apparent reason, Pat rubs minority groups the wrong way. Tried everything to overcome it. Does Jewish dialect: oy, oy, Abie trow de key to Ikey. Digga da ditch Tony." Hey, this is funny! Now, I need a closer—got it. "Pat has four stitches over right eye."

One of the strangest features of a visit with Lenny Bruce was the conversation conducted through the half-open door of the bathroom. Lenny spent so much time in the john that I was willing to credit the report which placed him there at the time of his death. The author of *How to Talk Dirty* was an obsessively clean man. Every day he would swill glasses of mineral water, administer enemas to himself, bathe several times and repeatedly change his clothes. He would dictate his legal correspondence from the john and, of course, he retired there to inject drugs. The association between drugs and going to the bathroom is a common one; in

Lenny's case it was obviously strong because he felt compelled to flush the poison out of his system with incessant irrigations. Even his use of the hypodermic syringe had an unmistakable anal character; instead of simply injecting the drug and removing the needle, Lenny would withdraw a little blood, then squirt it back in the vein, until finally he released the junk.

The use of "dirty" material in his act was not simply a strategy to shock the audience; it grew out of his own anal obsessions. The word "toilet" was constantly coming up in his conversation: second-rate clubs were "toilets"; when things went wrong, you went "into the toilet." The most powerful imagery of his fascinating comic picture book, *Stamp Help Out,* is anal. On the cover there is a remarkable photograph of Lenny stripped to the waist like a heroic frontiersman smashing a toilet bowl with an axe. Inside is a droll picture of him sitting nude on the toilet with a thoughtful expression on his face: the toilet thinker. The copy begins with a cry of anal anguish, as Lenny berates the "dopey, Commie toilet" and explains that it has no power to harm. This, of course, was his key insight: that dirt—of thought, language or substance—was harmless, indeed pleasurable. Smashing the toilet meant conquering the fears of pollution with which his mind must have been long obsessed.

As Lenny became increasingly obsessed with his legal affairs, he lost interest in his career. Like so many people in show business, he found the profession contemptible and the achievement of success unreal. One of the basic themes of his work was show business as the great imposture, the symbol of every form of hypocrisy, deceit and ulterior manipulation, from the campy antics of Adolf Hitler to the tent shows of Billy Graham and the solemn performances of Cardinal Spellman. The obvious question raised by this attitude was how Bruce could go on being a part of the business while regarding it with such profound contempt. The answer came with his first arrests for obscenity.

Originally, Lenny had no intention of conducting a free-speech crusade. He saw his first "bust" as excellent publicity and told his lawyer they should capitalize on the notoriety. Soon, however, he became aware of the real danger presented by the unfolding pattern of arrests. He began to take an active part in the preparation of his defense; from involvement he soon escalated to obsession. Being a great enlister and manipulator of people, he applied the same charm that had won him audiences to the recruiting of legal assistance. My role, for example, was that of academic ponce. I was supposed to line up attorneys from Columbia's Law School who would do Lenny's bidding. For once he really got into the act, he expected to receive top billing. Lawyers were simply straight men and fall guys who had to be kept in their places because, like all minor talents, they were jealous of the star.

I sometimes found myself at my office in Lewisohn Hall talking on the phone like some wheedling agent with an especially cranky client. "Lenny, this one is the real thing: Harvard Law, snᴄᴄ background, Supreme Court experience, only twenty-seven—thinks you're an artist!" "No, man," the funny nasal voice would come back, "I'm tired of breaking in these twerps. Get me somebody who swings with the First Amendment." And the search would go on and on and on.

Lenny's principal helpers were women. He was always surrounded by a galaxy of females, each of whom had her special role. Sally, his mother, and Honey, his wife, were the only permanent members of his stock company. They pretty well symbolized the two sides of woman without any third party. Sally's relationship with Lenny was always that of pal and playmate. During the war, while Lenny was in the service, Sally graduated from mistress of a dancing school to professional comic and M.C. "I just got up and talked," is her way of explaining a career that was a remarkable anticipation of her son's. When Lenny got out of the navy (by pretending to be a homosexual), he decided to follow Sally into the business. Sally was surprised by his decision: "That malted milk face! I never thought he had any talent." Whatever Lenny wanted, though, Sally tried to give him; she used her connections on Broadway and broke Lenny in on the amateur nights he described so amusingly in *How to Talk Dirty*. After Lenny's marriage to Honey Harlowe, a gorgeous Rita Hayworth-style beauty who worked as a stripper and drove around in a pink convertible with leopard-skin upholstery and her name blazoned on the outside, "Hot Honey Harlowe," Sally saw much less of her son. Lenny and Honey moved to the West Coast; Sally continued working in New York. But Lenny had to have his mother near him, so he arranged to have Sally come out to the Coast, where, changing her name to Boots Molloy, she joined Lenny and Honey at a really raunchy strip bar in Los Angeles called Duffy's.

Duffy's was the making of Lenny Bruce the comic—and Lenny Bruce the junkie. "Everything he ever did came out of burlesque," Sally says, recalling Lenny's first breakthroughs; "and what burlesque! A bunch of schlocky broads, the lowest." Duffy's was a rough spot, a real "bust-out joint." If the boss, Rocky, didn't like a customer, he would piss in his glass and then cover it with a little beer. Fights with crashing glasses and collapsing furniture were common occurences; Rocky would say, "All right, you're through for the night. Take that bunch of fag musicians and get the hell out of here!" A regular Serge Diaghilev!

The boys in the band were not "a bunch of fags," but they were mocking, cynical hipsters who lived "wild." Lenny was fascinated by them. He was like the new boy in a tough neighborhood; he soon found what tickled the gang and he gave it to them in every show. He delivered his lines into the house, but they were intended to register behind his back. The big duel was between himself and those "schlocky broads," the strippers. He was always making fun of them, putting them on in every key. One night he really surpassed himself. He introduced a stripper and left the stage. The girl went through her long, teasing, tantalizing routine, the whole big production involved in merely getting undressed. Just as she finished, Lenny came walking out on the stage—stripped down to the raw—clapping his hands mechanically and chanting, "Come on folks, let's give the little girl a big hand." It was the first of a series of kamikaze attacks on show-biz shams.

The boys in the band were so delighted with the new banana that they turned him on to hard drugs. Lenny passed the habit on to Honey, and their relationship began to deteriorate. Eventually, they were divorced and their child was reared by Sally. But Honey was part of Lenny's life till the day he died. He went through an enormous number of women, but he was never again in love.

Lenny's confrontations with the law were generally presented as David-and-Goliath conflicts; actually, it was more like caveman and computer. Lenny's mind had a primitive Stone Age concreteness that was perfect for farce and fantasy but absolutely incompatible wih the abstrusities of the law.

I never left Lenny's room without receiving instructions for legal research; "Uncle Al" (he would always do the baby bit when he wanted something) "go in the big library and look up Section 1121-a, little a"—and he would carefully write the numbers in the air with his finger. Spelling and legal jargon were obstacles even more formidable than the juristic formulas they encased. I remember looking with shocked disbelief at the first page of his appeal from the New York conviction; a year of hard work had gone into this document, but there in the first sentence was a glaring misspelling, "in *faumer* [*forma*] *pauperis*." Lenny had tried to play the Latin by ear and missed—just as he often did with his secondhand Yiddish.

Despite all these obstacles, there is no question that by the end of his life Lenny Bruce had mastered all the legal aspects of his cases and moved out beyond the confines of the obscenity law to explore the implications of the First Amendment, with its guarantees of free speech and action. A West

Coast journalist who specializes in legal subjects told me that he witnessed a fascinating discussion between Bruce and a friendly judge in San Francisco that left the magistrate shaking his head in amazement at Lenny's knowledge of the law. When the writer told Lenny that there was only one other man in the entire United States who knew more about the First Amendment, Lenny snapped, "You mean Justice Black. I'm going to see him next."

Lenny always said that he wanted "a bigger life" than the clubs offered, and the law with its theatricalism, its impressive ritual and liturgy, the endless opportunities it offers for fast thinking and analogical imagination became the theater of his dreams. He was almost sure that he would end by playing the Supreme Court. But he would have settled for a lower court. He had a fantasy about how his New York trial would conclude. He would become his own attorney (he did, in fact, try it) and after an eloquent, witty and learned summation, Judge Murtagh would turn to the jury and say: "Are you kidding? Arrest a man for this sort of thing?" Then, like Barry Fitzgerald in some old M-G-M movie, Murtagh would put his arm around Lenny and they would walk out of the court room forever—maybe to go fishing.

As the years wore on and Lenny's position became increasingly desperate, his anger began to build and he meditated more and more outrageous forms of legal action. He advised Ralph Ginzburg to sue the Supreme Court, just as Lenny had tried to sue the three judges who had convicted him in New York. His last great plan was to mount a spring offensive against the governors of five states—California, Illinois, New York, Nevada and Florida—launched from the courts of some Southern state to highlight the civil-liberties aspect of the case. Had he had the money, there is no question that Lenny Bruce would have initiated some extraordinary legal maneuvers to dramatize his predicament. He never lost his faith in the law as a magic weapon which, when properly wielded, would right any wrong. The law was his silver bullet.

Apart from the ambitions and needs that prompted his legal obsession, Lenny was motivated by a touching love of print and the paraphernalia of learning. He was childishly delighted by Magic Markers, staple machines and clipboards. The sight of a stack of fresh Xerox copies would make his day. Laboring over law books like some young student, he would rise early every morning and work until night in his "office," reversing the habits of a lifetime. In the last months of his life, he learned to type, and this simple skill so delighted him that he could not be enticed away from the machine. His last words were a legal formula tapped out on a typewriter.

Behind all this enthusiasm was the satisfaction of learning a real discipline. Lenny had conquered life with his fantasies, but he never believed in the victory. The development of one skill testified to the capacity to learn more and higher skills. "If I can master the law," he would say, "I can learn Latin and Greek." I knew what was behind Lenny's thinking. If you were brought up by an adoring mother who was more like a playmate than a parent, a mother who did not want to distress you by imposing real discipline and who could not disguise her amusement at your groping efforts at self-sufficiency, you might well develop in later years a damaging pattern of dependence on all sorts of people, coupled with a profound yearning for autonomy.

Lenny's childlike undisciplined temperament was at the root of everything that was splendid, and appalling, in his life. It gave him the charm to win audiences, the self-indulgent freedom to explore every corner of his mind and to play all sorts of amusing and delightful pranks. At the same time, it left him feeling that he was swimming around in a world without shape; it set him off on a lifelong quest for limits, for restraints, for a solid line of demarcation. When he discovered that his audiences would not restrain him, he had to seek control elsewhere; he found it eventually by coming into collision with the police, the courts and the *law*. The conflict was painful but no one who watched Bruce through his ordeal would ever believe that his arrests and trials were experienced without a peculiar sense of gratification. An arrest would stimulate him to wild flights of humor. When he was seized with narcotics in his possession in Los Angeles, his behavior astonished the police and the reporters. Faced with a charge that could put him away for ten years, Bruce could not stop joking. Asked where he had been arrested, he quipped, "At Lawrence Welk's pad." Reporter: "What's narcotics like?" Bruce: "It's a weird, dizzy, crazy scene" (giving big twitch). Judge: "Do you have any final utterance before you're put in a cell?" Bruce: "I just hope my mother doesn't hear about this." The press thought Lenny was high when arrested; he was simply exhilarated.

Many people believed that Lenny Bruce harbored a death wish and was actively working to bring about his own destruction. They pointed to the incredible accidents he suffered—like falling out of the window of a San Francisco hotel. Perhaps they were right. The problem was very deeply connected with Lenny's drug addiction, which had produced most of the serious trouble in his life. Drugs had broken up his marriage, drugs had undermined his health, and it was drugs and the crazy, malicious people that he met in the junkie world that sent him flying out that hotel window.

The story comes in several versions: but essentially it boils down to a typically irresponsible hippie girl who thought it would be great fun to see the fascinating Lenny Bruce out of his skull on LSD. She slipped the drug into his coffee, and soon Lenny began to feel strange sensations. His answer to any problem in his head was to take a shot; so he set to work and tried to inject some opium or cocaine. The drugs were not really soluble and Lenny, clumsy as always with a needle, could not find a vein. Finally, an old friend came into the room and jammed the needle into his shoulder. What happened after that is not clear; in any case, he went out the window and fell two stories fracturing his legs and pelvis. In the hospital his arm became gangrenous, and he came close to losing it. Among the members of the New York underground, it is still widely believed that the police taped Lenny's mouth shut to stop him from uttering obscenities after the accident, and that he was unable to complain of the pain in his arm—produced by glass splinters—until the infection was far advanced.

One summer, when I was visiting on the West Coast, I heard similar stories about Lenny's death. The rumors were fed by the fact that an autopsy had been performed and the results never released. Everybody had a different story: suicide, overdose, heart failure. The most bizarre tale had Lenny the victim of a mercy killing. The saddest story came from Lenny's mother. Sally had wanted to run to Lenny's side the moment she heard the news of his death, but her friends dissuaded her, saying, "Is that the way you want to remember him?" A year passed before she went to the morgue to claim the clothes he had been wearing when he died. As the attendant handed her the bundle, she reached out with both hands and suddenly remembered another scene from forty years before: a nurse putting into her hands a little yellow-faced baby wrapped in a blue blanket.

New York, 1968

The Comic Prison

MARCEL MARCEAU, the famous French mime, may have never heard a sick joke nor read a page of black humor, but he has danced the difficult truth of these ambiguous phenomena in his parable of the man and the mask. A little man playfully dons a comic mask. After cavorting about exhilarated by his disguise, he grows tired of the novelty and tries to remove the mask. Horrified, he discovers that he cannot. The mask is fixed to his face. A terrible struggle follows; his body writhes in agony while his face remains frozen in a grin. At last the false face is wrenched off, but the real face behind it is now simply a blank.

Marceau's clown could stand not only for the ubiquitous comic entertainers of our time but even more appropriately for the audience that increasingly has adopted sick, or black, humor as an important part of its own life style. The strident, caustic chatter of the sick comic is no longer confined to the little clubs, the downtown lofts and pads, the haunts of the underground. Now every neighborhood movie house, every suburban cocktail party, every college dormitory—

and child's bedroom strewn with copies of *Mad*—rattles with the yelping laughter of people whose tightly leashed anxieties and resentments are permitted to bark only on a comic cue. The sick style is probably the most frequently adopted social disguise of our day: it provides a badge of sophistication, a smoke screen for social withdrawal, a spotlight for self-assertion, an ambush for hostility, a Masonic handclasp of belonging and a palliative for prurience. Ultimately, it can become a blind compulsion to fling every disturbing experience or emotion into the comic trash can.

So common today is the use of humor as character armor that psychiatrists at Yale have already responded to it by inventing a new therapeutic technique called "banter." Instead of the traditional medical earnestness and sympathy, the therapist adopts a joshing attitude toward his patient and then analyzes the wisecracks that come flying back. The strategy should have wide applicability. Millions of people are now squirming behind masks with mirthless grins that conceal the blankness of personalities inadequate to openly express or withstand the angry energies of the "cool" world.

Paradoxically, these masks are the very same that once afforded a great sense of liberation. For when sick humor erupted in the early Fifties, it came as a catharsis of the anger, fear and rebelliousness brought to a boil during the McCarthy era. No mere fad, the new humor revealed the great depth and breadth of the need to sound off and purge the soul of perilous emotion. There were other sources: the atmosphere had been charged with comic potential by the surrealistic shapes of contemporary reality and by a widespread loss of emotional involvement with this reality. Once the subtle web of affects that binds us to life has been torn, everything looks slightly ridiculous. But ultimately it was *hate*—for the sick self as well as the sick world—that sent the satiric spark crackling across the gap of alienation.

We ought to ponder an equation, one that in time may become as decisive and as threatening as Einstein's famous atomic fission formula in postulating the likelihood of a disastrous explosion. In our society, as incitements to anger increase, the socially endorsed means for expressing this anger diminish. This begets another vicious cycle, for no one is less tolerant of hostility than those who have barely repressed their own rage. The final irony is that psychoanalysis, which has provided this diagnosis, has inevitably aggravated the condition by sensitizing us to even the most covert forms of hostility. As a result, we are compelled to adopt devious stratagems in order to express anger and yet escape punishment. Sick comedy, for a time, served us well as just such a dodge.

Then, several years ago—when the sicks seemed to be dying—a remarkable thing happened. At what were once considered the opposite ends of the cultural scale, first in fiction, then in film, sick comedy was reborn in a shape far more bizarre than anything seen in its first appearance. The treatment of war in a whole series of productions from *Catch-22* to *Dr. Strangelove* and the satire on sex from *Naked Lunch* to *Candy* made the old routines of Lenny Bruce seem as quaint as Jiggs and Maggie. But despite the enormity of the license assumed by some of these satires, the effects they produced were surprisingly weak. For true to the typical pattern of any novelty in American culture, the new humor has been overworked and underdeveloped, recklessly transformed in a few years from vision to *déjà vu*. At the same time its moral tension has been collapsed: for where the sick comic sweated and suffered and finally screamed forth the "unspeakable," the new slick sicks violate taboos with the lobotomized glee of Mickey Mouse. And where once there was the continual shock of surprise as one sacred cow after another fell over, impaled by a shaft of wit, now the satire has degenerated into the ritual slaughter of dead horses. Often the satirical intention is merely a specious cover for infantile sexual aggression and exhibitionism. Sick humor, in short, has turned into camp. Consequently, instead of providing that longed-for catharsis that was its original boon, it has become a soft, cheap substitute, both for immediacy and candor in personal relationships, and for freedom and integrity of imagination in the arts. Sick humor, like Marceau's mask, has become a comic prison.

But, even with its targets gutted wrecks like Mother and the White Liberal, its weapons rusty devices from the Fifties, and its ammunition pasteboard bombs that explode like party favors, sick comedy is today, as *Variety* would say—"Smash B.O." Every week the book page of the *Times* shouts forth the good news of the latest comic apocalypse, juggling its shrill adjectives like a 42nd Street movie marquee—"daring," "hilarious," "outrageous." This echo of Broadway ballyhoo is no accident, for the novel is fast becoming a branch of show business with its writers located in Hollywood, its favorite technique the parody of an old film, and its vision of life on a par with an animated cartoon. Listen to this spiel:

> There must be something more, this can't be all there is to life! *So reasons undergraduate basketball star Hector Bloom, who thereupon sets out to seek a pattern for the world in which he finds himself (a few years in the future).*
>
> *Militant espousal of non-conformism, "radical" thought, revolutionists, a mad race against death at a hundred-miles-an-hour down a parkway, love with a professor's wife, Zen, marijuana, sex, a stupendous extravaganza of a party at a millionaire's Long Island estate, do-or-die confrontations on the basketball court, strong protests against war—all these enter into Hector's search.*
>
> *Underlying this vigorous, controversial, mocking, fantastical, violent yet withal humorous satire, there is a solid foundation of truth and honesty. . . .*

Sounding like something one would read off a billboard in Times Square, this copy is from the jacket of Jeremy Larner's *Drive, He Said,* a book that was awarded the $10,000

Delta Prize by a jury of eminent American writers and
critics (Mary McCarthy, Walter van Tilburg Clark and Les-
lie Fiedler). The puff itself appears to be an incredible instance of commercial gaucherie, but the novel it pitches for
matches the sensationalism of the blurb. Larner's theme is a
farrago of the frustrations, failures, grievances and gripes of
the current generation. With patience, craft and penetra-
tion, he might have converted his catalogue of post-adoles-
cent thrills and chills into a novel; but being an impatient
improvisist, he surrenders to the mode and riddles off his
stuff with the nervous, compulsive rapidity and incoherence
of a Mort Sahl, keeping his audience off balance and his own
guard up high. Jazzing his jerky narrative with lurid gang-
ster-film horrors, hooking his reader into the next chapter
with the cliff-hanging suspense gimmicks of the pulp writer
—while always reaching for the never-fail Jewish gag—Larner runs on like a dying comic, too scared to wait for the
laugh.

What is so disappointing about this kind of performance
is that one knows that behind its trite grotesqueries there is
most likely a sensitive suffering soul. But to articulate imaginatively his most profound feelings and ideas, he has to
whip himself into an opening-night fever and flatten his
thought to the Stone Age scratchings of the funny papers.
Perhaps the moral is that the tawdry fantasy life of America
does not permit the artist to attack it in any but its own
sterile terms.

There are alternatives, however, to the crudely reductive
satire that has inundated us recently. One possibility is to
train our attention on the sick comic himself, not treating
him after his own fashion, but employing the conventional
craft of comedy to make him a character instead of a mere
target. A modestly successful achievement of this sort is
The Sterile Cuckoo by John Nichols. Embarrassingly square
at first sight for its evocation, through half-amused, half-
boastful reminiscence, of frat-house drinking revels, redolent of Dartmouth Winter Carnival—at second glance,
Nichols' book takes on a deeper dimension. With astuteness

and unfailing intuition, the young author has placed at the heart of his college recollections an absolutely unique yet broadly representative character named Pookie Adams. A comedienne, who has adopted the new humor as her personal life style, Pookie is the type of today's funny little old college girl.

The essential Pookie is engagingly depicted at the long overdue consummation of her first "affair." Having reeled in the narrator from miles below the surface of sexual maturity (when they met he was absorbed in studying beetle copulation), she is faced with the problem of easing him off the hook. After driving through a terrible blizzard in a fabulously dilapidated jalopy, they have found their bower of bliss in a tacky motel, as cold as a cabin in the Klondike. To help the boy, who is numb with anxiety, alternately freezing and sweating on the brink of his first complete sexual experience, Pookie starts to work the room like a stand-up comic. Her fist a make-believe mike, she does an on-the-spot broadcast from The Kozy Kabins, conjuring away with laughter the lumpy bed, the embarrassment of the visits to the john, the getting undressed "bit." And after urging her lover to peel off her sweater and skirt, and maneuver the inevitably troublesome brassiere fastener, she offers him his long-desired sight of the promised land, turning around and around like a mechanical doll in her glasses and her loafers, keeping up a stream of self-disparaging wisecracks.

Although Pookie often appears a fragile, childlike moppet encased in a gauzy pink cocoon of Disneyland fantasy (she writes a poem to the "Lavender Grella," and discourses on a whimsical creature called the "Long-Billed Sneet"), her actions and daydreams suggest pathological hatred. Actually, at eighteen, she is a veteran neurotic with a classic case history. Cut off from her classmates by a bad heart, remote from her parents for whom she has no respect, Pookie spent her childhood concocting fantasies of revenge, acted out with frogs, spiders and other little creatures. Unconsciously associating "real feeling" with violence, she is compelled to destroy things with ruthless vigor, starting with herself.

From one end of the book to the other, she is injured in a series of "accidents" that seem to pursue her with malignant fatality. In her eagerness to retrieve the body of a crow she has just shot for the fun of it, she lacerates her feet by running across broken glass remaining from target practice. Hurtling off the train to give her boy friend the hug she has been rehearsing for weeks, she knocks him to the ground in a fall that splits his skull. Some of the fantasies into which she escapes are masked by deliberate nonsense, but there is no mistaking the meaning of her favorite daydream: "to walk into a very crowded station some day with a machine gun and let everybody have it. She liked the idea of herself, skirt uplifted daintily, stepping over a rug of bloody bodies burping occasionally, sending honey-colored bubblish souls up toward the smoky ceiling." Spunky as her efforts are to exorcise fear with farce, their ultimate effect is to make her a "sterile cuckoo," cut off from life by the comic persona she originally adopted to protect her deeply damaged personality. Pookie Adams is an emblem of the extreme precariousness of the comic adjustment as a means of survival, and the utter insufficiency, indeed severely thwarting effect, of this strategy the minute we reach for the genuine intimacy of friendship or marriage.

Granting that people have always used humor to dispel tension, to conceal embarrassment and to win sympathetic attention, still it seems clear that the intensity, ubiquity and automatism of humor in contemporary American life goes far beyond anything known from history. As sick comedy has established itself as our accustomed way of seeing things, every man has become his own sick comic, with the result that whatever was not ridiculous in our world is now being made so by this uncontrollable mental tic. What an ironic and devastating criticism is implied by this single fact—that in ducking behind the comic mask, we actually believe we are boldly facing reality.

The Nation, 1965

Shaking Hands with Philip Roth

Τ HE PUBLICATION of a book is not often a major event in America. Most of our classics, when they first appeared, met with disappointing receptions, and even the much-ballyhooed best-sellers of recent years have rarely cut a great swath outside the lanes of publicity and journalism. But this year a real literary-cultural event portends, and every shepherd of public opinion, every magus of criticism, is wending his way toward its site. Gathered at an old New York City inn called Random House, at the stroke of midnight on the 21st of February in this 5,729th year since the creation of the world, they will hail the birth of a new American hero, Alexander Portnoy. A savior and scapegoat of the Sixties, Portnoy is destined at the Christological age of thirty-three to take upon himself all the sins of sexually obsessed modern man and expiate them in a tragicomic crucifixion. The gospel that records the passion of this mock messiah is a slender, psychotic novel by Philip Roth called *Portnoy's Complaint* (the title is a triple pun signifying that the hero is a whiner, a lover and a sick man). So great is the fame of the book even before its publication that it is being hailed as *the* book of the present decade and as an American masterwork in the tradition of *Huckleberry Finn*.

Heralded last year by several stunning excerpts in the serious literary magazines, *Portnoy* comes to us glowing not merely as a *succès d'estime* but as a *succès de scandale*—the scandal fuming up from the book's pungent language, a veritable attar of American obscenity; and from its preoccupations, foremost among which is the terrible sin of onanism. Presently the object of a cult, which passes selections from the sacred writing from hand to hand at sophisticated dinner parties so that all may have the opportunity to read aloud, *Portnoy* today is still an underground password. But the complete work is being readied for distribution by an international ring of literary agents who are cutting, packaging and peddling it like a deck of pure heroin. Soon it will be injected into every vein of contemporary culture: as hardcover book, as soft-cover booklet, as book club offering, as foreign translation and as American movie. The TV rights remain as yet unsold, but even without them the book has already earned almost a million dollars prior to the first press run.

A million dollars in publicity is what the book will earn next. A chain reaction of cover stories and profiles and critiques and put-ons and put-downs and pictures and cartoons and slogans and quips has already begun to build toward a blast that may set a new record for publicity overkill.

The book that is being blown up by all of this puffing is not so much volatile as it is intense, probing, incisive. A diagnostic novel by a comic Freud, it focuses its lens of a beautifully cut and brightly stained slice of contemporary American life—all sick, black and blue. The hero, an Assistant Commissioner of Human Opportunity for the City of New York, is a man who exemplifies the cherished values of the Kennedy years. Brilliant and precocious as a student, successful as a lawyer, dedicated and sensitive as a public servant to the underprivileged, Alexander Portnoy has devoted his whole life to being good.

Yet when we discover this nicest of Nice Jewish Boys, he is lying on his back on a psychoanalyst's sofa, like an overturned cockroach, spewing out a frenzied stream of angry, resentful and self-defensive words. Honking through his beaky nose a heavy Jewish blues, he reels off an endless chronicle of suffering, degradation and terror, interspersed now and then with little grace notes of pleasure.

Though Alexander Portnoy's complaint is directed in the first instance against his smothering and seductive mother, and in the second against the succession of maddening females who have poisoned his life, the ultimate truth of his condition is that he has fallen victim to American history in the same way that Oedipus fell victim to fate. For struggle as he will, and analyze as best he can, Portnoy cannot escape the appalling fact that in the Sixties Americans are seeking to live by two completely contradictory moral codes. Maintaining their allegiance to the traditional morality of monogamy, fidelity, self-sacrifice and the sublimation of sexual energies, Americans are almost equally sanctimonious about those "needs" and "rights" that include the license to experiment with every sort of sexual and sensuous behavior dictated by the most primitive instincts and passions. Walking about in a fallen world, with these two Edens warring in their heads, modern Americans are made borderline schizophrenics.

Something of this sense of the *Doppelgänger* that stalks us has been suggested in a great many works of contemporary literature and comedy. Indeed, the farcical gap between what all Americans are supposed to be and what they are has been the mainstay of our humor ever since this American dilemma found expression in the wit of the so-called "sick" comics of the mid-Fifties. Lenny Bruce, Mort Sahl and Nichols & May were the first to exploit the awkward, spraddling moral stance of the new American; after them the comedy of the Yankee *schlemiel* was developed much further by a whole succession of Jewish novelists, including

Saul Bellow, Joseph Heller, Wallace Markfield and Bruce Jay Friedman. For more than a decade these comic artists cultivated the themes and techniques brought to final fruition in *Portnoy*. For it has always been evident that, though this profound conflict between our better and worse selves might tear us apart, drive us to despair or make us crazy, it could never be treated with complete seriousness or with the literal-minded simplicity of the sexologists and the public moralists. Comedy alone could provide the lens through which this strangely embarrassing American predicament could be examined.

Philip Roth's achievement in *Portnoy*, therefore, is not the discovery of a theme nor the invention of a mode, but the final perfection of an art, the comic art of this Jewish decade. Purging the Jewish joke and comic novel of their lingering parochialism, Roth has explored the Jewish family myth more profoundly than any of his predecessors, shining his light into all its corners and realizing its ultimate potentiality as an archetype of contemporary life.

Portnoy's Complaint boldly transcends ethnic categories. Focusing its image of man through the purest and craziest of stereotypes, the book achieves a vision that, paradoxically, is sane, whole and profound. As intimate as the mirror on the bathroom wall, it affords its readers glimpse after glimpse of themselves nakedly living the truths and lies of their innermost lives. Looking into this mirror, the reader—Jew *or* Gentile—will be caught between old shame and new pride, between the instinct to cover up and the urge to bare all. Torn, yet relieved by successive shocks of recognition, he will murmur the healing formula of self-acceptance. "It is I."

So intense is the conflict between the two sides of Alexander Portnoy's fractured psyche, so classically clear is his syndrome, that he has been accorded by his psychoanalyst the signal honor of having his illness defined by his symptoms and labeled with his own name: "Portnoy's Complaint —A disorder in which strongly felt ethical and altruistic im-

pulses are perpetually warring with extreme sexual long-
ings, often of a perverse nature. . . . Acts of exhibitionism,
voyeurism, fetishism, autoeroticism and oral coitus are plen-
tiful; as a consequence of the patient's 'morality,' however,
neither fantasy nor act issues in genuine sexual gratification,
but rather in overriding feelings of shame and the dread of
retribution, particularly in the form of castration."

Portnoy's personality derangement derives, of course,
from his childhood relationship with his Jewish mother. Alternately rocked in the soothing seas of maternal solicitude
and swamped by the terrifying tides of maternal domination, the boy grows up pathetically seeking some one thing
he can call his own. Not until puberty does he discover what
he is seeking. Masturbation offers him the thrill of a secret,
rebellious and wholly self-indulgent life. Behind a locked
bathroom door, his head thronging with erotic images, his
ear alert for the terrifying knock and the unanswerable challenge—"Alex, what are you doing inside there?"—Portnoy
comes to identify sex with feelings of anxiety and remorse.
But the power of his secret pleasure propels him out into the
world in search of the beautiful, responsive creatures of his
fantasies. Gentile girls with silky hair, button noses and long
slender legs are what he seeks: little beauties redolent of the
perfume of America, the alien land that must be plowed to
be possessed.

Questing like a nervous knight-errant in search of an
erotic grail, he must pass through many encounters, many
trying adventures, before he discovers the embodiment of
his dreams standing at midnight on the corner of 52nd
Street and Lexington Avenue. Springing off the high-
board of life-as-fantasy with this girl, who is so lecher-
ous and ignorant that he calls her "The Monkey," Portnoy
tumbles head over heels in the most extravagant of all erotic,
romantic, neurotic relationships.

Their dreamlike fall into the depths of sexual debauchery
is at first thrilling—in this respect paralleling the stolen
pleasures of his boyhood. But gradually they come to de-

mand something more of each other than exchanges of erotic goodies, and the relationship splinters into angry words and exacerbated feelings. Finally, after having inveigled his mistress into a scene of climactic licentiousness, our hero abandons her as a crazy person who menaces his life and happiness.

Leaving the hysterical Monkey standing on the window sill of their hotel room in Athens, threatening to dash herself to death on the pavement below, Portnoy flees to Israel, where he meets a lady *kibbutznik*, a rugged, self-righteous amazon who reminds him of his mother. Attempting a crude physical seduction, he finds himself impotent. When he offers the lady an alternate form of gratification, she becomes enraged at his degeneracy and kicks him in the heart. Ending his sexual odyssey much where he began it, sprawling prostrate and helpless at the feet of a greatly desired but inaccessible woman, Portnoy concludes his long complaint with a protracted scream of pain.

Portnoy is not only a funny but an impassioned and angry book. Unlike every other Jewish writer since Heine, Philip Roth knows what's hurting him—and it isn't the *goyim*. He delivers his most soul-gratifying thrusts at those sentimentalized objects of mindless piety, the Jewish mamma and papa, the emasculators of generations of Jewish men. Yet his anger is crossed by love for its targets, and is distinguished even further by an "Arise Ye Brothers of ——" ardor, a rhapsodic sympathy for his fellow sufferers that bursts forth in passages of ironic eloquence. The crown of the book is his vision of a Jewish *Ship of Fools*, a boatload of Nice Jewish Boys rolling on the seas of guilt:

"I am on the biggest troop ship afloat . . . only look in through the portholes and see us there, stacked to the bulkheads in our bunks, moaning and groaning with such pity for ourselves, the sad and watery-eyed sons of Jewish parents, sick to the gills from rolling through these heavy seas of guilt—so I sometimes envision us, me and my fellow wailers, melancholics and wise guys, still in steerage, like our forebears—and oh sick, sick as dogs, we cry out intermittently, one of us or another, 'Poppa, how could you?' 'Momma, why did you?' . . . the retching in the toilets after meals, the hysterical deathbed laughter from the bunks, and the tears—here a puddle wept in contrition, here a puddle from indignation—in the blinking of an eye, the body of a man (with the brain of a boy) rises in impotent rage to flail at the mattress above, only to fall instantly back, lashing itself with reproaches. Oh, my Jewish men friends! My dirty-mouthed guilt-ridden brethren! My sweethearts! My mates! Will this . . . ship ever stop pitching? When? *When*, so that we can leave off complaining how sick we are—and go out into the air, and live!"

For many readers the strangest feature of *Portnoy* will be the fact that its author is the same man who wrote *Letting Go* and *When She Was Good*, books that reveal Roth's moral preoccupations and literary skills but in no wise prepare one for the high jinks of this latest work (though these high jinks do in fact mirror closely the style and wit I and other friends of Roth have enjoyed for years in private conversations and at parties). Indeed, since 1960, when at the remarkably early age of twenty-seven he won the National Book Award for fiction with his first work, *Goodbye, Columbus*, Philip Roth has given every indication of desiring to be counted among the handful of recent authors more concerned with the values of traditional literature than they are with the currents of contemporary writing.

Educated at Bucknell and the University of Chicago, active for many years as a teacher of English literature and creative writing at Chicago, Princeton and Iowa, a familiar figure on the college lecture platform and even behind the lectern of the synagogue, a contributor to *Commentary* and *Partisan Review*, Roth has clung through his whole career to the skirts of the university and has counted himself a member of the intellectual and cultural elite. It was to this audience in particular that his early work appealed.

With *Goodbye, Columbus*, a collection of canny, morally

sophisticated stories written in a scrupulously impersonal style—the antithesis of the verbal extravagance of *Portnoy* —Roth focused fiercely on the life of middle-class America in the postwar years, particularly in the American Jewish community, where all the traditional values were being submerged in the scuffle to obtain the good things of material prosperity. This volume was followed in 1962 by *Letting Go*, a long and thoughtful novel in which Roth articulated his moral obsession, the theme which underlies all his subsequent writing: the effort of the self to break the bondage of narcissism by renouncing all selfish gratification in favor of a self-sacrificing dedication to the happiness of others. This Christian theme he treated, of course, with a great deal of irony, steadily increasing the dosage, until in *Portnoy* the theme is totally inverted and the hero struggles, with the reader's covert approval, to cast off all traces of moralism and lead a life of guiltless self-gratification.

It was while he was working on his third book, *When She Was Good*, that I first met Philip Roth. Whether it was owing to some congeniality of temperaments or simply to the fact that he knew I had spent a great many years running with a pack of Jewish comics that included the late Lenny Bruce, our encounters soon assumed the form of spontaneous staging sessions with Roth out in the spotlight working the room like a stand-up comic. Typically we would meet by chance at Mayhew's, a little breakfast shop in Manhattan's East Sixties. I'd be sitting there enjoying the peace of the morning hour and the soothing influence of an egg and butter, when my mood would be shattered by a reproachful voice: "Albert, your father and I have been worried sick about you!" Looking up I would see, not my Jewish mother magically transported from Santa Monica to New York, but Philip Roth, glaring at me maniacally. Looking nothing like the picture on the jackets of his books—that beautiful fem-man face, with its cleft Cary Grant chin, bold intellectual nose and distantly gazing Mesmer-eyes—this was the comic-crazy Roth, the one lost soul on the pilgrimage, a jarring presence sending out hysterical waves in every direction.

Slipping into the chair next to mine, fixing me with a hooded maternal gaze, he would continue his exhortation in that guilt-inducing, this-is-not-your-mother-but-your-conscience voice: "Two weeks and not a word. How is it a writer, a person who sits all day behind a typewriter, can't put two words together to send to a mother who lives three thousand miles away?" Then a hyena laugh, fracturing that sorrowful maternal stare into the crazy lights and angles of a Cubist portrait. I'd be gagging, choking, caught between laughter at Philip and anger at my mother, wondering meanwhile (with an instinct as old as the race) what the *goyim* were thinking—particularly that thick-lensed cashier, who has stopped toting up his bills and is staring with astonishment at this strident newcomer.

By this time Philip would be too wound up to notice or to care what reaction he was getting. He'd be doing the Jewish Genet who has written this play called *The Terrace* in which there's a brothel for Nice Jewish Boys where you go every night and they dress you in Dr. Denton's kiddie pajamas and they bathe you and powder you and put mineral oil where it itches. Tucked into your bed, you fall asleep blissfully listening to a little radio with an orange dial. Next morning a voice calls softly, "Wake up, dear, it's time to get up." For that, Philip says, he'd gladly pay $50 a night.

Now the magic word "radio" triggers him into his "Blue Network" bit. "J-E-L-L-O!" He's doing all the voices from the Jack Benny show: smoothie Jack, fruity Dennis. Yes, yes, I remember them perfectly! But wait, he's reaching even further back for—wow!—*Mr. Kitzel!* Now he's sliding his voice way up in the air in an oral shrug, a vocal curlicue: "Mees-ter Benny!" Oh my pop epiphany, it's Schlepperman! "Awesome, Philip, awesome."

After fifteen or twenty minutes of this comic fuguing, the waiters would be throwing Philip looks, *Wall Street Journals* would be dropping and some old lady would be giving

him the top lens. Everybody would be asking himself,
"Who the hell *is* this guy? He must be some famous Jewish
nightclub comedian who hasn't gotten to bed yet. Wow!
He's really up there. Nine o'clock in the morning and still
flying."

After all my years with the funny men, my response to
Philip's antics was partly professional. I recognized in him a
type not of the stage but of the Jewish living room, the
candy store or luncheonette, where after school the kids
take turns driving each other over the edge into hysteria. He
agreed that he had learned to be funny when he was a child,
probably on those daily walks from Chancellor Avenue
grade school in the Weequahic section of Newark to the
little Hebrew school fifteen minutes away. In that precious
quarter of an hour, those highly regimented Jewish kids
could blow off steam and subject the pyramided pieties of
their world to a healthy dose of desecratory humor. For a
few minutes they could afford to be bad.

Being bad and being funny were much the same thing in
Roth's mind, and I often had the feeling that when he wrote
his fiction he was intent upon being very good. Having as
one of my own obsessions the ideal of a Jewish comic who
would be an artist and not just a theatrical or literary entertainer, I often urged Roth to exploit his comic gifts in fiction. I told him that his role was to be the comic messiah, the
redeemer of the Jewish joke. When I pressed my arguments
and exhorted him to write a novel that would match his
hidden talents, a book that would be black, sick, surreal,
Kafkaesque, unabashedly vulgar, obscene and Jewish, he
would say with a sigh, "Oh, Al."

In those days, *When She Was Good* was his primary obsession. He had worked on it for years and rewritten it
something like eight times. In his apartment were four big
cartons stuffed with manuscript. After so many years of
close-up work, he couldn't tell any longer what he was
doing; so one day he packed the latest draft into his brief-
case and left his rackety apartment for the calm of the 42nd

Street Library's reading room. There he read enough of what he had written to realize that, despite the enormous pains he had lavished on the book, it was still so defective that he could not think of publishing it. Walking out into Bryant Park with its pigeons and hobos, he contemplated the future. No longer was he a writer, he decided, nor would he trade off his literary reputation by taking a succession of teaching jobs. At thirty-three he was young enough to go into something else. What would it be? Well, he could always go up to Harlem and be a playground director and die.

Instead, he went off to Yaddo, a foundation-supported estate in Saratoga Springs, which serves as a work retreat for writers, artists and composers. (Roth's deep attachment to Yaddo owes something to the beauty of the place—it is set among lakes and woods, with a view of the distant Vermont mountains—but it is really its character as a sanctuary from city life, and more especially its comfort as a surrogate home, a home without the annoyance of a family, that explains his frequent and prolonged visits there.) Regulating his life for as much as six months at a time by the soothing routine of the place—they get you up early, feed you breakfast and pack you off to work in a little cabin with a lunch box full of cold chicken and a shiny apple—he was finally able to bring *When She Was Good* into order and to publish it in 1967.

A stylistic tour de force, *When She Was Good* turns the tone of *One Man's Family* back on itself to produce a highly ambiguous literary texture whose irony is as subtle and deadly as the ripple in a highly polished saw blade. The tension of the book is generated by counterpointing the most gracious of all pop American tones against the moral frenzy and insanity of the heroine, a Midwestern Medea who embodies the horror of the Protestant ethic run amok.

Expecting high praise—at least from the more sophisticated critics—Roth was dismayed to find the reviewers yawning over his novel and offering consoling phrases while they waited for his next book. Perhaps *When She Was*

Good was too subtle for those who sat down to write about it. In any case, as soon as Roth had finished it his mind righted itself and all the baffled energies that had blown this way and that during five years of mental doldrums now became a steady breeze which soon shaped itself into a voice— a voice rising and falling with the complaining intonations of an angry and neurotic Jewish boy.

For two years I had seen so little of Philip Roth that when I dialed his number last summer I wasn't even sure whether he was still living in New York. But having read the fourth installment of *Portnoy's Complaint* in *New American Review*, I had to toss in my penny's worth of praise. Always glad to hear from an old playmate, Philip invited me to his home in one of New York's tallest and baldest buildings. As I walked into his apartment on the twenty-first floor, a flat lined with brown metal bookcases like the stacks of a library, he greeted me with a routine, singing in the strident voice of a Broadway musical comedy star, "New York, New York, it's a wonderful town!" and gesticulating toward the huge plate-glass windows of the room. Holding a high note, he drew the blind to reveal a stunning panorama of city skyline.

Stepping offstage, he slumped into an armchair and began to talk. Immediately, I caught a new note in his voice, a lilting note of optimism.

"Wow, what a year I've had!" He reels off an incredible yarn. It starts with his going to a publication party for William Styron's *Nat Turner*. Standing there in his new British tweeds, nibbling on an hors d'oeuvre, Philip begins to feel this pulsing pang in his right side. He'd had the same pain months before and figured he'd licked it, but now it grows worse and worse. The doctors can't tell what it is, so they put him in the hospital and his fever goes up and up, and finally, this crazy scene: a big, handsome surgeon dressed for a black-tie party is pressing down on his abdomen and Philip is going through the ceiling. Appendicitis is the diagnosis and immediate operation the plan, but when they cut

him open they find that the cap blew off his gut days before
and his belly is flooded with pus. They stick tubes into him
from top to bottom and for days he wallows in delirium.
Every time he comes out of it, he finds this exquisite
woman, the woman he's been seeing almost every day for
three years, standing at the foot of the bed wearing these
strange sacklike dresses. "Get out of here!" he screams. "Go
home and put a short skirt on. You look like you're dressed
for my funeral." (And indeed, as he learned later, by the
time they cut into him he was just two hours' walk from the
grave—a shocking realization that flooded him with an awed
feeling of pride and elation. He had wrestled the *Malekha-
moves*—the angel of death—to a fall.)

Then there is his convalescence in Florida, an idyl of sun
and water, and the finishing touches on *Portnoy*, and the
growing feeling that he has his life back under control at
last, when one morning, in this same living room—he's up
on his feet now, showing me what happened—the phone
rings and he hears his stepdaughter saying, "Mother has
been killed." His estranged wife, Maggie, being driven
across Central Park at five in the morning, had been instantly killed when the car smashed into a tree. Philip is
stunned. He goes through the funeral arrangements in a
trance. Then, just as he starts to pull himself together again
—wham!—all the hullaballoo begins about *Portnoy*. Fame
he's known before, but now, for the first time in his life, he
has money—and everybody is shooting zingers into him. He
passes the man next door, who says, "Oh, my neighbor, the
millionaire!" But what can Philip say? Yesterday a messen-
ger came to his door and gave him a royalty-advance check
for a quarter of a million dollars. Philip gave him a tip.
What's the tip on a quarter of a million? "I gave him a quarter, Al."

Now he's into this new book. He doesn't know where he's
going: he has all these pieces of paper with one sentence on
each page. He's just writing this stuff and throwing it away,
groping for a new theme—some big semi-comic idea. And

he's haunted by this phrase, a simple little phrase: "A terrible mistake has been made." Just that. Now he thinks he may write a book which will stand Kafka on his head. Sort of a marvelous idea:

"Instead of having a guy who is more and more pursued and trapped and finally destroyed by his tormentors, I want to start with a guy tormented and then the opposite happens. They come to the jail and they open the door and they say to you, 'A terrible mistake has been made.' And they give you your suit back, with your glasses and your wallet and your address book, and they apologize to you. And they say, 'Look, people from big magazines are going to come and write stories on you. And here's some money. And we're very sorry about this.'"

Life, 1969

Mel Brooks Zaps the Movie Schmendricks

"**M**Y COMEDY is based on rage. I'll show those cocka-mamie *Cahiers* critics. I'll make a movie that'll bend their bagels. It'll be called *Un Film de* ———. That's all. The first shot will be from inside the girl's mouth. For the second shot, I'll point the camera through the guy's fly—or, better, through an enlarged pore!"

Ever since he peeled off his modish Norfolk jacket and got up on his feet like a boxer, shoulders hunched, hands going, blue eyes stabbing in every direction, Mel Brooks had been his old self. Not the charming pussycat of the late-night interview shows, where he does Fred Astaire and Gene Kelly and tosses off some mildly irreverent opinions; nor even the much grittier 2,000-Year-Old Man, who once defined tragedy as cutting his finger and comedy as watching someone fall down a manhole—no, this was the tough, funny, smart little Jewish boy from Brooklyn who had ventriloquized for years through the mouth of television's greatest comic, Sid Caesar.

The setting was oddly perfect. The most famous of all

parlor comics was working in a New York producer's office that looked like it had been floated down the river from Scarsdale. Miles of spotless white curtains draped one side of the room, back-lighting a showroom ensemble of elongated damask sofa and chairs with a coffee table crouching between them like a wooden dachshund. On the facing wall was the return mileage in expensive walnut book shelves, empty except for old copies of *Variety* and framed B'nai B'rith awards for the *Eleanor Roosevelt Story*. The only thing missing was a brand new Steinway. Mel Brooks would have played it furioso.

Anger is Mel's muse. His fast mental fugues, his timing calibrated like a stop watch, his beautiful comic footwork, the skeet-shooter's reflexes you need to nail a funny idea just as it lays its Kilroy nose over the edge of consciousness—all that comes with anger and an undying sense of outrage. And why shouldn't he be sore?

Here he'd brought his first picture, *The Producers*, into New York after months of successful showings and "sell" reviews all over the country, brought it home to his people —the brighties, the smarties, the hippies. And then these *schmendricks* that write for the *Times*, the *New Yorker* and the *Voice* had laid fingers to delicately palpitant nostrils and said, "It stinks." "Vulgar," "crude," "doesn't know where to put the camera," they had written. About the star they quipped, "Zero Mostel looks like a seal with a disease of the inner ear." Well, the truth was that the picture was crammed with goodies, with things that grabbed you and made you laugh. "Can't they see that this is the funniest movie in years, maybe the funniest movie ever?" Well, he would get them.

His whole life had been played in double-takes. Something was always coming along that pulled your *schvantz*— angered and obsessed you for days. Then one morning you woke up and—hey there!—it was funny, funny, funny. Every little detail was crepitating with Day-Glo Disneyland FUN. Like the time Mel saw that arty cartoon by McClaren;

you know, one of those abstract things where the triangle meets the rhomboid and they do parallelograms together. It bugged him so much, he decided to do a picture where some simple Jewish man, some old Yid with phlegm in his throat, would sit in the theater and expose this geometric hanky-panky with contemptuous common sense. That was the spark for *The Critic,* one of the cleverest little shorts ever filmed.

Now these Westchester country-club matrons and downtown cinemasturbators were asking for the same treatment, with all their gabble about the "art of film." How many funny movies—flat-out funny movies—were there?" "*Strangelove?* O.K. Good picture, but too much diddling in the cockpit like some scary documentary. *The Loved One?* Gorgeous book, cockamamie picture. Terry Southern? Good comedy bones but no meat on them—and no heart." That was the trouble with the white bread *goyim;* when they got funny, they freaked out completely, like Jonathan Winters. The Jews weren't the only funny people, but they were the ones who could laugh and still care. Look at Lenny Bruce. He went all the way. Gave up his citizenship. But he cared a lot. Lenny was a writer, a thinker, a rabbi.

Mel could have gone the same route as Lenny. He could have gone on missions, too. But he and Sid could never forget that there was a world out there, a wife at home and a kid. Yet, Mel had become famous performing his own stuff on records, and he wrote himself a great part in *The Producers.* That's right, he was all set to play the Nazi, Franz Liebkind. He would have done it like one of Sid's Krauts. But at the last minute Kenny Mars asked to read for the part; and before he was half through, Mel jumped up, ran over and shook his hand. "You've got it!" Kenny did a fine job, too; but those *schmegeggi* reviewers couldn't see it. "What is it with them? Can't they give a little credit for the *ideas* in the picture?"

Take the relationship between the old producer, Max Bialystock, and the young accountant, Bloom. Wasn't that beautiful? Somebody asked Mel, "Were you influenced by Saul Bellow's play, *The Last Analysis?*" Mel never even saw that show. Max was a real producer that Mel had worked for as a kid. The old boy used to walk around in one of those Berlin overcoats with a collar as thick as your face and lined with papers; he had his office in his coat. But he did have an office, too—and he slept there on a ragged black leather sofa with cans of Bumblebee tuna fish stacked underneath. He used to make it with lots of old ladies who gave him money for his shows. Once, one old lady arrived before the previous one had made her getaway. She screamed, "Who was that woman getting dressed in there?" You know what Max said? "That's my mother." Beautiful! But Mel wouldn't use that line in the picture because he has a thing about taking words out of people's mouths—it's like stealing their souls.

When Mel showed the "treatment" to the people at 20th Century-Fox, they said, "Where's the love story?" Mel told them, "The man and the boy—there's your love story." It's true, too; they love each other like a Jewish mama and her son. Yet they're so different. "Max is an animal: he likes grapes smashed in his mouth, white Rolls-Royces, big tits, fat cigars. The kid is delicate, transparent, he changes color like a pigeon's breast." They played it that way, too. Zero played orange—a pure Van Gogh color; and the kid played in pastel. "Such a beautiful instrument, that Gene Wilder—a flute, a dulcimer, a finger cymbal!"

Maybe there was a little of Mel in that part. He'd always been the little indulged dahlink of the family. Wow! had they pinched his *toosh*. They really overdid it because in later years he became a pretty obnoxious character. He just couldn't shut up. He had to grab all the attention. "I'd fight my way through a *farfel* blizzard to work for three old Jews on the boardwalk at Brighton 8 St." Once, at a story conference, he got Max Liebman so *fatutzed* that sweet, gentle Max threw a lighted cigar at Mel. Years later, after *The Critic* came out, Mel got another cigar from Max—a tribute.

Max had been the papa to one of the wildest family circles

that ever assembled, the writing crew of *Your Show of Shows*, the First International Festival of Film Parody. Mel was like the bad little boy that Sid brought home from school. Actually, they met up in the mountains when they were both musicians. Mel never thought he would work with Sid as a comic, but he loved to play with him. One night, when Sid was appearing in *Make Mine Manhattan*, Mel went backstage to demonstrate this little opener he worked out for his M.C. jobs. Sid made Mel go out on the empty stage and do it for Max. Opening wide his arms, Mel sang:

> Hello, hello, hello,
> I've come to stop the show.
> I sing a little, dance a little, say some funny things,
> In other words, I bring to you a feast that's fit for kings.
> Though not much on looks,
> I hope you'll love your M.C.—Melvin Brooks!

With the final line—you guessed it—he went down on one knee.

It was Sid, not Max, you can believe, who called him one day in 1948 and asked for some ideas to use in a new TV show. Mel jumped in and started writing a series called "Nonentities in the News." For the first one, he made Sid a jungle boy; that was a natural because Sid was the strongest comic who ever lived. "He could kill a Buick with his bare hands—punch it in the grille and kill it." Then he started writing the famous Professor—for fifty dollars a week that came out of Sid's pocket. Max wouldn't even recognize Mel as a human being. When there were conferences, Mel would have to stand outside in the hall and wait. Finally, he stood up for his rights. "I wanted credit. I wanted money. I wanted to be a man."

The years with Sid were an endless jam session. Every morning they would run from their analysts to Max's office in the City Center. They'd light their cigars, form a circle around Sid and watch him improvise like a one-man band until they were turned on. Then they'd jump up, start throwing lines, capping each other, doing business and screaming, until finally they fell down again, worn out with laughter. By the time they were through, Sid had the bit memorized and they would go on to the next *shtick*—six complete routines, a whole Broadway review every week. No wonder Sid threw up his lunch every day. Saturday they put the show together on the stage of the old TV theater on Columbus Circle. That night Mel would be standing in the wings as Sid worked, living every line, punching and pulling inside his gut as he laid the good ones over and shuddered at the bombs. A *schvach* line would so enrage Sid, he'd come charging off and threaten little Mel with violence. What a *shtarke* Sid was—and good-looking. "Sid had the profile of a silent movie star."

Then, after the show, it was Mel's turn to be the star. He and Carl Reiner would run around to parties and do the wild, inside stuff. That was how the 2,000-Year-Old Man was born. Carl had a tape recorder, and he decided to interview Mel. "You're a little candy store keeper in Nazareth, and I would like to know what happened that day when they crucified Christ on the mountain. Did you know Christ?" "Yes, thin, thin, nervous—wore sandals. Came in the store, didn't buy much, mainly water, wanted water—so I gave him water. Look! You have a business. You can't always make a sale. So when people want water, you give them water. But one thing I have to admit. He was a bit of a troublemaker. He beat up a couple of *rovs* on the steps of the *schul*—and *you know you can't do that!* But they didn't have to nail him up. They could have given him a severe lecture. I didn't agree with such a severe punishment. Oh, such a terrible day! All that yelling and screaming up on the mountain. I tell you it was very upsetting. In fact, it got so bad, I had to close up the store."

That's how it started, and then it got to be a thing. Every time Mel would meet Carl they would go into the bit. Mel never knew what craziness was coming; Carl made him a

Lisbon sailmaker who was angry because Columbus left without paying his bill, or he was a Greek wrestler or a Tibetan monk. Once Carl was interviewing him on Fire Island and he made Mel—zing!—a fag holy man. "Kiss iron, kiss iron," he said. "Even if it's rusty, brush it off, and kiss it. It will bring you all the luck you need. Besides, it's good if someone should bother you late at night; you have a piece of iron—you could stick it in his eye."

But the best was the 2,000-Year-Old Man. He was also drawn from reality, from Mel's mother and other old-timers who had seen the world change so much it seemed like centuries since they left the *shtetl*. Like a ventriloquist with a dummy, Mel would talk through that character—not trying for funny bits so much as the most basic level of truth, a primitive Stone Age literalness that undercut the dizzy spires of romance. He'd see his mother being asked about Cleopatra and the asp: "Nonsense, there was no asp. She was afraid of snakes. The woman died of a stroke. The woman was eighty-three. History! Romance! Romantics! Nonsense, she was an old woman. She gasped, they rushed her to the hospital pyramid. The doctor said, 'It's a stroke,' and she died. Like a person, she died."

Mel was always a literalist of the imagination. Once a writer came in complaining about the paper walls in the new building he had just moved into. They decided to make fun of new apartment buildings with big lobbies, music in the elevators and paper walls. The bit was composed like a fugue: three couples living in different flats speaking in closely interwoven dialogue whose questions and responses would work no matter who spoke. But they were stuck for a closer. Finally, Mel came up with the idea. Sid would break his lease by walking through the walls—through six or seven apartments with people eating, sleeping, shaving, brushing their teeth. What an image! Big Sid stalking through the paper walls.

The Jewish thing was fresh in those years; Sid and Mel were the first to use it—not as an inside gag but simply be-

cause it sounded funny. Their Japanese movies had characters like Takah Mischigah, Ganzah Mishpukah or, simply,
Prince Shmatah. In an English court-martial scene, Carl
would say, "Your lordship, in twenty-five years in the service, I never heard *such a mouth* on an officer." But the funniest use of a Yiddishism occurred in the classic take on the
$64,000 Question. Sid got into the Humiliation Booth, and
suddenly he began to faint—they had forgotten to turn on
the air. Then, after asking him all sorts of embarrassing personal questions about his sexual problems, they came to the
big question. $64,000 riding on the identification of a piece
of music. Sid got the first part right; it was *Faust.* Then they
asked him who wrote it and he was finished. He hung his
head sadly, shrugged his shoulders and said, "Oh, I don't
know—go know!" "Right! Right!" they screamed, "The
answer is Gounod."

When Sid went off the air, Mel was lost. For a whole year
he'd wake up at 6:30 every morning and bang his head
against the bathroom wall. He didn't know what to do. He
had no vehicle for his passion. Once he had wanted to be a
comic, but after working with Sid it seemed pointless. Sure,
he was a natural performer. Even as a baby he could make
people laugh. It was his gift. But if he went all the way and
gave everything to the public, what would he have left to
give to his wife, his children, his friends? Comedy for him
was a very intimate thing. It was a communion between
people who loved each other. He couldn't whore it all out
for fame. And who wanted to be like those nuts who are
always on? You meet them in the street and they do ten
minutes with you. They develop horrible insidious rhythms,
their motors are always running. Think of fat Jack E. Leonard and Sid Gould—tragic and obscene. The pity of it was,
you knew there was a living person imprisoned an inch
away from what you were hearing.

It was too bad Sid and he had never made a film in the
great years. Hollywood wouldn't have it. "Not family fare,"
that had been the line. But low-key comic titillation—that

they would buy. They were still buying it. And the critics loved it. He'd like to ask those reviewers, "Which would you rather have: a couple of liveried flunkies who come out with a big silver thing with flying cupids on it and pissing ducks; the trumpets blow; they lift off the lid—and there's an American cheese sandwich? Or better, some dirty, unshaven old *muzhik* comes *schlepping* out of the kitchen, scratching his ass; but he's carrying a tray with a roast beef that would kill you and *gribenis* and *knoedlach* and—a meal!" That's it. Do they really want to eat, or will an olive do? Zero Mostel was the greatest comic actor in the business. Mel Brooks was not going to spray him with fixative to flatter a lens. No graven images for this Hebrew—his only reverence was for life.

Yet, he had a lot to learn; this was, after all, only his first picture. He wanted something finer now, something that was more literate. He was fascinated by Gogol. There was a resemblance, like twins parted at birth, between the Jewish comics and the great Russian grotesques. And he was moving. "We Jews have upward mobility, you know. We're short people, but we know how to grow."

He would make more movies, and nobody would say "*shtick*" when they saw them. Because *shtick* gets to be story and comic gets to be character and pretty soon the whole thing takes off and shows its tail to these fastidiosos.

New York, 1968

The Return of the Naz

LORD BUCKLEY

THE ONLY good comic these days is a dead comic. Witness the cults of the dead—yet very much alive—W. C. Fields, Harpo Marx, Buster Keaton and Lenny Bruce, all of whom were of their time while being ahead of their time and therefore right on time for the present day with its schizzy habit of looking fore and aft at the same time. With all these ghostly jokers riding the air waves again, it might seem that history has given us all the laughs it can. But no, there is one more old boy coming through the time tunnel at this very moment, and he is—"My Lords and My Ladies of the Royal Court"—His Ebullient, Double-Hip, Non-Stop Grace, the late Richard, Lord Buckley.

Scion of the early Western settlers, tree-topper among the California redwoods, daredevil marathon entertainer in his Walkathons and tent shows and speakeasies of the Depression, Lord Buckley could be viewed a decade after his death as a legendary figure redolent of the vigor and gaiety of a vanished era. Yet no comic of the Thirties, Forties or Fifties belongs so completely to the contemporary scene as does

Richard Buckley with his philosophy of universal love, his keen relish for black beauty and his zooming aspiration toward cosmic consciousness. He appears to have vaulted over history with a mighty leap—just as he used to jump across vaudeville orchestra pits—and landed smack dab in the Aquarian Age, where he is now being royally welcomed by his shaggy spiritual descendants—or, should one say, avatars?

"The Naz" is no longer the name of a brilliant monologue: it is the moniker of a rock group, a sign over a fashionable men's boutique, a hip word the kids toss around. Lord Buckley himself is no longer an eccentric jazz comic heard late at night on jazz stations sandwiched between Miles Davis and Horace Silver; now he is a funny father figure whose bass-barreltone voice is heard as often inside the noise collage of some youthful genius as bellowing and mellowing in his own jazzy solos. To complete the illusion of resuscitation, Lord Buckley is now bringing out "new" records, like the recent one edited by Frank Zappa, that contain routines even his greatest admirers cannot remember.

Once past the astonishment of seeing the dead lord resurrected, one marvels again at the bizarre conglomeration of ill-sorted things that constituted his character and art. An apoplectic English aristocrat in appearance, posing onstage with pith helmet and imperious waxed mustache, Buckley spoke in pungent slum ghetto slang using an old-fashioned Amos 'n' Andy Negro voice. (Imagine anyone trying that today and getting away with it!) The pampered pet of the old Chicago gangsters (who loved to see him put on the suckers), a free liver, heavy boozer and fabled pot smoker (onstage, that is, with an elegant little pipe!), Buckley's favorite theme was sacred history, the soul of his art the mystic celebration of the universe. A born actor with a strong literary bent—illustrated by his hipster parodies of the Gettysburg Address and "The Raven"—Buckley was above all a *musician* who patterned his words and sounds into powerfully propulsive licks and riffs that exploited the rich black common ground between jive talk and jazz.

In his great monologue on Jesus of Nazareth, Lord Buckley achieves a virtual parody of Bach's *St. Matthew Passion*. Every time the beatified Naz speaks, an organ (from *The Eternal Light*) sanctifies his words like the violin halo that accompanies Jesus' words in the *Passion*. Though the effect of translating the life of Jesus into black hipster slang is occasionally reminiscent of *The Green Pastures*, Buckley's enormous gusto and joy in re-creating the miracles of feeding and healing—the Naz straightens one poor little cat's "bent frame" by thundering like an earthquake, "Straighten it!!"—raises the burlesqued gospel back up to the level of religious exaltation it occupies in the tradition of American evangelism and revival shouting. Indeed, Buckley is the very model of the modern nightclub preacher and black-mass celebrant. You can see Lenny Bruce emerging from one side of his head while out of the other pops Arthur Brown or Dr. John.

Even more congenial to Buckley's soul than the role of secular preacher was the love labor of recounting the legends of the saints, among whom he numbered both Mahatma Gandhi ("The Hip Gan") and the Marquis de Sade ("The King of Bad Cats"). The love-beaming sunshine warmth of Buckley's wonderful chant-fable about the great convocation for the Gan must be heard to be appreciated. Nowhere else as in this mad Mother Indian epic did his Lordship get it all together. Like a well-sauced old bard, he riddles off sonorous catalogues of nonsensical names and builds long lung-bursting crescendos of rhetoric, until at the end of the narrative he slips right over the line from speech into pure sound. Mr. Rabadee, the dhong-dhong player, has asked the Gan which is his favorite instrument; when his "sweet double-hipness" replies that his favorite has not been included in the festive symphony, Mr. Rabadee bursts into tears and demands to know what instrument is missing. The answer comes in a string of rhythmic riffs (Buckley breathlessly scat singing) that spell out the triumphant rejoinder—

"The spinning wheel!"

Comedy is obviously too narrow a label for the media-mixing, convention-defying art of Lord Buckley. Gaiety, fun, burlesque abounds always in his work; exuberant joy, wild fantasy and nonsense enough for anyone; but the soul of his show is something different: something very old and deep in the American grain. He is the echo of the old Southwest, land of tall tales and braggadocio, of strapping giants bursting with unbridled energy and blowing their minds as high as the heavens. America the infinite, America the intoxicated, the land that stretches to the stars—that is Lord Buckley's real religion, his evangelical mission. Now like some crazy planet, rising from west to east, he hangs above us beaming down the welcome beauty of his love and cosmic laughter.

The New York Times, 1970, and *Life*, 1970

That Laughter You Hear Is the Silent Majority

RODNEY DANGERFIELD

RODNEY DANGERFIELD walks out on the Sullivan, Frost, Carson, Bishop, Griffin shows like a glad-handing shingle man staking out a living room in Shantytown. Freshly barbered hair slicked back from balding temples, jowly face shining pink from the scorch of the sun lamp, Fresca-dieted belly worrying the button on his jacket; he's got that old-fashioned best-foot-forward (or is it one-foot-in-the-door?) business approach. Then the zooming camera sets you face to face with his moist, protuberant, bloodshot eyes, his impatiently pursed, irritably drawn mouth, his lugubriously heavy, self-pitying voice and suddenly—you're staring deep into the soul of the Silent Majority.

Rodney's nothing new as a comedian—his rabbinical meter, his set-'em-up, knock-'em-down laff pattern, his stereotypes of sissy Jews and punchy Italians have been breaking them up in the Catskills for decades—but as a comic symbol, as a comic spokesman for every middle-aged, middle-of-the-road, middle American who feels that he's out of the money, out of the fun, out in the cold while everybody else is getting *his*, Rodney Dangerfield is the show-biz counterpart of Spiro T. Agnew.

Rodney's whole act is *complaining*. He complains about pushy minority groups, exploitative women (even a hooker can make him say, "Please!," and when a nice girl consents, he says, "Think it over!"), snotty kids, unsympathetic wives, crooked business partners, larcenous employees and cars—Rodney never gets a break with his car, which has traveled more miles vertically on the rack than it has horizontally on the highway. When he steps into an elevator, the operator says, "Basement?" When he turns on the shower, he gets rust. When he drinks, he gets drunk. When he gets drunk, it's "stoopid time." The next morning, aching with a hangover and hating himself, he has to endure his wife's reproofs: "You danced, now pay the fiddler!"

Sometimes his complaints reach poignant intensities, as when he laments the days when he could eat three franks from the old man under the yellow umbrella and then go home to gorge on Yankee Doodles and Hostess Twinkies. Sometimes he swerves into surrealism, as in his recollection of a date with a manicurist who held one hand romantically while she dipped the other in his drink!

Whatever his theme—whether he be lamenting his loveless childhood or anticipating his unctuously phrased funeral eulogy—Rodney's refrain, the burden of his lament, is always *"I don't get no respect!"* That line is Rodney's trademark, his droopy-tailed escutcheon; it's just the sort of line that could go down in the history books as summing up the American people's basic attitude during their greatest spiritual crisis. Soon the line will be printed with Rodney's posterized face on sweatshirts ("I gave Mickey Mouse two per cent and now you want ten per cent?" queried the irate shirtmaker when Rodney flashed his business acumen). It's blazoned already on the napkins and match covers of a jam-packed East Side supper club, called Dangerfield's.

Just as anachronistic as its forty-eight-year-old proprietor, Dangerfield's is a quarter-million-dollar investment in a business that saw its last good days during World War II. Operating with a $7 minimum, twice the usual tab, the club is so popular that a weekend visit is virtually impossible. Once you do get inside its plushy interior and past the phalanx of maitres, captains, subalterns and lance corporals guarding the back room, you're surprised by the layout. It's dark, warm, intimate and heavily padded: just the sort of old-fashioned *boîte* that was once the East Side's entertainment trademark.

The patrons, however, don't look like a New York nightclub audience. They're obviously from Queens, Long Island, Jersey and points west. Most are solid, husky young men in dark suits with short hair and healthy complexions, sitting close to their girls and doing a pretty good job on the J&B. What really gets them is Dangerfield's locker-room frankness: "I haven't scored a broad out of this room in eight months." Or his portrayal of his Italian partner counting the club's take to the chant of "Beat the Jew! Beat the Jew! Beat the Jew!" Reminded by the comic that they'll never hear these gems on Ed Sullivan, the boys roar their approval.

As for the Loser-Winner, he's digging his success after thirty years of scuffling in joints like Vinnie's Boom-Boom Room and Cohen's Monte Carlo. Chatting with him recently in the bedroom of his Miami-in-Manhattan apartment, where he holds court in a red silk dressing gown, I heard a thousand and one tales of his battle to grab the stage: really humiliating stories staged in ghastly places like Bayonne, Staten Island and the Bronx. Rodney had plumbed the depths, swallowed endless insults, paid the band to play him on, paid the waitress to bring him an extra piece of chicken, been patronized by the critics, torpedoed by his own agency and once dragged out in an alley by two toughs while a third punched him out for making fun of him from the stage.

His history is a strange one. Rodney (then Jack Roy, a falso for Jack Cohen) had gotten into the business when he was nineteen, working a resort at Ellenville for $12 a week plus room and board. Plugging away in the minors for the next decade, he gradually hauled himself up to a Big Chance in Philadelphia. Then his anxiety got out of control, and he blew ten years' work in a single night's freak-out, peeling off his pants and running around the club in his shorts. (Exhibitionism has, as Dr. Freud divined, a rather primitive root.)

Another guy would have caved in: Rodney went right back to work, this time as a home-improvement contractor in New Jersey. As he prospered in his business of selling aluminum siding jobs to poor blacks and Italians, he hired all his old pals from show business, all the shadow comics who never had the nerve to walk out on the stage, the washed-up dancers and existentially hip jazzmen. He got himself a flying circus that took off half-potted from Broadway every afternoon and flew across the river into Jersey, where they divided neatly into canvassers and closers: the former to hook the suckers, the latter to reel them in. Never has the connection between salesmanship and showmanship been so clear as in the exploits of this crazy crew.

Despite the eccentricity of his employees and certain investigations into alleged business irregularities, Rodney's National Home Improvement Co. grew and grew. Eventually, Rodney had a sales force of fifty men, five offices and an income in excess of $80,000 a year.

He was wretchedly unhappy, however; everyone on Broadway knew him as an irritable, uptight, self-pitying and chronically dissatisfied man. When you'd meet him over a corned beef sandwich and a bottle of celery water at the Stage, all you could see was a blur of tension: the finger in the shirt collar, the restlessly shifting eyes, the steadily rumbling voice, starting and stopping abruptly like a taxi motor in heavy traffic. Though he was making money, Rodney wanted another shot at the clubs. He constantly thought up new gags, new lines and bits of material. He lived with a guy to whom he gave free lodging in exchange for his services as a comedy coach.

On weekends he would pick a cheap little club out of the *Daily Mirror*—a "shithouse," he called it—and drive out to the joint dressed up to go onstage. At the bar he would spend ten or fifteen dollars and ingratiate himself with the proprietor. At the right moment, he'd ask the guy if he could get up and tell the customers a few jokes, just for the hell of it. The owner would think, "Why not humor this nut? The place is practically empty and besides the guy drinks like an alky." So Rodney would get his shot, though he might only work to two drunks in a dark corner or be forced to throw his voice from the empty backroom to the juicers way up front at the bar.

Bit by bit he built himself up until, at the age of forty-three, he decided to fold his business and go back to work full-time as a comic. It was while working in the upstairs room of a little club in Greenwich Village that he got his incongruous name. He didn't want to use his old professional name in this joint, so he told the owner, make up something. The owner had read Donleavy's *Ginger Man,* so he dubbed Jack Roy Rodney Dangerfield. The unconventional name became just one more of his innumerable worries.

After three years of scuffling, Rodney worked himself into the Copa, where he was "discovered" by Ed Sullivan. At the age of forty-five on the Sullivan show, the comic who blew it at twenty-eight got his second Big Chance. This time he killed them. Overnight he was a fixture on the TV talk shows, a new voice in a dying business. Unwilling to go back on the road, Rodney drew on his business know-how to build himself a permanent base with his own New York club.

Now he's really ready to rip. He's got a movie coming out, called *The Projectionist,* in which he plays a real Silent Majority type, a petty, mean-spirited movie manager who's always craning his flushed, angry face at ushers, warning: "Dirt is our enemy and dandruff means dismissal!" He wants to write his autobiography in two years and call it *My First*

50. He's even working on the pilot of a weekly TV series to be filmed at the club and called *A Night at Dangerfield's*. Lots of good things are happening to him, and now some nights onstage, he goes out there to test his power. "Al, the other night, I looked at all those out-of-towners, and something came over me. Al, I gave such a show—I *faklamiched* them!" "Faklamiched them?" I gasped. "My God, Rodney, I remember when you just wanted to *kill* them!"

The New York Times, 1970, and *Life*, 1970

THREE

Jazz: The Art That Came In from the Cold

The Apple at Its Core

T HE DEATH of jazz has been predicted countless times since
its birth. Every change of style, technique or attitude has
convinced some anxious soul that the end was near. Now in
the year 1963, when for the first time the prophecy is likely
to be fulfilled, no one will believe it—no one, that is, except
those who are close to the jazz scene and conscious of the
very great problems that are plaguing the art and its practitioners.

During the past few weeks, two of the outstanding jazz
critics in the United States and Britain, Nat Hentoff (in the
New York *Herald-Tribune*) and Francis Newton (in the
New Statesman), have described the depressed condition of
the New York scene and endeavored to explain its causes.
Returning to the city after a two-year absence, Newton was
shocked to find the clubs dark or half-empty, the musicians
without work or gigging behind counters, and the much-
publicized avant-garde the victim of a club owner's lockout.
He summed up his impressions of New York—"the Apple"
in jazz lingo—by describing the city as an "ex-Apple . . .

wilted and shaking on its bough." Hentoff finds great irony in the present jazz "boom," which he views as largely the work of publicists and image-makers, and as merely a hollow thud for the dozens of musicians who have had to take demeaning "day jobs" just to survive.

Even more disturbing than the critics' descriptions of today's hard times are their diagnoses of the causes. Newton thinks jazz has lost its audience to folk singers and to suburbia. Hentoff sees the long-established favorites pre-empting the field, blocking the rise of fresh talent.

Reading these reports, I was troubled by several things: the almost exclusive emphasis on the problems of supply and demand, the implication (in Newton's piece, the actual statement) that things were especially dead this year, and finally, the tendency of both critics to envision the current problems of jazz against the background of previous eras when both jazz and the world were much different. As far as the present "crisis" is concerned, I do not find the situation in 1962–63 substantially different from what it has been for the past decade. Jazz has not prospered in the New York clubs since the war years when the spill-over from the big-band craze and the on-the-town serviceman made it profitable to book combos on 52nd Street. To take the exceptional conditions of that period as a norm is unsound; 52nd Street was just a lucky break that could not last.

Nor can one ignore the fact that when jazz enjoyed its greatest popularity, during the swing era of the late Thirties, it was still a Negro folk art with a broad social base. The bopper of the Forties gleefully alienated this mass audience, put it down hard and made jazz the exclusive art form of the hipsters: a small interracial in-group with very little money and a constitutional aversion to institutionalized entertainment. It has taken years to woo the public back after the inspired insolence of be-bop.

The current situation is, if anything, somewhat better than it has been in past years. For one thing, the number of clubs featuring modern jazz, though still small, is definitely on the increase. Ten years ago the whole jazz life of the city was centered on two midtown rooms, Birdland and Basin Street; today there are enough new clubs below 14th Street to make the Village and its environs a major jazz locale.

More important, the radio coverage of jazz, particularly by FM stations, is now greater than it has been at any time since the late Thirties. On a recent Saturday night, I found almost half the city's FM stations broadcasting jazz recordings until the early hours of the morning. And the recordings themselves continue to pour forth in astonishing volume from a host of small companies, many of which are obviously in search of novelty and unafraid of the risk involved in presenting musicians with little or no reputation.

These facts lead me to conclude that jazz is in fact experiencing a modest "boom," though not of the sort that is immediately helpful to the jazz musician in search of work. Jazz, like art music, must now adjust itself to the new mores of middle-class America, which favor home entertainment by means of hi-fi and radio over public entertainment, particularly the kind provided by nightclubs. Jazz is reaching a wider audience than ever before, but it is an invisible audience, tucked away in homes and automobiles, the real centers of American life.

Although this change is no help to the working musician, it will probably be a good thing for jazz in the long run. Years of experience in the clubs have convinced me that they are not the proper milieu for modern jazz. The usual arrangements frustrate everyone: the owners are unhappy with the lack of turnover in the room, the musicians complain about the mechanical regularity of the schedule, and the patrons often feel uncomfortable and dissatisfied with the "show."

The other alternative, the formal concert, is just as bad, perhaps worse. The musicians feel terribly self-conscious and the audience finds itself compelled to listen head-on for long periods to a kind of music that is not designed for such intense scrutiny. Jazz ebbs and flows according to the spirit of the moment; it requires a flexible arrangement permitting the audience to turn away when the musicians are merely doodling—but not so far away that the moments of inspiration are lost in the hubbub.

The closest approximation to ideal jazz conditions I have ever encountered was, oddly enough, an event of this past winter, just at the time of Francis Newton's visit. It was an informal concert sponsored by the Jackie McLean Fan Club at the Fraternal Clubhouse on West 48th Street. Jackie, one of the greatest jazzmen of our day, lost his cabaret card years ago because of a narcotics violation. Since that time he has been barred from the clubs. But the ban has done nothing to impair his playing; indeed, he never sounded better.

I doubt, though, whether he would have performed so brilliantly in a less congenial atmosphere. Here he was surrounded by people who loved and admired him, who understood everything he was trying to accomplish, and who were themselves so cheerful and relaxed that merely being among them was a source of inspiration. Free to sit or stand or stroll about, drinking and smoking and chatting with friends and relatives, this audience was totally responsive.

The one thing this concert did not do, however, was give the sense of a new or emergent jazz style. Jackie demonstrated the great vitality still latent in the bop style; at times he seemed deliberately to challenge comparison with Bird—playing "Be-Bop" or "Star Eyes"—but it was not a new direction for jazz.

No new style comparable to the bop of the Forties or the cool style of the Fifties has yet emerged in this decade because of the confusion of identity felt by most modern jazzmen. With or without opportunities to work, these men are bound to suffer from a conflict between the aspirations aroused by training they have acquired in schools of music and the radically different values and techniques of jazz. And this conflict is directly related to the drive for status and dignity that propels the whole Negro community today.

The Negro jazz musician has at last become totally self-conscious; he sees himself as an individual artist working in a highly developed form with a long and compelling tradition. His problem is to synthesize this tradition, created largely by men of different character and status, with various elements of Western art music developed within a completely different cultural context. The problem is a great deal larger than the men who are trying to solve it. It is even questionable whether it can be solved at all. But it is inescapable, and it explains practically all the faults of modern jazz—the eclecticism, the attitudinizing, the forced-draft experimentation, the general atmosphere of confusion.

Francis Newton concludes his article by remarking that the generation of Parker and Gillespie had its forum on the Street, whereas the present generation of Ornette Coleman, Eric Dolphy and others has no place to play. But when Coleman was sure of himself, when he knew exactly what he wanted to do, he had the Five Spot all to himself for fifteen weeks, with a full house every night. Had he wanted commercial success, he could have been booked all over the country. After starting off in this direction, however, he suddenly pulled himself up and went into a retreat, which may last for a long time. Today, Coleman is not in the mood to play; he is in one of those latency periods that are becoming characteristic of every serious jazzman's career.

The same pattern is evident in the recent history of Sonny Rollins, who returned to public performance last fall following two and a half years spent in study and practice. After a few months on the New York scene—months of good notices, heavy publicity, even the rare prize of an RCA recording contract—Sonny decided to break up his group and think again. It was my impression after hearing Sonny last winter at the Museum of Modern Art that his playing had become an elaborate pastiche of every tenor sax style heard for the last twenty years. Perhaps he thought so too.

These examples are decisive. The really dedicated jazz musicians who must provide jazz with a new soul are now engaged in a difficult struggle to find themselves amid the confusing cultural eddies of the moment. Instinctively, they are doing the only thing that will help—they are going underground. There, free from the demands of scheduled performance and the annoyances of an uncomprehending public, supported by their friends and disciples, they will study, think and play. If they do not find a coherent and viable modern style, independent of both tradition and the alien ethos of art music, jazz, despite its new popularity, will be dead at the core.

The New Leader, 1963

Bird Watching

CHARLIE PARKER

BOB REISNER'S *Bird: The Legend of Charlie Parker* offers a fistful of important biographical documents—recollections, letters, medical reports—in the form of an unassembled jigsaw puzzle. The original idea was sound: tape-recorded interviews with everyone who knew Bird, from his mother to his favorite cab driver. Unfortunately, Reisner never got beyond the stage of primitive acquisition. He filed his reports alphabetically, and, when the time came to do the book, he simply hauled the stuff out and sent it to the printer. Now the reader is stuck with the job of putting some eighty-odd pieces together to make a composite picture of America's greatest jazz musician.

One striking side-effect of Reisner's mindless method is the light it throws on the bizarre inconsistency of Parker's behavior. On one page, there is a Parker who was generous to a fault, giving his last dollar to an indigent musician, playing all night in a bar for drinks, or shoving one of his women into the arms of a startled but eternally grateful friend. Turn the page, though, and you see Yardbird through another pair of eyes: here is Parker coolly picking the last eight cents from the outstretched palm of an impoverished jazzman, breaking into a friend's dressing room to steal his horn, or bullying the boys in his band out of their weekly wages.

By turns vulgar and courtly, arrogant and self-abasing, gentle and cruel, Bird seems consistent only in his inconsistency. Studying the puzzle more closely, however, some unifying patterns emerge. Parker's personality was a seesaw weighted on one end by colossal pride and on the other by profound self-hatred. And many of the fluctuations in his behavior were due to his inability to handle momentary crosses or frustrations.

When things were going well, when he had his daily supplies of junk, lush, willing white girls and submissive colleagues, Bird could be generous, amiable, even charming. He liked to play Big Daddy, handing out advice, helping young performers gain confidence, and shedding a genial radiance of *joie de vivre* over the dismal jazz scene. But when things took a turn for the worse, when the pusher failed to show, when the management demanded its due, or some little squirt in another band tried to show him up, the veneer of Parker's humanity would peel off, revealing the ugly personality structure so forcibly described by the Bellevue psychiatrists: "A hostile, evasive personality with manifestations of primitive and sexual fantasies associated with hostility and gross evidence of paranoid thinking."

The repetition of the word "hostile" is significant. Bird had inside him a bottomless well of frustration, particularly oral frustration, the kind that leads to overeating, alcoholism, drug addiction. Since he could never attain satisfaction of his Gargantuan appetites and demands, he was often a desperately angry man, conscious of his anger, fearful of its consequences and therefore duplicitous and shifty in his dealings with people. He used the familiar one-two of the paranoid personality: first, the soft sell, all butter and bull; if that failed, he came in hard and low on the muscle.

Sometimes he ran up against guys who weren't afraid of him. Don Byas had his own knife, so Bird put his away; Charlie Mingus was as big as a pro tackle, so Bird decided to pay him after all. But generally, by mixing up his pitches— slow curves and hot ones down the middle—Bird put every- one away. His friends were either flunkies, victims or will- ing martyrs. As Ross Russell put it, "Bird was a guy who hung everybody up."

After his thirtieth year, Bird began to deteriorate; the anger he could not release he was forced to absorb into his own system. He abraded his guts into dangerous peptic ulcers, he suffered agonies of despair, he attempted suicide several times. He would have died long before his thirty- fifth year if he had not been surrounded by loving and faith- ful people who pulled him out of jams, lent him money, gave him food and shelter and held back the swarm of dope peddlers who descended on him like flies on a rotten carcass. Everybody from the Baroness de Koenigswarter down to the lowliest hackie divined an essential goodness in Parker; vainly they struggled to save him.

Like many psychopaths, Bird was extremely intelligent; he understood his condition perfectly. He knew he was kill- ing himself with drugs and liquor; he knew he was a genius with nowhere to go; he knew the answers to all the ques- tions he kept asking other people. But his knowledge did him no good: he could never transcend the terms established for his life by the nature of his personality. At best he could effect a momentary escape through the only avenue that was always open and always safe—music.

The relation between Parker's violent and erratic person- ality and his extraordinary improvisational art is close and obviously important. Unlike the deliberate artist who changes his material constantly and devises new styles and tech- niques to render each new theme, the improviser tells the same story over and over again, altering it in various ways to accommodate the inspiration and the insight of the moment. Throughout the period of his greatest creativity, from 1945 to 1950, Parker had substantially the same book, the same traditional form and the same individual technique. He was infinitely resourceful in varying the details and in discovering new connections in the material, but the basic elements never changed. What did change from one night to the next, even from one set to the next, was his *mood*.

Parker's moods were really the content of his art, the categories of his mind. Like the old Greek modes or the Indian ragas, these moods were highly charged with experiential significance; by slipping them over the familiar material like colored glasses, he profoundly altered the character of this material. In his two recorded versions of "Lover Man," for example, the notes are practically the same, yet the meanings are utterly different. Sometimes Bird would spend a whole evening playing everything in a cool, detached style full of wistful delicacy; other times, he would throw his weight around like a musical bully, playing coarsely, aggressively, crowding his side men to the ropes in combative four-bar exchanges.

Probably no other man in the history of American music so fully expressed his personality in his art as did Charlie Parker. He was like Beethoven in his passionate commitment to naked self-expression. His oft-quoted statement about the relation of art to experience has the familiar Romantic ring: "Music is your own experience, your thoughts, your wisdom. If you don't live it, it won't come out of your horn. They teach you there's a boundary line to music. But, man, there's no boundary line to art."

Until quite recently only those lucky few who were hip to the jazz scene of the late Forties had any real idea of what Bird sounded like when he expressed himself freely, heedless of the performance values stressed in the recording studio. Bird himself complained that his greatest music, the music he created in hundreds of sessions in clubs, at dances, or in private parties, had never been waxed. He was luckier than he knew: some of those faithful disciples who trailed after him wherever he went did succeed in capturing on discs a few of his most inspired sessions. This material has now been made available in a series of recordings that are the best as well as the most authentic evidence of the genius of Charlie Parker.

Particularly important are the three volumes of *Charlie Parker in Great Historical Recordings* and *Bird Is Free*. The first three discs present Parker at the height of his powers, circa 1948, with a backing that includes many of the foremost boppers. For the first time on records, for example, we hear Bird playing with Fats Navarro, the superb trumpet man whom Ross Russell describes as being closer to Bird on the horn than either Dizzy Gillespie or Miles Davis.

To those who have for years listened to Parker's numerous and brilliant studio recordings, these on-the-gig recordings come as something of a shock. Never have we heard Bird so powerful, so free, so daringly open. There is a sense of his being totally possessed—picked up and hurled about by the force of his own inspiration. Equally astonishing are the depth and solidity of his moods: the tragic, the ebullient, the resigned, the hostile-aggressive. For sheer self-assertion nothing can compare with the "Lester Leaps In"—six choruses at machine-gun tempo, all of them probably directed at the great tenor man's head.

Soon after these were recorded, beginning about 1950, Bird began to decline musically as well as emotionally. I suspect he had gone as far as he could go with the jazz of that period; probably he needed a new medium, a new synthesis. He did experiment with concerto-like treatments of pop tunes, using a string-and-woodwind orchestra, but this was a musical blunder strongly motivated by a naïve craving for extramusical status.

It was at this time, too, that Parker talked so much about studying composition and going on to greater things than jazz. In his way, he was repeating the same futile pattern that George Gershwin fell into in his last years. The geniuses of popular music never seem to realize that the only way for them to rise is to dig deeper into their native soil. In any case, it was certainly much too late for Parker to begin anew.

Even before his death in 1955, Bird was dead at the core. His last batch of studio records, made in 1953, show him a hollow colossus standing astride the world of jazz. The power, the virtuosity were his to the end; but having destroyed his own soul, he lost his ability to reach the souls of others. It is terrible to think that this man whose only escape from a life of emotional squalor was through his art found himself at last blocked even there. No wonder he wanted to drink iodine and die.

The New Leader, 1961

Un Poco Loco

BUD POWELL

EVER SINCE the mid-Fifties, when the racially inspired movement to "bring dignity to jazz" got under way, many critics have labored to dissociate jazz from the traditional jazz life. Not content with debunking the Hollywood and men's magazine version of the musician's life, these writers have tried to convince us that dope has nothing to do with the music, that the antisocial behavior of many jazz musicians is simply an accident of their race or class, and that the fierce, self-destructive drives of great jazzmen like Charlie Parker are merely regrettable instances of psychic infirmity fortuitously associated with artistic ability. Now one of our leading critics has taken the final step in this whitewash campaign by implying that the lurid features of the jazz scene are principally the creation of hopped-up hipster novelists.

In a recent issue of *The New Yorker*, Whitney Balliett decided that all jazz novels written by whites were "unrevealing and unwittingly condescending." What is more, he found these books (including one he had originally praised) basically inaccurate. "In the main," he writes, "jazz musicians are home-loving, television-watching, newspaper-reading innocents who dislike night clubs, late hours, buses, and all other discomforts their jobs force on them."

The operative phrase here is "in the main." For the fact is, neither the jazz novelist, nor the jazz listener, nor for that matter the jazz critic, is much concerned with jazz musicians in the main. It is the exceptional men, the men of genius who really engage our thoughts and feelings, and these men have lived and created in a world of pain. In jazz, suffering and greatness seem inseparable.

Fresh evidence of this old truth was recently provided by the sad news of Bud Powell's wretched life in Paris. Bud is one of the few giants of modern jazz. For almost twenty years he has lived a nightmare existence of paranoid fantasies alongside realities not much less terrifying. His has been a world of brutal cops; angry, jealous musicians; cruel, exploitative friends and lovers; mental institutions with assembly-line electroshock; and squalid hotel rooms littered with empty bottles.

Today Bud is stretched out in a Paris hospital with tuberculosis, the result of appalling self-neglect. Shortly before the onset of his disease, I have been told, he suddenly broke through the sullen stupor in which he has been wrapped in recent years and for several nights played brilliantly at the Blue Note in Paris. Everything in Bud's history vouches for the accuracy of the story.

Born Earl Rudolph Powell in 1924, one of six children of a Harlem janitor who played piano in his spare time, Bud received the usual city education, plus music lessons, until his fifteenth year. At that point, he quit De Witt Clinton High and started scuffling in the sleazy bars of Harlem, Coney Island and the Village. Though still a kid, he got in with the boppers up at Minton's and soon became the protégé of Thelonious Monk, who taught him the "advanced" chords and pushed him on the stand, much the way Charlie Parker encouraged Miles Davis.

Before long Bud was in demand for record dates and downtown gigs. In 1944, Dizzy Gillespie wanted to use him for the first bop engagement on the Street, at the Onyx Club. But somebody vetoed the plan, and instead Bud spent two years seasoning with the Cootie Williams band.

Bud's early role as a supporting player was cut out for him by history. In those days, many Negro pianists were self-taught naïfs who could swing and play melody but were harmonically crude. When sophisticated soloists like Charlie Parker began to call for "fat-boy" chords to feed their invention, only a handful of wiggy whites—among them, George Wallington, George Handy, Al Haig, Joe Albany and Dodo Marmarosa—had the training and the ear to accommodate them. Bud and John Lewis, another classically trained Negro pianist, were exceptions, though even then Lewis was a sucker for impressionistic prettiness.

Bud Powell tried to follow Charlie Parker wherever he led. On the air check of "Round About Midnight," recorded around 1948, Bud enters after Parker's grimly despondent statement of the melody. He has to take the tempo up to swing, and his style is an eclectic jumble of his own manner and those of Thelonious Monk and Errol Garner. But his flow of ideas is impressive and, significantly, he does not change the subject. Of all the boppers, Bud is most truly Bird's musical son and heir. He has Parker's power, anger and defiance and is infected with the same racial virus that embittered Bird's life. Both of them knew this, and until Bird's death in 1955 their paths kept crossing, often with disastrous results.

Bud Powell's long series of mental breakdowns began in 1945, with a scene in Philadelphia's Broad Street Police Station. Brought in drunk, he got salty with the desk sergeant and was busted. A month later he was committed to Pilgrim State in manic condition: "His thoughts were flying away with him," one psychiatrist remarked. In ten weeks, though, Bud was out and those flying thoughts inspired the great playing to be heard on the 1947 Savoy dates with Bird. Confined to one eight-bar chorus per side, Bud would come yeasting up out of the grooves, swinging hard with a loose-jointed, splay-fingered style that soon got a name: people said he played "funky" (the word means, roughly, low-down, dirty and dark).

The funky style anticipated by a decade the recent emphasis on "soul" and "roots." Unlike the deliberate racial stance adopted by the hard boppers of the late Fifties, however, Bud's down-home stuff, like "Collard Greens and Black Eye Peas," was played without a trace of self-consciousness. Yet, while the funky style provided a rich soil for musical ideas, its first growth proved too luxuriant. The critic Barry Ulanov once complained of Bud's work: "His solos sometimes have a fragmentary quality, like a series of boxes piled precariously on top of one another."

Ulanov was right. All through the Forties, Bud was under the influence of Monk; from this strange genius he had learned that the basic rule for the jazz performer was to hold his mind as wide open as possible to the spontaneous entrance of ideas. And because Bud's mind was swarming with so many ideas, each clamoring for expression, his work often had a tentative, sketchy outline. Apparently, Monk had not been able to impress on Bud the corollary of the rule: while you *think* everything, you play only what fits.

From 1947 to 1953, Bud Powell was caught in a crippling cycle of psychotic episodes. He spent as much time in mental institutions as he did out of them: eleven months in Creedmore with electroshock; a brief period back at work; three more months in Creedmore; seventeen months of freedom; and, finally, a terrible breakdown leading to a sixteen-month commitment to Pilgrim State with still more electroshock.

Despite the constant interruption of his career by mental illness, Bud's development as an artist, from the evidence provided by dozens of records, seems perfectly regular. In 1951 he suddenly threw off his old style and emerged as "The Amazing Bud Powell." The circus billing was appropriate; Bud now became the mad genius of jazz piano. He was obviously out to beat Bird at his own game of killing tempos, dazzling virtuosity and startling ideas.

Bud's manifesto was called "Un Poco Loco," a number built on an orgiastic 9/8 rhythm whacked out by Max Roach on a cowbell with stunning Latin syncopations. In the long introduction, Bud generated an atmosphere of gagging expectancy and then leaped off the deep end into the turbid whirlpool of a rolling bass. In three successive takes, he struggled to break into the clear in his solo, but each time he seemed to sink into the dark element he himself had created. It was not until several years later that he finally learned how to combine his hypnotic rhythmic bass with a brilliant top line of solo figuration. When he did, as in the *Jazz Giant* album, he achieved for a brief moment the most satisfactory jazz synthesis since the heyday of bop.

The formula for all the up-tempo tunes in this collection is simple: It is, in fact, a translation into keyboard idiom of the solo-plus-accompaniment style of many bop horn players. Comping hard with his left hand, backed up by drums and bass, Bud spins with his right hand a long unbroken line of single notes which cascade up and down the keyboard with effortless fluency. Brilliant as is the effect, I have sometimes thought that the culmination of Bud's art was a dead end, for the loss of his rhythmic looseness and funky flavor subtly reduced the interest and suggestiveness of his work, even though it increased its surface brilliance and impact.

From 1953 on, Bud began to decline in much the same way that Bird did. The art remained but the soul shriveled. At a recent benefit for Powell at Birdland, Oscar Goodstein, the club's proprietor and Bud's long-time friend and patron, told me that he is now out of danger with the tuberculosis, though he will have to spend a year in a convalescent home. One great difference between the jazz life today and that of twenty years ago is that now people care. Years ago Bud Powell would have died alone in Paris, and some nitwit in the Village would have scrawled on a wall—"Bud Lives."

The New Leader, 1963

Man, You Gotta Dig That Cat Thelonious, the Thinker, the Skull, the Long Medulla

THELONIOUS MONK

THELONIOUS MONK is a hard man to place. When you mention Monk to somebody who knows the jazz scene, they always give you the same bit: "He's the guy who started bop." Well, we all know that, but still you can't peg Monk as a bopper—he's too individual for that tag. Then, there are the cats who go into a thing about "Monk, the Genius of Jazz," the man who plays and writes and arranges, and does everything the end. Well, jazz has had lots of triple-threat men, but it has never had another Monk.

No, man, you gotta dig Thelonious as the thinker, the skull, the long medulla. Just watch how he sits there on the stand. He don't hump over the keys like them studs who just wanna rave on all night. Maybe he's got one leg over the other, sitting sidewise with his elbow on the rack while he flaps the keys with one hand. You dig right away the cat is thinking. He don't wanna play for anybody, he just needs an audience so's he can be alone and work things out for himself. Sometimes he gets so frustrated trying to get something down, he just gives up and lets the other boys rave on without him. Sometimes he's thinking so hard, he don't even bother to get a sound.

Monk's solos are the craziest things, because every two bars he's off on a new idea. He'll start in with some weird little blip he just picked up from outer space, and then, just when you're sure he's gonna make it, he gives the dial a twist, and his rig starts bringing in the funny old sound of some Harlem stride player, circa 1925. Two bars of that jazz and the set suddenly jams on an African time signal—one swinging note struck over and over again until you're ready to flip! You see now what it is when a guy is always thinking —he can't get himself together so's he can play.

Monk's ideas are mostly things he does with tonality and rhythm. He'll set his bass player going in one key, then he'll come on strong in another key. Or, maybe he'll make two different rhythms fight it out, drums against piano. That left hand of his is always feeling around, grabbing chords nobody else would think to play. Every time he lays a strange chord down, the music tilts to a different angle. Sometimes he tilts it so sudden and so sharp, like, the cat who's taking the solo comes tumbling down like a bottle off an upturned table.

Monk's right hand isn't worth much. He has a hard time playing what he hears in his head. Compared to a great piano man like Bud Powell, Monk sounds like a cat who needs lessons. That's why you always wanna catch Monk inside a combo where he don't have to do the big solo bit.

The cats who play with Monk are the most grooved men in America. He keeps feeding them crazy ideas until they're out of their skulls. Sometimes you'll see him play something, and then look up to see whether he reached the other man. Monk's always sending messages like that, trying to turn the other boys on. One night he got so far out he even tried to turn the audience on. He shuffled off the stand and started yelling at the people to dance! Now, there's a scene for you —imagine all those cool cats lobbed out in their seats getting up and firking around to that insane beat!

I guess what gasses musicians the most about Monk is this: no matter how gone he gets with his atonal jazz, he never loses a strong racial sound. You see, most of the modern cats are pretty well hung up between jazz and the classical stuff. They all took a little vacation up at Juilliard after the war, and before they got away they were hooked on Bach and Debussy. Now, a man like Monk is good for these cats. He's like some old oil well that keeps pumping up the good black stuff when all the new rigs have gone dry.

Even the Modern Jazz Quartet has picked up on Monk. Milt Jackson, their vibes man, used to play with Monk years ago. I guess some of those rough chips must have stuck in his brain, 'cause every so often I hear a nutty sound in his playing, and I say to myself, "Now, there's a man that digs Thelonious!"

The New Leader, 1959

Big John Bends East

JOHN COLTRANE

BIG JOHN COLTRANE, looking more like an aging athlete than a leader of the jazz avant-garde, solemnly mounted the low stand at Birdland one night in June of 1964. After carefully parking a gleaming Selmer tenor on an adjacent chair, he raised to his lips a straight little soprano sax, the once-despised symbol of Mickey Mouse band leaders. Astonishingly, the beautiful theme-melody of "My Favorite Things" emerged from the instrument with the haunting sound of an English horn.

Playing against a sweet new time, the syncopated waltz, Trane repeated the melody, and then—just as we braced for the expected improvisatory flight out across the first eight bars, around the back track of the release, and then home again by way of the initial chord progression—an even more astonishing thing occurred. Ascending abruptly into the instrument's piercing upper register while never leaving the first two chords, now sounding in the background like a tamboura drone, Coltrane began to improvise brilliantly in the oriental manner. Soon the air was full of exotic Arabian

Nights figures—hard and bright, an elaborate filigree of metal sound. It was a thrilling effect, and it instantly created the cleanest, coolest musical atmosphere New York has breathed in years.

After a minute or two of oriental glitter, Trane stepped back and his piano player, McCoy Tyner (not so much supported as inundated by the dervish drumming of Roy Haynes) slipped effortlessly into double time and carried us far out into the endless American night. It wasn't the notes the man was playing that so enthralled us—he had no story to tell, just those two hypnotic chords. It was something in the musical atmosphere, some mystery of tonal sound and rhythmic motion that made us rock from the waist, like old Jews in a synagogue. The entire number lasted ten, perhaps twenty minutes; I lost track of time, but I distinctly remember a pang of regret when the first notes of the theme returned and broke the spell.

Having swept around the cool side of the jazz world in "My Favorite Things," Coltrane came out on the hot side in "Impressions," a fast, hard-driving number that sounded to me like a derivative from Ferde Grofé's *Grand Canyon Suite*. (Unless the performer plays the release or bridge of the tune—which Coltrane often skips—it is usually impossible to pin the source of a jazz line because so many pop tunes use the same chords in their choruses.) For this heavy action Trane unlimbered his big soul horn. His solo consisted of an unending succession of riff-like phrases blown with an intensity that recalled the frantic excesses of the old jump bands.

But even here, in this basically familiar style, one detected the oriental influence in the chorus structure. Instead of zipping along from one chord to the next, welding the whole chorus into a sleek, seamless sequence, Coltrane chopped up the chorus into little segments, each chord sustaining a flourish of notes. The result was a series of complicated but discontinuous statements.

Discontinuity is, of course, one of the hallmarks of contemporary jazz. Men like Thelonious Monk and Ornette Coleman often produce asymmetric, disjunct patterns because they are constantly pausing to catch the scent of a fresh idea. But Coltrane is different: he is a compulsive performer who plunges relentlessly on for fifteen or even twenty minutes at a clip, playing in patches but never pausing for thought.

The over-all pattern of his enormously long, hot solos is that of the jam session: a strong, I-know-just-where-I'm-going beginning; a period of diminishing returns as the original inspiration wanes; mounting excitement as a new goal comes into sight ("catch it! catch it!"); and then the cruel orgasmic climax—the eyes closed, sweat streaming down the face, the body bent in pain as terrible cries (screams, really) are wrenched from the horn. As he comes to the finish his listeners, some of them straining as hard as their hero, hoarsely chant: "Trane! Trane!"

It is the music of the hot, heavy belters, back again after the long freeze of the Fifties. Only now the players are more daring, because more desperate, than they ever were before. The struggle to break the strangling grip of jazz convention has driven even the most sensitive and highly accomplished musicians, like Coltrane, to the final limits of musical brutality. Hence the paradox of modern jazz: an extraordinarily sophisticated technique, as often as not cultivated in conservatories, combined with some of the most menacing, atavistic sounds ever heard outside the Chicago stockyards.

The other tactic in the effort to break out of the current bind is the flight away from jazz to the folk music of other lands. And here we come back to "My Favorite Things," with its obvious oriental flavor. But first, lest I appear to be going overboard on what may seem to some listeners no more than a pretty tune, I want to explain that the original record of this piece does not have the same impact as the 1964 version [released in 1970 in a live-at-Newport format]. Several things made the recording less than great. It was done too early, before Coltrane had fully worked out the concept or really gotten his new instrument down; Roy Haynes had not yet joined Trane, and it is a studio recording, with all that implies in terms of expressive inhibitions.

With the success of "My Favorite Things" and its sequel, "India," it is now clear that jazz is going into an oriental phase. When Ravi Shankar, the famous Indian sitar player, toured the United States in 1963, he found that some of his most appreciative listeners were jazz musicians; in fact, some of the boys went back to India with him. Had Shankar come to this country even as recently as ten years ago, he would not have exerted the same strong influence. At that time the cool movement was just beginning, and you have to be very cool to make the Indian style.

Indian music is closely analogous to jazz. It is made up of a freely improvised solo performance against a steady rhythmic background. Instead of chord sequences, the Indian improvisation is based on ragas (scales with one set of notes going up and another set coming down) and talas (rhythmic patterns with a fixed number of beats).

The conventional arrangement of the Indian performance has been adapted by Coltrane in "India." First, the mood is established by the drone instrument (in Indian music the tamboura, here the string bass); then the solo instrument (flute, sitar, soprano sax) enters, meditatively exploring the mood, playing scale figures, arabesques, and curlicues; finally, the rhythm tightens up and the soloist really begins to blow. Actually, it is a good deal more complicated in Indian music, but Trane has got the drift of the thing.

Apart from the purely musical affinities of jazz—the cool and Indian music—one discerns behind this *drang nach Osten* the now familiar yearning of the American Negro for a proud, strongly marked cultural identity that owes nothing to the white man and his civilization. We had the first experience of this tendency in jazz many years ago, when some of the boppers embraced Islam, changed their names to exotic monikers like Sahib Shihab and even turned up on the gig wearing Arab costumes. At that time the whole business was treated as a crazy camp, both by the musicians and the jazz fans. Today, Negro Moslems like Yusef Lateef are deeply serious about their religion and punctilious about its observances ("You don't walk into Lateef's pad with your shoes on, Dexter!").

Even if the Negro did not have compelling social and political reasons for cutting out of Caucasian culture, the Negro jazzman would still be receptive to foreign influences. The native American resources have been pretty well exhausted. The choice facing the jazz musician now is either to assimilate the essences of other folk cultures or submit to the exacting discipline of avant-garde Western art music, itself practically bankrupt.

Coltrane's excurions into oriental jazz are certainly more satisfying as art, and ultimately less subversive to the basic character of jazz, than are most of the experiments of the atonal-oriented Third Stream, the movement that seeks to combine jazz with certain elements of art music. Most Third Stream compositions sound like products of an advanced composition class spiced with a few hot licks. Efforts to revive hot jazz in something like its traditional form—the vein of "Impressions" and much of Ornette Coleman—strike me as regressive and self-defeating.

It so happens that the night of Coltrane's big blast at Birdland I met Ornette Coleman walking down Broadway at two A.M. Ornette is a sweet, friendly guy with none of the usual hip mannerisms, and I didn't hesitate to ask him for an interview. "Nothing happening, man; save the print." That was the word. Then, fearing I might be offended, he added: "I'm still your friend." I know, Ornette, I thought, it's bad all over.

Listening to Jive Talk

THE ASTONISHING SPREAD of jazz slang demonstrates how a tiny, offbeat minority can dictate terms to an entire nation. Many years ago this most potent strain of American slang began to ooze from its original sources: the brothels and barrel houses where the music and the sex shared the common name *jazz*. Down into the sewer-like labyrinth of the underground it flowed, where it became the lingua franca of the pimps, pushers and B-girls; the hookers, hitters, hipsters and beats. Then from these subterranean channels it worked its way out into the open via Broadway, where it passed easily into the mouths of thousands of urban teenagers eager to offend. As those man-sized adolescents, the disc jockeys, whipped each wave of the jazz fad to its crest, the mass media scooped up the froth and spread it across the country with countless articles appearing in *Life*, *Time* and *Newsweek*.

The efforts of these cultural pushers met an answering appetite. Words like *cool*, *hip*, *square* and *hang-up* were gobbled up by a society that increasingly yearns for that

little "edge," that trifling verbal distinction that signals sophistication. But on the long haul out to the provinces the
smoky flavor of the words often evaporated. When Smiley
Smith in Boise tells someone that he "had a ball," chances are
that he doesn't intend any sexual innuendo; when Dawn
Jones croons "funky" while listening to the Animals, we can
be pretty sure that she is as innocent of the original association between her adjective and sexual odors as her mother
was of the connection between "boogie-woogie" and syphi-
lis. Once these words get into general circulation, they're
not hip any more. By the time the "fays" have caught them,
the cats on 125th Street are tapping out their messages on a
different key.

The first code books of jazz slang, or jive talk, appeared in
the Thirties. They bore the names of such ancient culture
heroes as Cab Calloway and Benny Goodman, and they
touted the reader on the meaning of wild new words like
alligator (a swing fan), *jitterbug, cutting a rug* and *cooking
with gas* (*with both burners wide open!*). Then in the Forties and Fifties the "wigs" took over from the musicians:
critics and hipsters like Leonard Feather, Bob Reisner and
Elliot Horne peddled paper-bound booklets adorned with
"Bop Jokes and Cool Cartoons." Eventually, the heavy-
weight lexicographers came clanking on the scene, and the
language was embalmed in bulky compilations like the
American Thesaurus of Slang (revised 1953), and the *Dictionary of American Slang* (1960). At this point it looked
like the job had finally been done—but it hadn't. At a conservative guess, four-fifths of the entries in the *Thesaurus*
are inauthentic neologisms culled from disc jockeys, gossip
columns and teen fadists; the compilers even commit the
howler of spelling Louis Armstrong's name "Lewis."
Though the *Dictionary* is much better, it, too, reveals exces-
sive dependence on printed instead of oral sources, and it
mindlessly echoes the mistakes of earlier glossaries (accepting "hep," a word never used by musicians, as an earlier
form of "hip") while dealing prudishly and often inaccu-

rately with the idiom's jarring obscenities.

The final codification of jazz slang has had to wait all these years for someone with the uniquely blended qualifications of the academic lexicographer's thoroughness and linguistic science and the hipster's on-the-turf intimacy with the jazz scene. Robert S. Gold, a professor of English at Jersey City State College and a veteran observer of the jazz world, has produced the first fully satisfactory treatment. Exhaustive in its entries, accurate in its definitions, discriminating in its selection of authentic terminology, arranged according to the historical method of *The Oxford English Dictionary*, *A Jazz Lexicon* (Alfred A. Knopf, 1964) easily supersedes its predecessors. Yet it will probably suffer their fate and sit forlornly on the reference shelf in the library awaiting the clandestine clasp of an adolescent hand. This is a pity, considering the insight this volume provides into a world more often exploited than understood. For jazz slang, jazz music and the jazz life are (or *were*) simply different expressions of the same spirit, each being a mirror in which the others are reflected.

The vocabulary of the jazz musician is vivid and powerful, but his speech is often vague, monotonous and unclear, because a few key value words usurp in each period the functions of an entire spectrum of language. In the bop period of the late Forties, everything that was "in"—beards, glasses, fancy speech, as well as the musical style—was "bop." When "cool" came in with the early Fifties, this monosyllable assumed every grammatical function, operating as verb, adjective, noun. Now the same thing is happening with "*soul*"—the effort to get back to the racial roots of jazz in country blues and gospel music: Harlem is *soul city;* Southern cooking is *soul food,* fellow musicians are *soul brothers.* The history of jive talk, then, is just the history of the death and renewal of this limited vocabulary as—in every era—its coinages are pounded flat by overuse.

One of the interesting ways to read *A Jazz Lexicon* is to watch how the words bunch around the prime values and how they spawn generations of synonyms that often presuppose an earlier form which has been truncated or parodied in the latest version. Thus, to take an obvious example, no language in the world has a higher proportion of superlatives than has jive talk. And when all these different ways of saying "wow!" are sorted out, they fall into lots, depending on which primary value is being evoked. One strain derives from the idea of transcendence, as in the old phrase *out of this world*. Later this was shortened to *out*; lengthened again to *out of sight*; parodied as *gone*; and understated as *somethin' else* or, as a coolie would say today—*different*. Another superlative shows the common association between fantasy and madness: *crazy, insane, nutty, wild*. Still another shows the great value placed on violence: *kill, knock out, fracture, knock a hole in, break up*. But the most numerous class of superlatives are those whose connotations are sexual: *hot, swinging, rocking, riding, smoking, burning, balling, up tight*.

There is also a heavily used vocabulary to express suffering, frustration, failure; but it is significant that these words understate, minimize or shrug off troubles too familiar and too distressing to require dramatization. Thus, all the hardships of maturation are written off as *paying dues*; a situation of grave danger or humiliation is dismissed as a *bad scene, a drag, a hassle*. Even death is treated jocularly: when a jazzman dies, he *rolls a seven, calls off all bets* or simply *checks out*. One thing the language does not have is a word for comfortable mediocrity.

The values of the normal world are defiantly inverted in the world of jazz: *bad, terrible* and *tough* are synonyms for excellence, while *sweet* and *pretty* are terms of disparagement. But even when the values of the upper and the underworlds coincide, the emphasis is not the same. Sophistication, knowledge, alertness and awareness are obviously good things, but where the white American sees these qualities as means of enhancing life, the Negro prizes them as protection. Gold writes: "The way [hip boots] protect the wearer from bad weather or dangerous currents is analogous to the way in which *hipness* arms one against social perils."

The language's principal obscenity has an amazing number of forms: *mother, motheree, motherferyer, mother fouler, mother hugger, mother jiver, mother lover, mother superior, mammy jammer,* etc. Though this phrase appears to be an outrageous insult (as it was long ago when it was hatched in the primitive game of abuse called the *dirty dozens*), its customary usage among Negroes today is as a term of grudging esteem or affection. An explanation of this paradoxical use not mentioned by Gold is related to a peculiarity of Negro family life: since many mothers live with men who aren't their husbands, this typical epithet—in addition to its obvious reference to incest—may describe the ambivalent blend of resentment and respect felt by a Negro boy for his mother's lover, part father, part interloper.

If Gold's *Lexicon* has a substantial shortcoming, it is the unavoidable limitation of the word list as a method of representing a living speech. Even though he has been careful to include entries obtained from oral as well as printed sources, all the citations are from articles and novels in which jazz language is necessarily stylized to intensify its flavor. More Boswell and less Johnson would have given us a more authentic and original specimen of the jazz idiom. Here was an opportunity for a sane man to pick up on the late Joe Gould's fantasy of an Oral History of the World by throwing in a generous handful of jazz talk in vivo.

And this brings us to the "nitty-gritty" of this whole question of jive talk. Just how live is it today? During the years Gold was preparing his book, the jazz age was running down to its end. What was planned as a key to a living language has actually become its monument. The *Lexicon*'s jacket calls it the history of "America's most successful nonconformist minority." Ironically, the very "success" of this minority has resulted in its elevating itself out of its citadel in Harlem as it strains for the sophistication of the international avant-garde. Most of the words in the *Lexicon* would be spurned by today's young jazz musician, who is well educated, refined and sophisticated, alienated from his people, self-conscious when he attempts "soul music." Harlem will go on spewing out new words and launching new fads for years to come, but the jazzman will not—as in the past—stand in the midst of this yeasty action, "sending messages" from underground.

The New Republic, 1964

Hot Dogs

T HE LATE Professor Marshall Stearns was a scholar errant who divided his mind between medieval English literature at Hunter College by day and American jazz at Birdland by night. The author of the standard history of jazz and the standard work on the fifteenth-century Scottish poet Robert Henryson, Stearns lavished on both his loves the same precious gifts of painstaking research, sympathetic understanding and carefully matured judgment. Only in his prose was there sometimes visible a conflict between the academician and the journalist: he wrote in a feature-story style through which the reader could often discern the ghostly outlines of his innumerable three-by-five cards.

For the seven years immediately preceding his untimely death (in 1966) at fifty-eight, Stearns and his wife, Jean, devoted every day and week they could snatch to a project of heroic proportions: nothing less than the first full-scale history of American popular dance. Not surprisingly, they followed the path beaten by Stearns's *The Story of Jazz* and

defined American "vernacular" dance as "dancing that is
performed to and with the rhythms of jazz." Both the considerable merits and the no less obvious faults of *Jazz Dance*
(Macmillan, 1969) are due to this restricted perspective.

The jazz slant enables the Stearnses to marshal an un-
wieldy mass of material along the lines of a familiar tale: the
story of how the American Negro patched together a hybrid culture, part African and part European, out of which
sprang the vigorous and increasingly sophisticated jazz arts.
But even the analysis of jazz dance leads back to the days
before jazz; as the Stearnses themselves explain, virtually
every step that has been popular during the last ten years
was cut first on the rough floors of some Southern church or
barrel house around the turn of the century. The frug, for
example, harkens back to the old shimmy, the jerk is close to
the shake and the monkey is derived from the heebie-jeebies.
The mashed potato and Charley bop are spin-offs from the
original Charleston and the twist is an ingredient of two ancient dance routines called ballin' the jack and messin'
around ("Twist around with all your might,/Messin' round,
they call that messin' round").

Seeing everything from the jazz angle also obliges the authors to slight or ignore all the American dancing inspired
by other kinds of music: not only the country and court
dances of the early white settlers but the more important
Spanish-American styles that in modern times have formed a
countercurrent to the jazz tradition, a black Latin style
vying in each period with a black American style: the
rumba with the Charleston, the mambo with the Lindy and
the bossa nova with the boogaloo. Nor do the Stearnses take
sufficient notice of the progressive blending of Latin and
jazz styles, a process that now has a country bluesman like
Albert King playing a thing he calls a "bent rumba," that is a
rumba whose 6/8 time has been accommodated to the blues'
4/4 by rhythmic "bending."

The origins of black American dance are hopelessly ob-
scure, but they include elements as diverse as the Irish jig

and the Lancaster clog. Actually, it was not until the mid-nineteenth century—and then only through the performances of white minstrels like the famous Daddy "Jim Crow" Rice—that Americans got their first look at "plantation" dancing. The Negro minstrel (who blacked up his black face in deference to tradition) did not emerge as an important figure until the end of the century, when he inherited the worn-out tent shows that white performers were abandoning for vaudeville. By the Twenties, however, the familiar stereotype of the dancing "jig" with his flashy clothes and rakishly tilted derby was well established on the Broadway stage, and slumming parties were going up to Harlem to see the snake-hips "jungle" dancer with his hypnotic stare and tassel-bedecked midriff.

The emergence of the "class" acts—such as Bill Robinson and Bill Bailey—impeccably tailored soft-shoe and tap dancers with graceful floating styles, signaled finally the black man's bid for the status of the cool and exquisitely poised gentleman: a stance that profoundly influenced Fred Astaire and a whole generation of film and stage dancers who worked in blandly engaging white face. This early cool was soon blown away, however, by the hot breath of a bunch of kids who seized a corner of the Savoy Ballroom in the Thirties and touched off the Lindy hop, the first jazz dance to become a national mania.

As the Lindy swept the country, behind the scenes, at the Hoofer's Club in Harlem, on Garfield Boulevard in Chicago, the dancing counterparts of Charlie Parker and Dizzy Gillespie were carrying jazz dance to it ultimate levels, developing the ultrafancy footwork demanded by the convoluted rhythms and stuttering-stammering phrases of bebop. Improvising with unheard-of ingenuity on three feet of hardwood floor, these hipster hoofers rapped out the valedictory tattoos of the jazz age.

When rock rolled in with Elvis "the pelvis," the day of the professional dancer was done: either he became a coach for adolescent rhythm-and-blues groups working in banana-skin suits or he opened a "studio" and taught secretaries the latest mating moves for their weekends at Grossinger's. The last great figure in the history of Negro dance, James Brown, is not even mentioned in the Stearnses' chronicle, presumably because he belongs to the rock and soul worlds and not to the jazz tradition.

The omission is barely pardonable because on the Stearnses' own showing the steps Brown executes are a virtual anthology of Negro dance. What better way to conclude the show than to bring on "America's No. 1 Soul Brother," dressed in an old-fashioned frock coat, flashing a big white grin, doing skate heel glides, dazzling double shuffles, knock-kneed camel walks and high-tailed, chicken-pecking atavisms in the crisscrossed spotlights of Madison Square Garden, while an invisible pit band snaps out the whiplash beat of "Poppa's Got a Brand New Bag" and the last of the song-and-dance men gasps:

> He's doing the jerk, he's doing the fly,
> Don't play him cheap, 'cause you know he ain't jive,
> He's doing the monkey, mashed potato,
> Jump back Jack, see you later Alligator.

With every raspy phrase, every flashy movement, the shoeshine boy sublime laces present to past in a Double Dynamite-Out of Sight-Righteous Wrap-Up of nearly one hundred years of hot-dogging it in America.

Newsweek, 1969

Jazz: The Art That Came In from the Cold

ABOUT THE TIME I started listening to rock in the mid-Sixties, I stopped listening to jazz. I was fed up with the bad vibes, the arrogance, hostility and craziness of the jazz scene. Guys getting knifed to death at the pimp bar in Birdland. Hysterical Jewish managers right out of the old Berlin cabarets. Arrogant spades sticking it up every white man's ass. The tone of that day was set by Miles Davis. He consummated its contempt. Every black musician modeled himself after Miles, working behind shades, turning his back on the audience, walking off the stand when he wasn't soloing, and receiving the press with all sorts of booby traps ranging from put-ons and lies to outright threats of violence.

Jazz was sick to death in those days. Some of the musicians, like Bud Powell or Charlie Mingus, were simply crazy. Bud was an electroshock zombie who had been brought back to New York from Paris by Oscar Goodstein, the owner of Birdland. He could barely get his hands together to play his old stuff. The last time I saw him work, he had a couple of scared-looking kids on bass and drums.

Somebody asked him, "Who are those two little twerps?" "I dunno," mumbled Bud. "We never been introduced."

Mingus was another story. A huge man mountain, always smoldering with paranoia and weight pills, he sometimes erupted with terrifying violence. One night in the Village, he spotted a man walking into the club with two old sabers tucked under his arm. Divining instantly that this elderly antique dealer was an assassin, Charlie lunged wildly toward the man's table and seized one of his swords. Tearing the curved blade out of the sheath and brandishing it maniacally, he sent hundreds of customers screaming and scrambling for their lives.

It was easier for a white man to put up with the stupor of Powell or the physical menace of Man Mountain Mingus than it was to withstand the withering contempt of Davis. Miles was a soul man, a sound, a black Bogey. He was also an insufferable prick. Posturing onstage in his shades, continental suits and bantyweight boxer's physique, he played the role of the jazz genius. "Miles could spit in his horn and it would get five stars in *Down Beat*," quipped one A&R man. Actually, the spitting was more likely to be aimed at the audience.

Putting down the house was one of the classic mannerisms of the be-bop musician. Miles had studied the art with the masters. Yet the contempt that rolled off a real genius like Charlie Parker had a very different feel than the poseuring of Monsieur. Miles was a paper panther. His power was almost entirely the power of the press. No matter how hard he hit the bag at Gleason's, his trumpet tone remained the puniest in jazz. He could never do a Buddy Bolden and "call the children home" by sticking his horn through a ballpark fence. Miles stuck his horn right into the mike—and even so amplified it hardly had the punch of a champion.

What Miles did possess in superlative degree was the art of mime. He was jazz's Marcel Marceau. With a single gesture he could signal an attitude; with a single note, precipitate a deep mood. Listening to him was like watching

Balinese shadow puppets. Everything was a dark profile, a tenebrous outline, a stylized stretch-and-dip that closed into itself with ritualistic finality.

When Miles was a jazz kid with Charlie Parker, his role was that of femme foil to Bird's aggressively thrusting horn. The classic picture of the pair shows a heavy-shouldered Parker hunching forward while beside him trembles a skinny kid whose body is bent back in a supple S-curve. Like Frank Sinatra, who commenced his career a softly crooning femme-man, then turned into a middle-aged belter, Miles Davis had to go through a change of life before he could become the musical embodiment of black power.

In the process he produced some remarkable playing. Foreshadowing the obsessions of the rockers, Miles created the first psychedelic music (we called it "hypnotic" in those days). The modal scales, static stance, cool, silver-frosted atmosphere of an album like *Kind of Blue* anticipated by many years the fusion of blues and drugs in the spookier kinds of soul and rock music. Miles also gave the impetus to John Coltrane, his tenor player, to create a more dynamic type of psychedelic music with his "Arabian" style. Here, as elsewhere, the jazz of the Fifties and Sixties prophesied the moods and essences if not the actual sounds and styles of the later pop period.

What Miles lacked most conspicuously was the compositional talent of a great improviser like Parker. An editor not a writer, an abstracter not an expatiater, a man who spent his whole life trying to sound the ultimate blue note, Miles could not move off the pedestal he had fashioned for his pose. His solution to the problem of what to play was to enlist the services of the arranger Gil Evans, who contrived for him elaborate and beautiful settings based on paraphrases of *Porgy and Bess* and various Spanish materials. The albums were brilliantly scored and breathtakingly executed by jazz studio bands. They carried the art of arranging for jazz orchestra to unrivaled heights. But they also raised the question of how far you could go into concerto treatments of semiclassical stuff without losing the whole sense of jazz as a hot, existential get-it-off music.

This was precisely the question raised by the work of the Modern Jazz Quartet in the same period. The MJQ spear-headed a movement called "Third Stream" which sought to fuse jazz and classical music in loose, suite-like compositions with fancy names like "Milano," "Versailles," "Vendome" and "Concorde." Though the members of the MJQ were all first-rate jazz musicians, the tendency of their work under the direction of composer-pianist John Lewis was away from jazz toward the Frenchified, faggotized art music that has always been the black jazzman's idea of "class."

Few critics have cared—or dared—to discuss the failures of taste exhibited by the jazz masters in their flirtations with the European classics; most writers have preferred to casti-gate European composers for their failures to capture the jazz spirit in their written compositions. As far as I can see, the treatment of jazz across the whole range of serious compos-ers from Stravinsky and Milhaud to Gershwin and Gunther Schuller has been much more successful and far less embar-rassing than the efforts of black jazzmen to cull the flowers of European art music. Since the days of Duke Ellington, jazz musicians have made themselves look foolish every time they have ventured in the direction of classic beauty. Their Affected Elegancies, the Modern Jazz Quartet, were simply the culmination of a wretched tradition.

If jazz was not to borrow from the classics or the contem-porary avant-garde, where was it to go in the course of its greatly accelerated development? This was the problem posed by bop. When Charlie Parker and the boppers were youngsters, jazz was only half musicalized. In the Thirties, pure-music patterns mingled on equal terms with material that was anthropomorphic. Drawls, shouts, growls and squeals—the whole rich rhetoric of Negro speech—issued from horns stopped with mutes or fanned with toilet plungers to make them mimic the sounds of human voices. Even when the illiterate stammer of Cootie Williams went

out of style and a certain certified casualness and sophistication came in with swing, the great soloists like Lester
Young and Coleman Hawkins continued to speak through
their horns. With them it was "sweet talk," the burbling,
lisping, attitudinizing speech of city men, but still the listener
could say to the jazzman, "I can hear ya' talkin'!"

All that died when Bird and Dizzy began to machine-gun
their way down 52nd Street. Overnight, jazz was kicked up
on a plane of abstraction comparable to art music. Bird was a
Bartók who sublimated a potent folk essence without losing
any of its pungency. He raised jazzmen's sights and made
them aspire higher than ever before. When the war ended,
hundreds of musicians enrolled in music schools under the
GI bill. There they discovered affinities between Bird's linear designs and the writing of J. S. Bach; they also found the
source of Bird's "advanced" chords in the harmony of the
French Impressionists. For the first time in the history of
jazz, most players could read music and approach expressive
problems with the resources of trained musicians. The time
seemed ripe for a great leap forward.

Sad to say, nothing of the kind happened. In fact, the very
opposite occurred. By the time of Charlie Parker's death in
1955, the bop synthesis had been destroyed. Jazz was either
regressing toward its roots or whoring after strange European and Oriental gods.

It took me many years to figure out how bop could have
killed jazz when bop was obviously the greatest thing that
ever happened to jazz. Eventually I realized that bop was a
terminal product, that Charlie Parker had taken jazz to the
end of the line. Though Parker was hailed as a revolutionary
and his music treated as the jazz of the future, the truth was
precisely the opposite: bop had simply one-upped the jazz
of the swing era, leaving its materials, techniques and con-
ventions essentially unchanged. Even in his most daring forays, the great Yardbird had remained firmly locked within
the circular walls of theme-and-variation form. Round and
round he had gone, pouring out brilliant ideas, tossing off

dazzling phrases, suggesting rhythms, harmonies and counterpoints that no one had ever dreamed of in this little world. But all his creative brilliance had been poured into one of the narrowest and most constrictive of musical forms.

When Bird got through with jazz, he had exhausted its traditional resources: nobody could play faster, think more ingeniously or further sophisticate jazz rhythm. A whole generation would con Bird's exercise book, assimilating his ideas to the common stock; but while they did so, the art of jazz stood still. Worse, it fell into a state of crisis trying to find a new direction in which to grow.

Part of the hang-up of the Fifties, therefore, was simply the struggle to break out of this bind; that accounted for the experiments with classical music and the alliances between improvising soloists and structurally sophisticated arranger-composers. The other basic problem was the bleaching out of the jazz essence, a process which had begun with Parker's radical musicalization of jazz. Bird and Diz were steeped to the lips in jazz essence. They never had to worry about "soul." Their epigoni, however, were men of a different stamp. Instead of abstracting their music from the black experience, they abstracted it from the playing of the bop abstracters. The result was a Whiteyfication of jazz leading eventually to the spectral sophistication of Paul Desmond of the Dave Brubeck band.

Loss of the black essence meant not only a weakening of jazz's emotive force; it meant a loss of homogeneity and purity in the jazz idiom. Jazz is an art of taste. Everything the musician hears must be tested against a mental touchstone, a black Kaaba that dictates this *is* or this *is not* jazz. Lots of things that were not jazz originally have been brought into alignment with jazz tradition, but many more have been rejected. By the early Fifties it was becoming harder and harder to know what would work as jazz. Men were toying with Afro-Cuban, Arabic, Spanish and other folk essences. They were attracted by Impressionism and atonalism. They were into remote periods like the Baroque. How could anyone speak convincingly in such a quotation-ridden tongue?

The answer came in the mid-Fifties with the funky, hard bop regression. Musicians like Horace Silver, Bud Powell, Thelonious Monk and Charlie Mingus began to play music that was strongly flavored with traditional blues and gospel sounds. All these men were black and their embrace of the Negro roots was given a political or social interpretation. Fundamentally, however, their motives were musical; they were simply getting back to basics.

At first the soul sounds were more decorative than functional. After an old-fashioned cottonfield "shout," the players would start to run changes in the conventional figuration of be-bop. This meant that the so-called hard bop school was really further from coining a new style than the despised soft boppers of the West Coast. Gerry Mulligan, Shorty Rogers and that gang had at least gotten their thing together; the heavy swingers in the New York clubs were just reheating what had been cooked in the previous decade —with a little country salad dressing. Yet they reminded jazz of its roots and suggested its future. Within a few years you could see soul glimmering on the horizon.

By 1959, jazz was desperately in need of its next messiah. The art was split right down the middle, one half effete artistry, the other funk and gospel. Some big man was needed who could pull these pieces together in a genuinely contemporary style. It is testimony to the incredible vitality of jazz that even at this late date, when so many expressive resources had been exhausted and so many jazzmen were up against the wall, jazz did cast forth one more genius and make one final effort to adapt itself to contemporary sensibility.

Ornette Coleman was cast in the classic mold of the jazz hero. He came out of the Southwest like a black Parsifal, innocent of everything save his mission to find the jazz grail. Appearing at a time when the breakdown in jazz tradition plus the crisis of Negro history had focused keen atten-

tion on the black essence, Ornette proved himself the ultimate soulman. He had actually worked for many years right
down in the dirt of the Texas rhythm-and-blues scene,
honking a tenor horn and lying flat on the floor with feet
and instrument pointing skyward like a trussed hog. He was
as much a shouter as any big mama in a sanctified church.
He had an almost Russian sense of suffering, especially the
suffering of an abandoned female, like the one portrayed in
his greatest composition, "Lonely Woman."

No mere primitive, Ornette was an avant-garde composer
and theorist with novel ideas about pitch, time and timbre.
He said that pitch was relative to musical motion, meaning
one thing when you were going up a scale and something
different when you were descending. Subsequent scientific
analyses of the playing of symphony violinists proved he
was correct. Ornette was a believer in total improvisatory
freedom. Jazzmen had always prided themselves on being
free (a value especially precious to the descendants of
slaves); but they had all worked in strait jackets compared
to Ornette, who advocated absolute freedom, whether for a
soloist or a whole group of musicians playing together. It
was the amorphous, anarchic, undisciplined character of his
playing that prompted the scandal of his first stand at the
Five Spot. Many musicians accused him of jiving, faking—
an odd word for a man who killed you with sincerity.

Basically, Ornette's esthetic was that of abstract expres-
sionism. Instead of parodying or paraphrasing the pop tunes
of the day—as did the boppers with "How High the Moon"
or "What Is This Thing Called Love,"—Ornette carved
powerful new shapes from the raw stone of his musical imagination. He played odd numbers of bars, odd numbers of
beats and sometimes wandered off the chord patterns implicit in his expositions. Like the country bluesmen of his
native Southwest, he played by instinct and created sophisticated effects by naïvely following the promptings of his
soul.

Gathering a circle of brilliant disciples around him, he

established a style called "The New Thing." No more pre-
cise label could be stuck on a music that refused to commit
itself to any rule or tradition save that implicit in the word
"freedom." "Soul" would have been a much better title, because Ornette was closer to James Brown and Ray Charles
than he was to Charlie Parker and Dizzy Gillespie. He had
the soulman's faith in publicly stripping himself bare. He
had the soulman's piercing cry of agony.

Though Ornette gave his pieces pious titles like "Peace,"
"Congeniality" or "Focus on Sanity," the content of his
music was often nightmarish. His world was bleak, cold,
desolate, full of frightening violence and the lonely presence
of death. When Ornette talked about his life back home—
where he had been a proto-hippie with thick, matted hair
and bushy biblical beard—he recounted scenes of humiliation and ostracism. Down in nigger-hating Texas he had
made trouble for himself, as he did later in liberal New
York.

Trouble was Ornette's middle name. When he could have
been out on the road making money for himself, he was
being evicted from his apartment. When he should have
been blowing his horn and making friends for his talent, he
was sawing away on a fiddle which he bowed as though his
arm were in a cast. Once he went into a club after a long
retreat and drew rave notices from all the major magazines
and newspapers. By the time the stories ran, however, he
had decided that the club owner was unfair to jazz artists.
When the magazine-reading public arrived, Ornette had
pulled his band out of the club. Then the following week he
decided the club owner wasn't so bad after all and returned
to play out the engagement before skimpy houses.

What was most appealing—and appalling—about Ornette
was his *innocence*, the quality he possessed of seeing things
unmediated by experience or disillusionment. This was a gift
of imagination, not a quality of his own soul. When you met
Ornette, you found him a bitter and dispirited man who
contemplated his life under a tragic aspect. In his art, how-

ever, he was perpetually young. He had an awesome faith in openness, honesty and directness. He never knew the meaning of shame.

The greatest of all Ornette's statements was a remarkable concert he staged in December of 1962 at Town Hall. After programming a very bad string quartet of his own composition, and a series of jazz compositions in which he soloed on one emotional note, Ornette capped the evening with a bizarre performance entailing a frightened-looking rhythm-and-blues group out of some uptown bar, an incredibly fast and complicated black drummer and a virtuoso white bass player of symphonic caliber. Setting these forces in motion and jamming along with them on alto, he produced one of the most cacophonous uproars in the history of music. As the notes came pouring off the stage, all you could do was try to listen first to one, then to another of these simultaneously sounding groups and soloists. The effect was not the saints at Pentecost. It was Babel. When it was over, everyone was asking, "What the hell was that all about?"

Not till several years later, when I stumbled upon an interview with Coleman in a jazz book, did I grasp the meaning of that strange symphony. When I did, I was amazed at its symbolic significance and synoptic scope. Coleman's crazy composition was actually an allegory of his soul. The rhythm-and-blues band represented the past, all the years he had played with such groups in Texas. The white bass virtuoso was the future, that world of classical string music from which the Negro has always been excluded and toward which he may now aspire. The drummer was, of course, the present, the still vital, still developing core of the jazz tradition. The possibilities suggested by this grouping were four: the regression to earlier, simpler forms like rhythm and blues; total assimilation of the values and capacities of the white world exemplified by the bassist; continued maintenance of the black tradition at its point of maximum development, as symbolized by the drummer; or—what must have been Coleman's ideal—a synthesis in which past, present and future might triumphantly merge.

What resulted, of course, was a fifth possibility—*failure* due to radical incoherence. Though Coleman had set forth honestly the ingredients of his soul, though he had hurled himself courageously into the battle to weld these disparate voices together, he had been at a loss to know how to compose or direct them. As the uproar mounted that afternoon, his only recourse was to lift his anguished and lonely voice in what sounded like a scream of pain.

During the heavy rock years, from 1966 to 1969, I hardly thought about jazz. I was trying to swallow the ocean of new sounds rolling in with rock. I had one close friend who was a devout jazz fan—Robert Gold, the author of *A Jazz Lexicon*—and sometimes he would drag me down to a jazz club where we heard the same old stuff the guys had been playing for years. It was an embarrassing scene. Jazz had lost its audience and was talking to itself.

Then one afternoon, chewing over story ideas with my editor at *Life*, Dave Scherman, I got into a conversation about jazz and the younger generation. "My boy Tony wants to be a jazz drummer," growled Scherman. "He complains that you never write anything about jazz." "Wow! That's a strange kid," I said, "I thought they all regarded jazz as a dirty word." Then I recalled an exchange that had occurred in the *Village Voice* some years before. Mike Zwerin, the *Voice*'s feeble jazz critic, had written a namby-pamby article about jazz and rock, one of those why-can't-we-get-together things. The next week the inevitable letter turned up on the *Voice*'s inside page. Ronnie Schlub from Nowhere Blvd. in the Bronx was replying. "Rock music," he wrote, "is far from perfect. It needs many things. The only thing it doesn't need is some dumb bop trumpet noodling in the background." Wham! That took care of jazz and rock.

Now here was my editor asking me to play Mike Zwerin and get my balding head clobbered by those sarcastic kids out there with their deeply impacted hatred for everything middle-aged, beginning with J-uice and ending with jaz-Z. "Well, what does your son think I should be writing about?" I cautiously replied. (No sense getting too heavy here—maybe I was getting a signal from *them*.) "He's crazy about this drummer Elvin Jones, but he's never seen him and nobody can seem to find him. Tony thinks he's in Japan."

"Japan!" (What fantasies these kids have, I thought.) "I know who Elvin Jones is," I said, "he worked with John Coltrane for many years. He probably toured in the Orient, but I can't imagine him living there. I wouldn't be surprised if he were living in New York." A couple of calls later, I discovered that I was right. Jones was living five minutes away from me on the West Side and was scheduled to play a date in New York that weekend.

My memories of Jones were not all that happy. He was jazz's last super-drummer, an artist of extraordinary power and fluency with a funky uppercut that could knock a fumfering soloist right on his ass. Virtuoso-genius-heavy that he was, Elvin impressed many of us as being too damned *loud*. You got an unpleasant feeling that he was not so much supporting Trane as burying him and his little piercing soprano sax. Especially during the last years, when Trane had gotten deep into The New Thing and would go on for a quarter hour at a crack honking and squealing and clawing at some invisible but palpable prison wall, the incongruity between the blockage in the so-called soloist and the raving freedom of his totally liberated drummer was distressing to a listener of conventional sympathies. I used to have a fantasy that I was watching the jazz spirit sinking back into the jungle soil from which it had risen, the articulate, individualized voice of the jazz hero being swallowed up in the faceless roar of the drums. That was long ago, however, and Elvin was a leader now; so with an odd mixture of excitement and misgiving, I went down to the joint where he was playing, a place in the West Forties called Danny's Backroom.

Danny's turned out to be a crummy, cruddy brownstone

with a bar up front and a drinking-listening room in the back. The hatcheck girl was a big, tall, voluptuous blonde with everything hanging out. I handed her my coat and hat, eyed the whole show, fore and aft, took the ticket and said, "Thank you." In a deep, masculine voice, she replied, "You're welcome," giving me a long, moist look. Suddenly it hit me—this must be a transvestite joint! I began to cast suspicious looks at people going to the ladies' room. Was everybody here in drag? Were they all into something I was out of? Whew! What a weird scene!

The back room was Howard Johnson motel modern with a thin coating of evil. The dim lighting gave the place the atmosphere of a sunken bar and grill. All around me were young hippies with beards and jeans, nursing the obligatory beer but passing joints from hand to hand. It didn't look like a jazz crowd or a rock crowd. It was a strange seance. Up on the stand was Elvin doing his thing. I had forgotten how he looked—or maybe I never really saw him when I concentrated on Trane. He was a striking figure crouched behind his set of beautifully polished walnut and chrome drums, his small, bullet-shaped head raised with the eyes closed, like a blind man staring at the sun, his forehead beaded with perspiration and the smoke of a mouth-socketed cigarette curling up his face in gray swirls. He seemed to be straining away from his arms, incredible blacksmith's arms with big, protuberant veins, and his hands, huge, splayed hands that could cut through a drum head with a flick of the wrist. He looked like he was in a trance, and the sound that was pouring out of those drums made it seem like he was summoning up a hurricane or directing a typhoon across the South Seas.

I had forgotten the incredible energy level attained by the greatest jazz musicians. I wasn't accustomed to those fast-as-thought tempos, that crowding profusion of ideas. Instantly, I began to feel the old despair about describing this stuff to people who hadn't heard it. Rock was a snap to write about. The music was all symbol and archetype. It had the exaggerated, black-and-white outline of a caricature. Jazz was real music. Abstract, complex, *sui generis*, it was a bitch.

Nothing in jazz was harder to describe than the playing of the greatest drummers. A late-model percussionist like Elvin Jones has the mental processes of a computer. He has developed a revolutionary technique that allows each of the four playing limbs almost total independence of action. Doing effortlessly with one hand what was traditionally done with two, Elvin constructs patterns of polyrhythmic complexity that are hard to hear and impossible to remember. Nobody could do them justice in the zippy prose of the slick weeklies. "God damn!" I thought. "How did I get suckered into this mission impossible?"

When the seven-hour set finally ended, Elvin rose from his drums and wavered over to my table, stalking on stiff, skinny shanks and flashing a big toothy grin. He had a fascinating face with very dark skin, flaring cheekbones, a crude, leonine nose and eyes that opened so wide you could see white all around the pupil. He was drenched with sweat and dying for a drink. He ordered a vodka and beer in a voice that rasped tightly, like there was a peg in his throat. As we began to talk, I marveled at the emotional transparency of his face. One minute his grin was like a sunburst, the next his face was clouded over, with heavy-lidded eyes appraising you and an air of menace coming up from his smoldering cigarette.

Musicians are supposed to be inarticulate, but black jazzmen generally talk their heads off. Elvin was no exception. He was a great talker with a vocabulary that was peppered with impatiently inflected obscenities and pungent proverbial phrases. "Why, he thinks he's the greatest thing that ever shit over two heels! . . . Why, he was as happy as a sissy at the Y! . . . Why, tryin' to get him out of there was like coaxin' a houndog offena' garbage truck!" His basic note was that of a man who couldn't understand why things weren't better managed in this ridiculous world. Difficulties were things you should be able to slice through like butter. When I complained the beer was hot, he said, "Put some ice in it and drink it down. Don't fuck with it, Al."

The next day I went up to his apartment in the West Eighties off Central Park. His Japanese wife, Keiko, met me at the door, and Elvin asked me to slip off my shoes in the house. He was strolling around barefoot with a careless rolling gait. He had a little room-and-a-half with the mattress on the floor, a tiny table for eating and a kitchen in the wall. The place was plastered with pictures and awards and plaques and statues commemorating his achievements. At forty-three he was widely acknowledged as the world's greatest jazz drummer. Yet he had nothing to show for it except this little pad, which, they told me, was the first apartment they had had, the early years of their marriage having passed uncomfortably in a Greenwich Village hotel room. The only reason he had this apartment was that one of his sidemen, Joe Farrell, owned the building (left to him by his father-in-law) and the apartment was dirt cheap.

Jazzmen have never been prosperous, but in the old days it was often their own fault. They made money and blew it supporting their habits. When Charlie Parker was making the huge sum of $900 a week at Birdland, he had a runner who plied back and forth between the club and Dewey Square in Harlem scoring dope for him. Elvin had once been into drugs, too, but now he was straight. He drank beer all afternoon out of a jelly jar clinking with ice cubes, and bobbed his head with a shy grin saying grace before dinner. Though he always made his gigs and took care of business, he was just as poor as any old junkie. He did enjoy one great luxury. He didn't have to get up at eight in the morning to go to the studio and record jingles and make a whore of himself. He played only jazz and was resigned to never having a nickel.

That first afternoon in his pad he really won my heart. I found it hard to believe that there was anyone with his talent who was still dedicated and pure. Everybody I knew was peddling his ass to the highest bidder. Painters made money, writers made money, photographers made fortunes and every little rock twerp had clothes and cars and dope and travel and fancy chicks. Here was a guy who had more talent than any ten of those amateurs, and the only thing he owned was a set of drums which he had gotten for free.

The other quality that appealed to me was his amiability. Jazz fans of my generation were brought up to regard jazz-men with a mixture of awe and dread. They were notorious pricks, lunatics, smackheads and knife-toters. If they didn't put the make on you in the first twenty minutes, it was only because they were busy putting you on in some other key. Now this guy was obviously pretty tough; he was a notorious brawler who had once crowned a French nightclub owner with his bass drum and then wrapped up the bartender and the rest of the club. He wasn't pulling any punches in his personal relationships either. He said just what he thought about everybody. But you felt a strain of beautiful disinterestedness in his personality. He was in command of his life and he knew his own worth. He didn't have to make compromises and he scorned those who did. As he talked I could feel a current of moral strength rising in my tired backbone. Knowing Elvin was going to be an inspiration.

Finally, we got down to cases. I had come up with a gimmick to rationalize his appearance in *Life*. He was going to do a jury on the leading rock drummers, some of whom regarded him as the grand old master of the skins. He had a little phonograph of the sort you'd give your twelve-year-old daughter if she were deaf. I put Santana on the table and waited for his reaction. Elvin was a heavy listener. It was work for him, just like playing drums. He lowered his head, sweat beaded from his brow. Zeus was checking out the pygmies. "Fiery"—that was his word for the Frisco kids. But I could tell he thought their music was electric wallpaper. Then he was listening to Keith Moon going full-blast during the "Underture" to *Tommy*. "See there, where the tempo started to die, how he picked it up! The man is a drummer. Everything they play, he *contains* it." That was interesting. Now the big test. Ginger Baker in an enormously long solo on Blind Faith's "Do What You Like." This was the drum break that brought down houses from coast to coast and convinced millions of kids that Ginger Baker was a genius. Jones liked the opening; then he began to cloud over and his head withdrew between his shoulders like a turtle. After what seemed an hour of ominous silence, he raised his head and rasped, "Nothin' happenin'. Cat's got delusions of grandeur with no grounds. Know what, Al? They should make him an astronaut and lose his ass!" "Oy," I thought, "how can I print *that* in *Life?*" I went home, wrote up what he said, sent it in and put my fingers in my ears. A few weeks later the piece ran without changes.

Then the fun began. About a week later, the phone rings and it's my agent, or rather one of his girls calling me. She's all excited, the Coast is calling, something about Elvin Jones on the Coast. I said, all right, let's talk to them. So a guy calls me up, he's a Hollywood producer. What happened was they were just about to start shooting a film called *Zaccariah*, a rock, shlock, cowboy musical turn-of-the-century thing starring Ginger Baker, when the drummer OD'd and had to be replaced.

I discovered later on that they had called up a thousand different people and asked them if they wanted to do this movie. James Brown, Jimi Hendrix, Little Richard, et al., baby. I don't know why they tried so many blacks, but apparently the only thing you can substitute for Ginger Baker is a black man. Anyway, they hadn't gotten too far with it—most people were already commited. Finally one day they were sitting in their office, uptight, hung-up, looking through *Life* and they saw this article about a guy who was a drummer. The whole scene was a repeat of Lenny Bruce's routine about the talent scouts who have to find a "dictator type" and come up with Adolf Hitler.

The Coast was nervous. They had a million questions: is this guy on dope? Does he hate whites? Does he really look the way he looks in that picture? In short, is he going to fuck us up? I said, "Oh, he's incredible-looking and he has this sexy way of moving and he's a genius." So they sent a lawyer with a contract and flew Elvin out to Mexico with his wife, his drums and his Zildjan cymbals. (A Zildjan cymbal is a big hunk of Turkish brass with a hole punched through the center. Elvin Jones's way of testing the cymbal is to stick it on his thumb and then give it a clonk with his thumb while he holds it next to his ear. One day at the factory, he told me, he went through a couple hundred cymbals. His ears didn't stop ringing for a week.)

When Elvin got out to Mexicali, Mexico, he found that he was playing the part of a tough, mean gambler. He wore a blood-red shirt with a silver vest, rode a horse up onto the front porch of a bordello, played a long sweaty drum solo and in one scene was challenged to fight by another tough. The director saw great dramatic possibilities in this scene. He said to the other actor, "Ad lib something about Elvin's color. Say, 'Come out of there, you black bastard, or something like that.' " So the white actor does the line, and Elvin pulls his gun, comes up to him, gives him one of his death-ray looks—and the actor had a nervous breakdown! Broke into tears, refused to continue, had to be replaced. Elvin killed him with a glance!

When Elvin came back to New York, I could hardly recognize him. He came into my apartment wearing a thickly fringed Daniel Boone jacket of expensive suede. Putting his arms around my waist, he lifted me straight up in the air and gave me a big kiss, the way you would a baby. Making the movie had really given him a charge. Now he was full of new plans and ambitions. For one brief moment it looked as though he might really take off. There was talk of another film, of a tour, of renaming Danny's "Elvin's."

Within a few weeks, the old jazz luck started to drag him down. The movie was just talk, the concert tour failed to materialize and Danny's was closed for unknown reasons, its liquor license revoked. Elvin didn't bat an eye. He was accustomed to wipe-outs. They were just part of his job. He went to work organizing a new group, which played very successfully in all the old joints.

During the same winter that I met Elvin Jones, I began going down to Half Note, a legendary jazz club near the Holland Tunnel in the dockside warehouse district of Manhattan. The Note looks like somebody broke a little piece off the old 52nd Street and dropped it on the way to Jersey. The outside is a 1940s streamlined, plate-glass window, a cupola awning and a corny neon sign with four skinny half notes on it. When you get up close, you see a hand-lettered bill in the window. By now it could be printed because it always announces the same guy, Zoot Sims. Zoot's been playing the Half Note for twelve years.

If you hit the Note on a bad winter night, you feel like you've stepped into the ultimate loser's bar. It's somber, shadowy, Saroyanesque, and it's virtually empty, with a neighborhood drunk slumped across the bar, a couple of bird-dog regulars in a corner and maybe two bronzed Texas loudmouths shouting at the band, "Let's dance!" If you hit the club on a good night, when it's doing business and the vibes are right, you see it as the supreme setting for jazz. Glowing red walls tiled with nostalgic album covers, oil-cloth-covered tables crowned with flickering candles, a whole maze of seating, serving and playing areas focused comfortably on the musicians, who stand above the bar in the classic situation where they can shower music down on the patrons who lean and drink or those who sit and eat the good, wholesome, gutsy Italian food. What more could anyone ask from a room designed for listening to jazz?

When I first started going down to the Note in February 1970, the club was clearly dying. Apart from a few devotees, like my friend Bob Gold, there was no one who would brave the black streets down there at the end of the world just to hear a couple of jazz licks. The proprietors were into the Shylocks for thousands of dollars. The piano was way out of tune. They had nights when they did $40 business.

Hatcheck girls used to make that.

Zoot Sims seemed to embody the mood of the club. The last of the great swingers had gained weight over the years. He looked now like a youthful Lionel Barrymore with bushy brows and a burgeoning bay window. Zoot's note, once bright and pealing, was full and deep and tinged with sadness. As his superbly modeled phrases emerged from the dusky light of a bossa nova, you realized that he had become a master of musical chiaroscuro. He had also become a clockwork figure on that tiny stage. As soon as he finished playing, he would retire to the stage steps and stand there impassively, a carved statue in a niche, one hand resting on the crook of his grounded horn while the other negligently held a half-empty glass of whiskey.

At another time the scene at the Note would have put me off. Generally, I prefer places where the action moves at up-tempos. That was what had drawn me into the rock world· its crackling energies and the sensation of being swept up out of yourself into new realms of being. But now I was ready for a slow movement, for the delicious indulgence of reverie and self-pity. I slipped into the Note's glowing crimson interior with a soul-sighing sense of satisfaction. As I sat there night after night, scarfing up the pasta and cheese in the flickering light of a candle, feeling the good dry Bardolino making high harmonics on my palate and waiting patiently for Zoot to appear, I enjoyed a rare feeling of public peace and harmony. It was a restorative experience, like lying passively in the bosom of your family.

The Canterino Brothers, Mike and Sonny, who had operated this club for years with their father Frank and their mother Jean and Mike's wife Judy, were a classic Italian-American family. You had the feeling that the whole world could perish tomorrow and they would build it up again like Noah after the Flood. It was they who had fashioned this fascinating room and filled it with its mellow atmosphere. They were like the owners of family-operated bistros in Paris; you were their guests and they offered you the hospitality of the house. Unlike the high-strung Jewish proprietor of the typical jazz club or the spaced-out young operator of the typical rock club or discothèque, these were people who exuded human feelings and a sense of human concern. I decided I would try to help them by writing a piece about their club. They welcomed the suggestion, but I noticed something wistful about their manner. Something was always going wrong with their efforts at self-promotion, they explained. They had the luck of jazz people.

They weren't pessimists either—as experience showed. When I handed my copy in to *The New York Times*, for the first and only time in two years the editor slashed the piece to bits and reproved me for mentioning the proprietors by name. I was annoyed and embarrassed and quickly turned the rejected portion about the Half Note into an article for *New York*. The piece was accepted and printed, but the day the magazine was mailed, a general postal strike commenced and the subscribers got their copies weeks late. Finally, I decided to help in a more direct way: I took the whole club for one night and gave myself a big birthday party with fancy invitations, an open bar, food from antipasto to cheesecake and the Zoot Sims band onstage. The party brought us all much closer together, and from that time on I began to regard the club with an almost proprietorial interest.

By the spring of 1970 I was deeply involved again with jazz. I could see that my own drift back to the jazz clubs was being paralleled by an unexpected revival of interest in the music by the rock world. When Blood, Sweat and Tears struck gold with their plastic Bop 'n' Basie, rock bands began dropping chunks of jazz into their arrangements. Similarly, the purveyors of hot buttered soul were feeding ever-increasing amounts of jazz improvisation into their ethnic mulch. Soul-jazz was just like the Memphis Sound before it: a skillfully contrived synthetic that distilled the most potent aromas of blues, funk, gospel and jazz into an attar of blackness. In New York it came pouring out of an excellent radio station, WLIB, "The Black Experience in Sound," mastermilded by a very intelligent disc jockey named Del Shields. Black broadcasters had an audience that was almost as ignorant of jazz as were white listeners. But in the ghetto there was a feeling that jazz ought to be heard and studied because it was part of the black heritage.

Neither jazz-rock nor soul-jazz is the pure, uncut stuff of mainline jazz; both belong to what an earlier, more idealistic age would have called "commercial" music. Yet their value to pure jazz cannot be exaggerated. Without broad popular styles, like those developed by the big bands of the Thirties and Forties, jazz is doomed to dry up and die. Pop jazz provides good-paying, on-the-job training for young musicians who may someday elect to starve with the masters. It entices young people onto the jazz scene and allows their listening tastes to develop at a normal pace. Most importantly, the pop styles feed the master jazzmen with fresh folk materials which they can parody and paraphrase up to the taxing altitude of their most sophisticated selves.

Obviously, there can be no revival of the jazz scene of earlier years; most promoters and record makers are reluctant to even use the good old four-letter word. What is happening now is the return of jazz *in disguise*. Everybody on the crashing pop scene is picking up on jazz licks, jazz voicings and (in the studio, where they don't show) veteran jazz hands. Laura Nyro slips Zoot Sims into one record and arranges to make another with Miles Davis. Astute operators like Herbie Mann and Les McCann develop pop styles that sell hundreds of thousands of albums and boost them way up on the charts. Rock critics even begin to hail jazz as the savior of the beat!

As I saw these signs of a jazz revival all around me, I began to push hard both in my writing and through my professional acquaintances for a new deal in jazz. I saw the opportunity opened by the death of rock, and I didn't want to have it wasted by the middle-aged jazz establishment.

Alas! there was little you could do with these old curmudg-eons. George Wein put together a wretched collection of washed-up old-timers and flashy soul acts for the fourteenth annual Newport Jazz Festival. When I complained that there was very little hard-core jazz on the program, he re-plied that jazz was hard to define these days. I offered to write him out a list of real jazzmen, but he wasn't interested. Bill Graham was willing to book a few jazz acts into the Fillmore, but he picked the wrong ones. His big draw was Miles Davis, who had sneered at rock during its best period and now was trying to climb aboard the sinking ship to re-gain his lost star status. Miles played his usual sneers and fleers in front of an electric rhythm section that chattered mechanically, nervously, like it was playing the holes in computer punch cards. His greatest appeal, as usual, was his physical appearance—mauve leather pants and body shirt. His biggest boost, as always, was from the press—no longer *Down Beat* but *Rolling Stone,* which gloated in full-page photos over his semi-naked encounters with a punching bag.

One day I had lunch with George Marek, a big shot at RCA records. He had been reading my stuff and was inter-ested in hiring me as a record producer. The record business was in terrible shape now that the pop bubble had burst. They were combing the woods for new talents and clutch-ing frantically at the pop pulse. I wanted to make records with great jazz artists like Elvin and Zoot, but I didn't want to make them in the old way. My thought was to treat the tapes just the way a film director treats his raw footage: as material to be cut, spliced and palimpsested into final form. Rock bands had achieved wonders in the recording studio, while jazz musicians had learned nothing from fifty years of record-making. Far more than rock, jazz demanded editing. Typically, the musicians hit their peaks only at certain in-spired moments and then doodled their way through the balance of the side.

Actually, jazz musicians rarely feel comfortable in the studio. Though they play hard and scrupulously for the engineers, they fail to attain the spontaneous brilliance of their best club and concert dates. Yet live jazz albums, like live rock albums, are not the answer because they provide only a peephole view of events at which the listener should be present. My thought was to approach the problem differently: rig a club like the Half Note with studio equipment, record Zoot every night for a week, pull out the best parts and put them together in a free-form sound-track pattern. I would scrap the archaic ritual of exposition, solo 1, solo 2, solo 3 and recap (with or without a final exchange of "fours"). It was tedious in a club where you could watch the men work; it was even more tedious on records. Jazz fans and new listeners were entitled to a fresh perspective on the old art.

You could put the matter even more drastically by saying that implicit in every jazzman was an archetypal chorus or concert. Most of them spent their whole lives playing essentially the same material, sometimes getting one part perfect, sometimes another. An experienced listener-editor could see the immanent outline and bring it to light in the developing bath of the studio. It was the familiar tale of the undisciplined, off-the-top writer, like Thomas Wolfe, and the careful, constructive editor, like Maxwell Perkins. Jazz was all Wolfes and no Perkinses. Wasn't it time for a change, especially now in this age of abbreviation and essentialization?

Marek heard me out beside the pool at the Four Seasons, tossing the waiters clipped European commands; then I never heard from him again. When I talked over my recording concept with musicians, they agreed it was the best approach, but warned that it would be slow and costly. For my part, I couldn't get involved in learning a whole new skill at that point in my career, so the idea was ditched. Jazz recording needed a good shaking up, but there was no one to do the job.

As soon as people began to pay a little money and attention to jazz, the whole scene brightened. Every night the Half Note was jammed, and Zoot came out of his winter slump to bat .400 for weeks on end. He not only raised his energy level to a point higher than anyone could recall, he dipped into jazz history to bring back all sorts of fascinating material from the Thirties (when he was just a kid). The night Duke Ellington was elected a member of the National Academy, Zoot paid him an unannounced tribute with tunes like "Rockin' in Rhythm" and "Do Nothing Till You Hear from Me." He captured the quavering, querulous vibrato of Johnny Hodges and the heavy, burbling sound of Ben Webster. Then he wrapped up the set with Fats Waller's cascading, lilting "Jitterbug Waltz."

That performance showed how perfectly the great jazzmen have assimilated their own history, how Proustian is their enhancement of the past. Jazz is eighty years old. Its history is terraced back and up, layer after layer, like ancient vineyards in the Rhineland. A jazz artist can move you strangely by journeying across this sharply demarcated, indelibly colored time map, by drawing the past into the present or by rolling the current style back toward its roots. Far more sophisticated and beautiful than the silly, campy antiques the rockers fabricate in the name of nostalgia, the time trips of jazz are, however, only to be appreciated by those who have the listening experience to recognize the stations along the line.

This has always been one of the limits on jazz's popularity: the knowledge demanded for initiation into the cult. In earlier periods, the self-involved complexities of the music were received as a challenge which many young men and women rose to meet; today, in the age of passivity, the reign of terror of standards, such demands are almost certain to be refused. Yet there is no real reason why the kids can't get with jazz. Jazzmen are, after all, their true fathers. Who knows more about drugs than jazzmen? Who has experienced more social alienation and ostracism? Who has known more of poverty, harassment and despair? Jazz was "loose," "groovy," "hip," "ballsy," "funky," "soulful," down to the "nitty-gritty" long before the current generation was born.

To treat it as an artifact of the uptight, three-button older generation is to evince not only colossal ignorance of American history but the kind of ears that would disgrace a donkey.

Jazz can never again mean to America what it meant in previous periods, but it can continue to act for years to come as a standard of musical and spiritual integrity in a society whose most radical members are soonest corrupt. It can also serve to pull the generations together in an atmosphere that is irresistibly cheerful.

Some nights now in New York's oldest jazz clubs, like the Half Note and the Village Vanguard, you can witness a spectacle almost unparalleled in contemporary American society. You're down in some low-ceilinged, smoke-blurred basement, and you look around and dig—what would you call it?—a hip church social! It's college kids and middle-aged hipsters and gray-haired couples who first heard jazz on a Stromberg-Carlson tuned to *The Fitch Bandwagon*, all sitting together, all eating and drinking together; and up on the stand is this band of old men and young, black and white, playing our greatest American music and really getting it off, rewriting the charts as they honk. Suddenly you flash: Hey! this is my music, my people, my scene! And you feel so great, so proud, so possessive, you could almost walk up to the bar, like the old-timers used to do, and growl: "Give those boys a drink—they're blowin' pretty hard tonight!"

FOUR

Sex Pop Psych Scene

Pop Is Mom

TODAY POP ART winks coyly at us from every newsstand; the Pop heroes of the comic strips, emblazoned on posters, stare from the walls of offices and bedrooms; and Pop-influenced ads offer, with the intense focus of a voyeur, tantalizing portraits of lovely but lonely frankfurters and cheeses. The translation of Ian Fleming's sophisticated British thrillers to the screen—increasingly a Pop operation—culminated in *Goldfinger*, a giant, stunningly colored crime comic for adults, crammed with violence, perversion and luxury. Our infatuation with the banal, the childish and the commercial has reached now such astonishing intensity that Pop has begun to dictate the personal life style of thousands of people, who seem themselves to have stepped out of the funnies or an old copy of *Silver Screen*. In Pop society (the new cultural elite comprising an odd lot of fashion photographers, magazine illustrators, models, hairdressers and aristocrats) the lady of imagination buys her costume in a thrift shop and turns up at a penthouse or loft looking like a movie queen of the Thirties, wearing a Garbo hat, a beaded dress, a

feather boa and those old-fashioned shoes with thick heels
and a strap across the instep. Indeed, nothing could be more
Pop than making life imitate art, since Pop consists in making art mimic the most tawdry and trivial features of
modern living.

Pop got its name a few years ago, when a handful of artists shocked the public by setting up in immaculate East Side
galleries monumental hamburgers and pie slabs, funerary
casts of worried bus drivers and obsessively repetitive
friezes of Marilyn Monroe and Campbell's Soup cans.
Though these artists established Pop as an upper-case, avant-
garde movement, they did not create the sensibility that is
amused and charmed by the obsolete artifacts of mass culture, nor were they the first to exploit such phenomena in
"art." In the late Fifties, the Pop sensibility was already
manifest in the sudden reversal of interior décor from functional modern (pole lamps, blocky foam-rubber sofas, plastic seats) to the Third Avenue antique style of Tiffany
lamps, curvy, velvet-covered Harlow chaises, and chairs
composed of bentwood scrolls. Even earlier the "myths" of
the mass media had been extensively explored by a whole
generation of comic entertainers, ranging from Sid Caesar to
Lenny Bruce. Indeed, throughout the decade of the Fifties,
a tremendous wave of nostalgia was mounting in this country as the first generation ever to receive its magic visions
and fairy tales exclusively from late-afternoon radio, evening newspapers and Saturday movies gradually recalled—
with embarrassed joy—the emblems of its unrelinquished
childhood. What the Pop artists did was blow away the
mists of sentiment surrounding—and disguising—this regressive movement. Pop turned what seemed a harmless flir-
tation into a front-page scandal.

Stripped of its aura of faddism, its disarming air of fun
and games, Pop emerges as the startlingly nihilistic conviction that anything that has character and vitality is art, and
that all art is equivalent in value. As in America nothing has
more obvious identity and energy than the products of Pop

culture—the cars, Cokes and cowboys that have conquered the world—it follows that the role of the Pop artist is simply the selection, replication and mounting of these products. And as the Pop credo proclaims that things shall *be* and not be used (as metaphors, symbols, as expressions of something else), Pop technique consists of devices for intensifying the object's existence without altering its form. Through enlargement, simplification, repetition and, above all, *isolation*, the object is popped into focus.

Pop esthetics sounds like an innocent stratagem for giving the impression of creativity without making anything new, like children doing tracings. One minute in a Pop gallery will convince anyone who keeps in touch with his feelings that no matter how simple-minded the Pop process and product may be, the Pop effect is anything but simple and innocent. Mindless energy and disquieting ambiguity are the dominant impressions. Detached from its normal environment and set up in the neutral white space of the gallery, a pub shot of an open-mouthed Marilyn Monroe becomes not simply "visible" but overwhelming, obsessive, hypnotic. The intense focus makes the image more real—but it also makes it more illusory. The incongruity between the vulgar object and its sacrosanct surroundings produces an effect of violation. The effect is heightened further by the ambivalent attitude of the educated American toward the beloved yet despised artifacts of mass culture. Seeking uncomfortably to accommodate himself to an art work that refuses to declare an intention, one spectator sneers "hoax," and another snickers at an imagined "put-on," but the most honest and defenseless feels the unhappy embarrassment of a man left out of a private joke.

Considering the force and ubiquity of the Pop impulse today, one naturally wonders whether it has affected literature. Is there such a thing as a Pop literature? If so, what is it like and who are its authors? Since Joyce and Dos Passos, literature has parodied the pulps, newspapers and newsreels, cutting out and pasting up montages of jingles, slogans,

headlines and typographic gimmicks. Especially in comedy
and satire, the material of Pop has played a conspicuous part,
which is precisely what we find it doing in the new genre of
the Jewish comic novel—I am thinking of books like Wallace Markfield's *To an Early Grave* and Bruce Jay Friedman's *A Mother's Kisses.*

Recollections of childhood and youth spent in a cultural
ghetto centered around "three rooms in Bensonhurst," the
candy store on the corner and *mischiganah* intellectuals who
quiz each other about the minutiae of B movies, comic strips
and radio serials—like kids rattling off baseball averages—
these books do contain much of the data of pop. Markfield
particularly has a tendency to cartoon his characters; one
can almost see the expletives—"Whoosh!" "Gaah!" "Choopie bar choopie!"—coming out of the characters' mouths in
comic-strip balloons. Markfield's total recall of the lore of
"Jujubes, Charms, Mary Janes, Hopjes"; his ear for the
cockeyed convolutions of Jewish English; his pastiches of
verbatim conversation; and, most important, his tendency to
simply lay this stuff on the page, expecting it to produce its
effect without authorial intervention—all bring him into
close relationship with Pop. The work of Friedman, a more
gifted and original writer, is not so close; but his characteristic tendency to focus in each book on a single character
whose imaginative intensity becomes so great that he seems
totally disengaged from reality—floating, as one critic has
said, off the ground like a Chagall figure—reminds one of
the isolation technique of Pop.

Yet, despite such important similarities, the Jewish comic
writers like Friedman and Markfield are not really Pop artists; the intensity of their ambivalence—a love (or envy)
that pursues through mockery—gives their work a depth of
resonance that is essentially different from the deadpan detachment and thin-skinned verisimilitude of Pop. These
books—not so much "novels" as literary entertainments—
remind one much more of the oral urban folk humor of
Lenny Bruce, especially his ghostly Brooklyn, where little

old Jews with phlegmy voices sing "Shicker ist der Goy" and complain because the "super" painted over the mezuzah.

Since literature, unlike the graphic arts, deals primarily with morally determinable actions, any useful analogy between Pop art and writing must eventually entail a bold esthetic translation. To my mind, the literary equivalent of the Pop artist's refusal to respect cultural values and to give his work "meaning," his isolation of his subject and his intensification of its energic essence—all this equates with a writer's decision to treat violent, perverse and criminal actions in a style of such illusory detachment that the reader is unable to react morally or sympathetically, but is invited instead to respond amorally and empathetically, almost but not quite the way he responds to the lower-case pop of detective thrillers, gangster movies, horror comics and the most explosive animated cartoons. The manic intensity of the comics and cartoons, their "cheery nihilism" (to borrow a convenient phrase of Susan Sontag's), is, in fact, characteristic of several recent novels; chief among them is Terry Southern's and Mason Hoffenberg's *Candy*—the prototypical Pop novel.

Southern and Hoffenberg started off (I am sure) in a direction diametrically opposed to Pop, with the intention of satirizing the moral illusions and clichés of the mass media. The focus of their anger is revealed by Candy Christian's one great line, "To give of oneself is a thrilling privilege." But the strategy for this well-justified attack held a fascination that soon prevailed over the satiric purpose. Disposed more to desecrate than to criticize, the authors became obsessed with their naughty game of compelling all the nice mass-media people—the American dream girl, the white-coated doctor, the wise old prof and the ideal suburban couple—to perform fantastic acts of violence and perversion, like the figures in a pornographic comic book. The result was that *Candy*, far from being another *Candide*, turned out a *Terry Toons* version of the Marquis de Sade, in which even the most insane acts of sexual cruelty had the exhilarating effect of good clean fun. Or, to put it another way, the authors of *Candy* found a formula for safely violating the taboos of civilization by treating perversion in childish terms appropriate to its psychological origin in infantile sexuality. *Candy,* therefore, was a giant step along the current road of cultural regression. Though written in 1957, its absolute contemporaneity can be gauged from current sales of 2.5 million copies.

Candy was suggested in part by William Burroughs' *Naked Lunch*: both books share the anthropophagous metaphor (Pop repeatedly associates sex with food), the flat, impersonal style, easily flexed into parody; both are organized as a string of improvised "routines," which in *Naked Lunch* pass from an uneasy humor into a region of fractured, hallucinatory, psychotic cruelty and perversion totally devoid of passion. Burroughs writes as a sinister voyeur, Southern and Hoffenberg as hysterical exhibitionists; but both are buffered by the use of fantasy and humor which disarm the reader's moral judgment. When reading Burroughs, one wonders whether there might not be such a thing as a tragic cartoon, or even a tragic reality that inspires the same reactions as a cartoon. A naturalistic parallel to the psychopathic fantasies of Burroughs is a pretty good description of Norman Mailer's *An American Dream*, a book which its author puffed as "the first Pop novel."

Mailer, like Southern and Hoffenberg, is not, of course, a product of the world of Pop; but for years he had been brooding over an idea that proved—like the concept of *Candy*—remarkably prescient. As early as 1957, when he published "The White Negro," Mailer made it clear that he intended to embrace as hero the psychopathic personality described in Robert Lindner's *Rebel Without a Cause*. The psychopath, Lindner explained, is not "crazy"; he can operate with great cunning, resourcefulness, intelligence—but he has no moral sense, no guilt for his evil acts, and no fear of consequences because he is insulated by an illusion of invulnerability. Amoral, impulsive, hedonistic, homicidal, the psychopath is an authentic personality type who lives like a comic-book desperado. He is the tragic hero of Pop.

The first installment of *An American Dream* is a great psychopathic roller-coaster ride; from a dead start of apathy and suicidal self-loathing, the hero climbs through provocation, retort and rage to the peak of wife-murder. Then, poised before the bathroom mirror, he experiences a moment of exalted peace as he gazes admiringly at his beatified countenance. Suddenly he is seized by an onrush of irresistible amoral energy. He hurtles downstairs, enters the maid's room and rapes her with the same wild zest that the comic-strip characters of *Candy* display. But Mailer, having chosen unwisely a naturalistic medium, is in serious trouble by the end of the first two chapters; the problems of real-life consequences come crowding in, and with them, apparently, the novelist's own irrelevant guilt. The book soon stumbles into incoherence as the psychopath behaves more and more like a neurotic, and the plot strains to hoist him out of his difficulties through a clumsy *deus ex machina*.

Mailer, one concludes, is not the man for the Pop novel, despite his intentions. For one thing, his tragic portrait of his psychopathic personality is constantly being smudged by his own personality. For another, his GI novel technique is not suitable to the requirements of a subject that must be distanced both from the demand for probability and from the demand for moral responsibility. To bring off the Pop-art thriller, a writer would have to have the mastery of artifice possessed by such genuine innovators as Vladimir Nabokov and John Hawkes. The moment Mailer joins the avant-garde, he becomes a casualty because he has never gotten beyond basic training.

The hero of *An American Dream* ends his mad career in Las Vegas; and there against the neon skyline of "the American Versailles," the Boswell of Pop, the journalist Tom Wolfe, takes his first lap in that lurid vehicle, *The Kandy-Kolored Tangerine-Flake Streamline Baby*. Wolfe chronicles and celebrates a society of caroming, mechanical, highly styl-

ized teens and toffs who lead a paper-thin existence trying to sustain their "image." Half his book enthusiastically
portrays Teen society, with its demolition derbies, stock-
car and drag races, mastoid-rattling radio, stretch clothes
and puffball hairdos; the other half sarcastically presents its
nominal antithesis, the sophisticated Pop society of New
York City. But as Wolfe demonstrates, the two societies are
virtually one in their cultural pastimes because Pop society,
composed of deracinated individuals lacking a culture of
their own, has borrowed from the teens such essentials as the
twist, the Peppermint Lounge, long hair, rock music, decal
eyelashes, Levi's and jukeboxes—the ultimate status symbol
for a Pop apartment.

As the check-vested, leather-lunged barker of this manic
two-ring circus, Wolfe reels off article after article in an
astonishing prose ("Baroque," he calls it), a riot of screaming jargon collected from every conceivable source—from
the Jet Set to the Jersey Teens, from effeminate hairdressers
to grimy pit mechanics to jivey Negro boxers and Southern
yokels. Wolfe's technique is the journalist's equivalent of
Pop art; leading off with the radio interviewer's "I am here
on the third floor of . . . ," he places his mental mike under
the victim's nose and lets him (or preferably *her*) talk himself into a devastating self-parody. Wolfe's manifest intention is to make his reader empathize completely with his
subjects; but in his portraits of Pop heroes and heroines—for
instance, his flaring poster of Baby Jane Holzer, "The Girl
of the Year"—his knack of impersonating appalling people
often feeds back, and one turns away disgusted more by the
ventriloquist than by his dummy.

Reading Tom Wolfe, however, does make one realize
how much of American culture is automatically excluded
by the deep but narrow scan of most artists and intellectuals;
one is also made to feel the immense breadth and power of
the impulse that has finally forced its way up through the
narrow crust of art and high culture to erupt in Pop. For
years we have known that mass illusion was becoming a sec-

ond reality, steadily encroaching on the primary validity of immediate individual experience. Now for millions of Americans this displacement is complete, and life has become the moment-by-moment effort to stay in touch with the transmitters of cultural signals. "Philco Baby," a brilliant story by Irvin Faust (included in *Roar Lion Roar*), offers the double experience of empathy with this new consciousness tempered by simultaneous understanding.

Morty, a young stock boy, is glad to work hard all day stacking boxes in an empty room, because he has "Baby," a tiny transistor radio, in his breast pocket. "Baby" monitors every move and moment of his day from waking to sleeping, while providing an endless stream of instructions on how to guard his health, shield his teeth, keep his armpits dry and fragrant, his breath sweet, his mood cheerful. Cool, clean and secure, Morty is narcissistically intact until a slightly deformed, overbearing female comes into his life, smashes "Baby" and reduces Morty to an obedient child, playing on the beach under his "mama's" watchful eye.

The ironic equation Faust establishes between "Baby" and "mama"—or between Pop and Mom—provides a perfect formula for the current cultural condition. Sexless, mindless, without feeling, Pop man, physically vigorous but emotionally frail, sustains a precarious existence at the breasts of the "media," which provide him with the measured routines, the soothing sights and sounds, and the benignly looming presences of the nursery.

Faust's story is at once the epitome of Pop and its antithesis: its flat, slick surface, often a tight mosaic of brand names and product slogans, its cool detached tone, its essentially banal subject, all fit the Pop esthetic perfectly. But the story, virtually a parable, is the carefully focused image of a profound idea, hence a work of traditional art. It would not be difficult, however, to imagine a literature composed with the same care and practically the same technique that would simply contemplate Morty's life, refusing to explain it or judge it. The fact is that some of the most sophisticated modern writers have been championing in recent years an ideal of "objectivity" that has made it almost impossible to locate the moral center of their work; indeed, Alain Robbe-Grillet has repudiated the whole moral function of fiction.

Pop art has been fed not only from below but from above—by existentialism, by Zen, by the "New Wave." Pop is ultimately the point of convergence, where art and entertainment, literature and journalism, sincerity and fraud, engagement and alienation, even art and life, meet and mingle in profound ambiguity. This ambiguity reflects in turn the confusions of a society that struggles still to affirm its traditional values while being steadily undermined by a powerful regressive drift. If this cultural retrogression continues unchecked, unabated, it will soon bring into being the society already glimpsed by Pop—a society in which people hurtle about like atoms in the void, pure energic essences, without affect, without gender, without mind, wedded to machines like half-human, half-mechanical centaurs. The literature that will mirror this society will be cool, detached, ambiguous, no longer even mocking. Its authors will stare back at an obscenely winking neon world with the huge vacant eyes, the adenoidal mouths and the blank faces of baby dolls wearing "shades."

Polymorphous Eroica

JIM MORRISON

WHEN JIMMY DEAN smashed up his car in 1955, he tore a hole that hasn't yet been patched in the American pantheon. Sensitive, introverted, deeply pained, stammering inchoate protests against a blindly demanding parental generation, Dean focused the anguish of youth in his day so sharply that the after-image of tousled hair and furrowed forehead still haunts the national conscience. But the youths he represented are no more; their kind has been succeeded by another and vastly different race. No longer sullen, injured underdogs caught in a wrenching struggle for understanding, today's youth has won so many of its battles and imposed its mystique so successfully on the older generation that nothing is left of the old diffidence. A messianic generation demands a hero of classic proportions—such a hero is Jim Morrison, the leader of America's finest new rock group, the Doors.

Abundantly gifted as a singer and songwriter, Morrison is, above all, a powerfully seductive public personality, at his most entrancing onstage. The three other members of the

Doors hang back deliberately at the fringes of the spotlights to allow Morrison to exercise his fascination in glorious isolation. Tall, lean and loose in the West Coast manner, his body sheathed in black vinyl bared at the chest and neck to show off his strong, classically formed head, Morrison is a surf-born Dionysus. With his heavy ash-blond hair curling luxuriantly around his neck and shoulders, his eyes wide and avid, his sensuously curved lips parted in anticipation, he embodies a faunlike sexuality that is both beguiling and menacing.

Morrison drifts onstage with the floating gait and bemused look of an open-eyed sleepwalker. Oblivious of an audience intent on cannibalizing him every possible way—with flashing cameras, whirring tape recorders and ducking, bobbing forays against a cordon of anxiously covering cops—Morrison waits limply as the other musicians go through their electronic countdown. As they tug at cables, flick switches and lay their heads against ominous-looking black boxes, he slumbers. But then, as the first deafening wave of sound rolls across the stage—making the audience cower as if a lash had been laid across its shoulders—Morrison stirs, seizes the mike with both hands, hauls it up to his open lips, squeezes shut his eyes, and, with a start, gives an anguished scream.

In the performance that follows he evinces an elusive being. Snarling one moment like an aroused panther, the next he subsides into a shy little boy with a tiny self-deprecating smile turning up the corners of his mouth. Sometimes he recalls the dangerously high, madly self-destructive jazz genius; at other times he seems the perfect embodiment of the serious, hard-working young artist devoted to creative integrity. Then again, Morrison can suggest a vulgar male hustler as he tosses his hair and runs his tongue around his open mouth before descending on a phallic mike. These mannerisms suggest how misleading is the common comparison between Morrison and Dean: the inarticulate and shambling Jimmy seemed scarcely sexually competent (love-starved but awkward and shy); Morrison—in any of his aspects—is energized by a ferocious eroticism. Totally uninhibited he appears to be always in a state of smoldering and eruptive sexual excitement.

Most of Morrison's songs are addressed to girls, but, far from being romantic, they are mocking and minatory, acrid with ashes from the cigar of Bert Brecht. (The Doors do a brilliant musical paraphrase of "Alabama Song" that makes the tune turn like a transistorized merry-go-round.) Morrison's mode is not satire, however, but mock-romantic Pop-art facsimiles that get bigger and bigger, closer and closer, until they scare you out of your mind. "Moonlight Drive," for example, sketches an old-fashioned love scene, a June moon spin along the oceanside that is right off the cover of some yellowed page of sheet music. But the singer's invitation to the familiar romantic encounter contains the lurking threat of something sinister. His voice taunts and teases like Sportin' Life's, an electric guitar laughs loonily in the background and the pounding, demanding, demented beat of the music suggests a thrill much wilder than a midnight skinny dip. Commencing in the coaxing tones of the boy next door, Morrison's voice rises by the end of the song to the wail of the demon lover who woos not with promises of tenderness and joy but with the lure of unearthly adventure. He beckons to his female prey and she follows him into the terrifying unknown.

The appeal of this mingled sexuality and demonry to today's young women is certainly not difficult to explain: they are sufficiently self-assured to be excited by the dangers of a bizarre sexual challenge. But Morrison is not just another "sexy" singer. He is one of the most admired figures on the American rock scene. He embodies more than anyone that free-floating longing for revolt, for breakthrough and transcendence that lies so close to the heart of the present moment. As an implicit anarchist operating on a histrionic level, he violates deliberately the decorum of male performers. Though his essential masculinity is never in question, Morrison's image incorporates blatant touches of the feminine. Complementing his dangerous virility and bestowing upon it an appealing aura of voluptuousness are his long wavy hair and beautifully formed features, the way his heavy silver pendants shine against his soft bare chest, and, above all, the sinuous, suggestive movements of his body and lips while he is performing. What Morrison represents in sexual terms is a fluid montage of male and female. He appears a sexually autonomous being, like one of those breast-and-phallus-bearing gods worshipped by the ancients.

The androgynous sex ideal is now a glaring feature of the culture of contemporary youth; but it was first enshrined by the fashion industry. Indeed, Jim Morrison might best be understood as the flip side of Twiggy. Just as she sprouted from the neutral zone between the sexes, he has emerged—like the Hermaphroditus of the classic sculptors—from the confluence of each sex's erotic outlines. Twiggy embodies the calm, epicene beauty of the fashion plate, the muted elegance of the dandy; Morrison the primitive eroticism and Dionysian frenzy of the rock ambience.

Both conform, however, to the paradoxical esthetic of a beauty that is carved and shaped by cutting against the sexual grain. In her famous poster picture, wearing Edwardian men's clothes, Twiggy revealed herself as the archetype of all the beautiful English boys. Cool, relaxed, handsomely turned out, she is an opulent aristocratic loafer—with just a suggestion of the Duke of Windsor. Yet the picture brings out—far better than any of those shots of a giddy girl camping in high fashion—Twiggy's exquisite beauty, her lovely eyes and lips, the whole aura of the young Garbo in her face. Morrison, too, is most breath-taking as the hippie Adonis when he is posed in the languorous semi-nudity of the female model. And he reaches the acme of his erotic appeal when in the heat of performance he abandons himself to the rock music with a woman's capacity for ecstatic surrender.

Ultimate realizations of a whole generation's drive to

overthrow the traditional restrictions and taboos on sexual behavior, Twiggy and Morrison represent the two polarities of sexual identity in the new society. One is without sex and the other is consumed by it. Twiggy's level of emotional development was suggested by the film that showed her fondly stroking and cuddling a newly hatched duckling; the subsequent death of the bird was described by Twiggy's manager as "the only real thing that has happened to her since she came to America." By contrast, Morrison's passion seems so extravagant that no fulfillment can be imagined that would still its insistent demands.

Inevitably, the rise of the androgynous sex ideal has meant a decline in the value of romance. Both Twiggy and Morrison are figures of solipsistic isolation. With their idolization, the era of sexual closed circuitry may be said to commence. And those who are unable to free themselves of traditional amatory ideas had best beware. The editors of *Vogue*, for example, are generally very alert to the style of their subjects; yet they made an obvious blunder when they photographed Jim Morrison with a girl pressed against his bare jewel-bedecked breast. Even though the photographer discreetly veiled the girl's face with her hair, the young god's beauty was offended and diminished by her presence in the picture and by the silly, old-fashioned suggestion of romance. Bad as that combination was, can anyone imagine the effect of a picture that showed the embrace of Morrison and Twiggy? Splinters and vinyl!

When the polarities of sex are refocused along narcissistic lines, a new pattern of sexual intercourse emerges. Antonioni satirized this phenomenon in *Blow-Up* with the scene in which the photographer virtually rapes Veruschka with his camera. The passionate encounter between the demanding, intently staring photographer—his whole being squeezed into the tiny world of his lens-finder—and the wildly excitable female model—fully aroused by the man's obsessive, fetishistic attention—should not be interpreted glibly as a substitute for coitus. Rather it should be seen as an exaggerated statement of another form of erotic union in which one person is aroused by watching the excitement of another, who is, in turn, aroused by the act of being admired.

Whether it be the model and the photographer, the rock musician and his audience or the dancers in the discothèque, the intercourse of voyeur and exhibitionist sparks into passion by arcing across a highly charged but absolutely maintained distance. The tension can rise to unbearable limits, but the fulfillment can never be more than masturbatory.

All of these developments can be regarded as approximations of the ideal of "polymorphous perversity" proclaimed by Norman O. Brown ten years ago in *Life Against Death*. Brown's argument that man was committing suicide by pursuing his traditional goal of sublimating bodily energy into spiritual power culminated in a powerful plea for the reversal of this process. What Brown urged was not, as is commonly supposed, a return to the mature body with its demands for unrestrained sexual union, but a far more drastic, almost unimaginable, retreat to the condition of the sexually undifferentiated and narcissistic infant. Brown imagined that the path of regression would lead to a new Eden; he dreamed of an exuberant and joyous sexuality that would grace man with the "lineaments of satisfied desire."

One half of the prophecy has been fulfilled: the new sex hero is a beautiful and fascinating creature who evinces the anarchic eroticism of the id. But he is also an ominous figure who oscillates between *atonie* and frenzy, exuding the chill of apathy and the fever of madness. His extravagant efforts to achieve an absolute freedom appear to produce a murderous sense of frustration. And, inevitably, he is alone. The harshest irony of all is that he appeals less to our love of life than to our infatuation with danger and death.

Like all hero cults this latest one is deeply shadowed with morbidity. Every week it fosters false reports from all over the country: reports that picture Morrison blind from drug abuse, maimed from the waist down, locked up in an insane asylum or simply—as the UPI flashed across its wire service recently—"JIM MORRISON DEAD. MORE LATER."

The worshipers are growing impatient. They want to get on with the rites of mourning.

New York, 1968

At Play in the Circles of Hell

S*tory of O*—notorious as an underground novel, remarkable as a rare instance of pornography sublimed to purest art—appeared first under mysterious circumstances at Paris in 1954. Bearing the name of an unknown, evidently pseudonymous author, Pauline Réage, and the endorsement of an eminent critic, now a member of the Académie Française, the book was greeted with a mixture of respect and perplexity, receiving the Prix des Deux Magots and touching off a lively discussion (as well as a police investigation) concerning the author's identity and intentions.

Regarded simply in terms of its material, *Histoire d'O* belonged to a familiar genre; as André Pieyre de Mandiargues remarked in a brilliant notice: "Madame Réage uses the tried and true formulas of more than a hundred volumes sold under the counter. The black leather, the little wasp-waisted corsets, the whips and riding crops, the rooms soundproofed to muffle the cries, the brandings with a red-hot iron"—all this paraphernalia of the *genre sombre* offered no surprises. What was astonishing was the art and sensibil-

ity that had infused these tired and ugly properties with
meaning and beauty, reviving their erotic energy even while
transforming them into the symbols of a profoundly religious temperament.

Story of O is neither a fantasy nor a case history. With its
alternate beginnings and endings; its simple, direct style (like
that of a fable); its curious air of abstraction, of independence from time, place and personality, what it resembles
most is a legend—the spiritual history of a saint and martyr.
Yet, by virtue of its formal design, it also participates in the
tradition of the novel of amatory intrigue; commencing with
the simplest of situations, the story gradually opens out into
a Daedalian maze of perverse relationships—a clandestine
society of sinister formality and elegance where the primary
bond is mutual complicity in dedication to the pleasures of
sadism and masochism.

O is initiated into this world by her lover, who one day
takes her to a secluded mansion (reminiscent of Sade's cha-
teaus) where she is trained through the discipline of chains
and whip to be totally submissive to the men who are her
masters. After several weeks, her chains are replaced with an
iron finger ring (lined with gold and bearing the device of
the triskelion, or triple-spoked wheel) and she is returned to
life a changed person, humbly prepared to dispense with
privacy, dignity and her own will.

During her subsequent progress, she is subjected to every
sort of sexual debasement and torture, only to be returned
in the penultimate stage of her education to a still more
brutal institution, a "gynaceum" where she not only endures
the cruelest torments but begins to fulfill the sadistic lesbian
underside of her own nature. Finally, O is symbolically
transformed into an animal and, fearing the loss of her lover,
requests and receives permission to die.

Despite its sensational action, O's history maintains the
sweetly solemn tone of a female martyrology. This paradox
is representative of the book's imaginative texture, a tissue
of intricately woven ironies whose consolidating theme—

implied by the religious symbolism of the convent-like schools, the iron ring, the flagellations—is a perversion of the Christian mystery of exaltation through debasement, of the extremity of suffering transformed into an ultimate victory over the limitations of being.

The more O is brutalized, the more perfectly feminine she becomes—the more *o*pen, *o*bedient and willing to *o*ffer herself. At the same time, this exaggerated feminine submissiveness leads her, goaded on by her master's voyeuristic lust, to adopt herself a masterful, almost masculine attitude toward various women whom she seduces or tortures. Eventually, this acting out of apparently contradictory sexual impulses culminates in total realization of the potentialities of femaleness: O comes to embody all three aspects of feminine being symbolized by the triskelion—the modest maiden (Diana), the inviting woman (Luna) and the sinister crone (Hecate).

Not until the final scene, however, does the full extent of O's transcendence become apparent. First, she is presented at the nadir of her debasement, arriving at an all-night party naked except for an owl mask and led on a dog leash by a young female attendant. Then, in an awesome peripety, the figure O—seated under the full moon of a midsummer night, "smooth and peaceful as stone"—slowly assumes the mysterious grandeur of an Egyptian deity, and we realize that this victim-animal-object has become the Triple Goddess, the apotheosis of primitive woman.

That Pauline Réage is a more dangerous writer than the Marquis de Sade follows from the fact that art is more persuasive than propaganda. Though at first Sade compels our admiration by his daring and fantastic invention, he soon alienates us by the madness of his method—the alternation of encyclopedic descriptions of sexual outrages with long stretches of defensive rhetoric.

Pauline Réage, who is not protesting against anything or sounding a call to arms, produces precisely the opposite effect: aiming only to reveal, to clarify, to make real to the reader those dark and repulsive practices and emotions that his better self rejects as improbable or evil, she succeeds in drawing us irresistibly into her perverse world through the magnetism of her own selfless absorption in it. Like some exquisitely balanced, gently undulating instrument, she carefully inscribes the cruel shocks inflicted on her heroine's refined sensibility—and we believe.

But believing, even grudgingly admiring, we are not happy with the triumph of her heroine—nor, for that matter, with the success of her book. Our situation is rather embarrassing; for men pick up pornographic books, as they do prostitutes, intending to take their pleasure and then repudiate the instruments that provided it. But this moral stratagem will not work with Réage. Indeed, she seems to have envisioned long ago the response of her American readers. In the final scene of the book, she describes a drunken American who comes up to O and, laughing, pulls on her leash. When he sees that the leash is attached to a ring in her flesh, he suddenly sobers up and backs away, his face expressing horror and contempt. Many of those readers who will purchase this expensive little volume for the titillation it affords will pay again in another coin before they put the book down.

The New York Times Book Review, 1966

The Old Smut Peddler

BARNEY ROSSET

HIS THEORY goes something like this: The movie industry! Mohair tycoons worrying about films that cost millions, worrying about moral-ratings codes, worrying about how to please everybody. It's time to scale the movies down to human proportions. The moving picture camera today is just a very expensive typewriter. A Hollywood director can go home, like the young writer used to go home from the ad agency, and knock out a very good movie for $50,000. It's possible to take that movie and squeeze it into a cassette videotape the size of a book. And then one evening, when the kids are in bed, you can slip that cassette into your TV set and, without getting dressed or driving the car, you can watch *Tropic of Cancer* or *Story of O* right in your own living room—where the censor can't go.

That's Barney Rosset, "Grove Press" Rosset, the old smut peddler himself, turning his dubious attentions to home movies and the debauching of the American family. Good old Barney, always gnawing away at the props of middle-class morality, always springing trapdoors under the square toes of the bourgeoisie. First he changes the rules of the publishing game by winning the right to print *Lady Chatterley's Lover* (remember that lace-covered valentine?). Then he dips into real filth with the Marquis de Sade's *120 Days of Sodom*—799 pages of excremental sex acts that ended the critic Edmund Wilson's lifelong habit of reading during breakfast. Finally he pollutes the very shrine of American culture by smearing the silver screen with the meat-rack obscenities of *I Am Curious (Yellow)*.

For these repeated and deliberate offenses against public decency, (1) Barney figures to make $3 to $4 million from *Curious* alone: (2) Barney's Grove Press stock has more than tripled its value recently on the exchange; (3) Barney is now being described by certain movie people as the First Tycoon of the new International Cinema. It couldn't have happened to a more persistent guy. In ten years of charging the forces of censorship and the devil, Rosset has never missed a chance to pick up a little yardage whether by publishing a banned book or straight-arming some local censor in the courts or backing up some other freedom fighter like Lenny Bruce, say, or Malcolm X. The result has been the total liberation of the printed word, and a place on the bestseller list for books like *Portnoy's Complaint* (published by a rival but grateful house).

Running out of track in publishing (just how many "ribald classics" are there, Barney?), Rosset has swung determinedly into films. The basic situation is pure *déjà vu*: a major culture industry imposing censorship on itself out of the mistaken notion that it is conforming to public taste—precisely the condition of publishing when Rosset entered it years ago. The messiahs of "underground movies" tried to fight the censorship battle before Rosset came along, but they proved to be a clique of solipsistic, self-defeating amateurs. In New York five years ago, they attacked the problem of censorship by assembling an audience in a Greenwich Village theater on the promise that they would show an *am strengsten verboten* movie: Jack Smith's *Flaming Creatures* (limp perversion in campy costumes). The cops moved in and busted everyone from the ticket taker to the projectionist. The underground messiahs turned up at court in full beatnik regalia and on the stand harangued the court with the ideals of Cinema, Art and Freedom, offending everyone in sight with their strident self-righteousness and their obvious contempt for the law. It was a soapbox show, not a fight, and when they were done the problem of film censorship stood just where it was when these kamikazes first attacked.

Now consider old Barney's performance on the same track as epitomized by the history of *I Am Curious*. Barney is at the Frankfurt Book Fair in September 1968 pricing the latest continental anti-novels when he hears about this fantastic new Swedish film that goes all the way with sex but treats the subject with "distance." What a marvelous opportunity, thinks Rosset, to challenge the whole censorship code for films! Why, the picture could do for movies what *Lady Chatterley* did for books—make "film," as his ad later smirked, Grove Press's new "four-letter word." Grabbing his teeny wife Cristina, he hops a plane for Sweden, hustles the Swedes for the American distribution rights—a steal at $25,000—and within a week he is preparing to kick some more teeth out of the mumbling bite of the censorship laws. As soon as the film arrives in the country, U.S. Customs begins a heavy schedule of screenings in its cinder-block projection room on Varick Street (for "explosive" pictures evidently). In march New York's professional dirty-book/picture witnesses, all the familiar names from education, law, criticism and, of course, the ministry. (There must be a mailing list of these names by now.) Documents are printed, testimony is solicited, press releases pour across the media's desks; Barney's lawyers plead, his sexperts testify, the judge gapes at the erotic smorgasbord, but the verdict comes through right on schedule: innocent, redeeming social value, no appeal to prurience, put it on the screen and let the mobs start lining up at eight A.M.

The week that *I Am Curious* started wrapping them

around two theaters in New York, I meet Rosset for lunch on the top deck of Grove Press's tree-shack office warren on Eleventh Street, a maze of bias-angled, high-ceilinged, tangentialized chambers that proclaims the Dickensian eccentricity of its principal inhabitant. Barney emerges from his office, bent forward from the waist like some old geezer clomping across a furrowed field. His tight, mustard-colored pants are a little too short and his yellow-and-black plaid a little too loud for a small, gray-haired man of forty-six. What he mostly reminded me of was one of those cranky inventor-type college professors who stare fixedly through their bottle-bottom lenses and address the air as if it were filled with invisible presences. As we exchange the initial pleasantries, I marvel at Rosset's fascinating body English, the unconscious mime of tics and twitches, head slaps and exclamation-point laughs with which he accompanies his words. Nicking and nodding his long, spare head, jouncing on invisible strings like a wire-dangled marionette, Barney leads me down the shiplike stairs of his aerie, and into a plate-glass Greenwich Village restaurant.

Rosset wants to be famous and he knocks himself out to cooperate with the press. It is strange that so many people mumble words like "enigma" and "masked" to describe him when, after many years of psychoanalysis, Rosset treats the intimate recesses of his private life as if they were matters of public record. His publicity man doesn't know what to do with him; he works hard to build his client an image as a solid, businesslike man, and then the boss goes out to lunch and shoots his mouth off about sex and drugs and political revolution, and—bam!—the whole thing is shot to hell. Rosset couldn't care less. His greatest horror is being considered a phoney—and besides, what's there to be ashamed of? The owner of Grove Press embarrassed by a few indiscretions—shame!

Still, even Barney has his limits. Take the time the *Saturday Evening Post* did a story on Rosset and the "underground." They wanted the old mole to pose crawling out of a sewer with a stack of Grove Press filth classics piled up around the hole. Barney fretted and squirmed; he wanted to be a good guy, but this was too much. Couldn't he just jump into his swimming pool with his clothes on? Or pose in the subway with one of Grove's authentic art-nouveau Communist May Day posters? No, the *Post* wanted the sewer, and finally had an artist draw a caricature of Barney clambering out of a manhole like some crazy old gopher. Just to make sure the readership got the point, they put next to the cover illustration: "How Barney Rosset Publishes DIRTY BOOKS for Fun & Profit."

How would you feel, Clarence? Dirty deal, right? So Barney simmered into action. He wired all the papers that he was *buying the Post.* Nobody figured he was kidding because people knew the magazine was in trouble and they thought, "Sure, there had to be some rich sucker who'd want to save her before she goes down the drain." Next day every big paper played the story. Over at the *Post,* the machinery was set—after much financial planning—to liquidate the magazine. And now comes this little twerp Rosset. The *Post's* president, Martin Ackerman, pooh-poohed the whole idea of an offer from Grove—who-the-hell-are-they?— Press.

Cut back to Rosset scrunched over his desk with a pitcher of martinis at his elbow and the plot thickening by the minute. Barney had a hunch that he was on to a good thing. You have to understand that this guy is a real plunger. He does everything on impulse and then figures out afterward whether he's made a smart move or was just kidding. Sure he goofs. He buys books that don't sell, houses that flood, vehicles that break down, movies that can't be shown, newspapers that don't reflect his views, wives that he can't live with—but sometimes he lucks one in there that makes him a millionaire, or, what is more important to a guy who's been a millionaire all his life, that makes him legendary. With the *Post* he suddenly stopped joking. Overnight he put together

a prospective editorial staff and worked out deals with print-
ers and paper manufacturers that would have enabled him to
keep the *Post* running, he says, on a reduced scale, for years.
But plans for the liquidation—and its corporate advantages
—were all made and Rosset never received the courtesy of a
reply.

As Rosset carefully unfolds his reminiscences, talking
slowly and firmly to the area just below the knot in his
orange knit tie, you wonder at the self-absorption that
makes him look and sound in the lunchtime uproar of the
restaurant as if he were alone in his office. He's like the old
guy in *Krapp's Last Tape* (by his favorite author, Samuel
Beckett) who passes his life in endless soliloquy, pausing
only to play back some fine moment from his past, some
flash of passion or of beauty now forever lost. Rosset is very
deep into his own past; everything he does derives directly
from his bizarre upbringing, his remarkable education in
nonconformity and alienation.

His parentage was one of those American mix-ups that
produce new strains of humanity. Imagine a wealthy Jewish
banker married to an Irish Catholic girl (who didn't stop
hating Jews just because she married one) sending his kid to
the most progressive, permissive schools of the 1930s. Imagine a grammar school where the kids stand in the playground wearing Greek laurel wreaths and reciting classic
odes; where the eighth-graders read *Man's Fate*, hold strikes
for peace and picket *Gone with the Wind* because of its
bigoted attitude toward Negroes. And imagine little Barney,
alternately adored and ignored by his parents, burning with
indignation and rancor, cranking out a little paper called
"The Anti-Everything" or "socom" (Socialist-Communist).
Skinny little Barney with his thing about his size and his
glasses and his being Jewish (what is the use of being Jewish
when you've never been inside a synagogue and your
mother hates Jews?). The kid is a battler, though; by the
time he is seventeen, he is president of his class, star of the

football team, holds a new state track record *and* the best-looking girl in the school. How do you cap that?

The answer is you don't. Rosset still regards his seventeenth year as the happiest moment of his life. When he reached Swarthmore, the first of several colleges he attended, he registered instant disappointment. The Quaker puritanism of the place appalled him, as did its provincialisms. Still, it wasn't a total loss because freshman English got the kid into forbidden books. He decided to write about Henry Miller's *Tropic of Cancer*. Not realizing it was banned, he strolled into the Gotham Book Mart one day and asked the lady in the Victorian leg-of-mutton sleeves for this notoriously dirty book. She stared at the boy and asked why he wanted it; when he explained, she reached under the counter and handed him his passport into the underground.

Still, it was years and years until Barney Rosset discovered who he was and what he wanted to do in this world. The price of total freedom can be total confusion. Luckily, a holy war commenced against the Fascists and, pacifist that he was, Barney could serve in the World War II crusade with a good conscience.

The Army should have been the last place that would please an intransigent and rebellious kid, but somehow it pleased Barney Rosset. He was exiled to a remote town in China, and that suited him right down to the good earth. Next to that town in Asia, the only place that has really satisfied Barney is a room in an abandoned firehouse on the Brooklyn end of the Brooklyn Bridge at No. 1 Fulton Street. He loved it so much that he is now building a rich man's mansion—equipped with an elevator and a four-car garage—in another slum, on Houston Street in downtown New York. The house doesn't even have a street running by its front door; Barney will have to fight City Hall for the paving job.

Five years in the Army followed by five years of floating around postwar America, trying one school after another, one job after another, going off to Paris with a Chicago society girl who wanted to be a painter, becoming a millionaire when his father died, becoming a father himself, entering analysis, going through a divorce and never, never, never knowing what to do with all those cramped competitive energies once released so easily on a chalk-striped field— Barney Rosset got to be a pretty sad guy. Perhaps that was when he started giving off the personal atmosphere that suggests Beckett characters standing in pools of light with the words coming out of their mouths as if suspended on slender strings. (Rosset carries in his wallet a strangely disturbing symbol of this alienation: a picture of the bottom half of a man, himself, seated in a chair, and underneath the chair, its eyes glowing crazily in the flash light, an obviously frightened and ferocious German shepherd. "That's the thing I feel closest to in the whole world," he confides—a frightened, vicious dog at bay.)

Finally, Barney blundered into publishing. He bought a tiny firm that had published just three books and stored the stock in his room, where he wrapped the orders for Henry James's *Golden Bowl* and Richard Crashaw's seventeenth-century verse in bundles that he hauled to the post office in a laundry cart. Publishing didn't offer Rosset any clear path for his energies, however, until he got the idea of putting out an unexpurgated edition of *Lady Chatterley's Lover*. The story of his carefully planned, skillfully executed court battle, of the first great breaching of the censorship code and Grove Press's subsequent notoriety is by now a major chapter in American publishing history.

Riding this initial success, Rosset has put together an empire that includes hard-cover and soft-cover books, college texts, a magazine, an off-Broadway playbill, a movie theater, a bar and, lately, films. Now he is eying that ultimate stronghold of imposed standards and inhibitions—television. His plan to use the new cassette technology that will convert every TV set into a home movie projector has run into difficulties. CBS, which has been out front in development of this technology, plans to control the programming of the cassettes. But with the aid of some other company—and several are working on the project—it is entirely possible Rosset will win this last fight, just as he has all the preliminary bouts (a recent Supreme Court ruling upholding the individual's right to possess pornographic materials would appear to strengthen his case).

What is not clear either to Rosset (who is not concerned with the consequences of "freedom") or to anybody else is the effect on modern life of this ultimate revolution in the media. Will transforming the book into the cassette put a period to the print culture? Will substituting *Story of O* for Johnny Carson put an end to the smutty *double-entendre?* Nothing is clear save the irony of the censored medium becoming the funnel to pour pornography into the American home. Asked whether he would care for such spectacles in his home, Rosset replies that there is nothing he reads or sees which he would deny to his fourteen-year-old son, Peter.

Most of the millionaires of Easthampton live in thirty- or forty-room "cottages." Barney Rosset lives in a quonset hut. Of course, it isn't an ordinary quonset. In the first place, it was built by the painter Robert Motherwell and finished inside with lots of hand-fitted wood; in the second, it lies in a delightful maze of willow trees and pools and tennis courts —all wrapped around this pink house with deep blue shades extending down over its long glass side. Inside, the place is casually decorated with Grove Press posters on the walls and lots of books on the shelves; on the floor are toys for Barney and Cristina's little girl, Tensey, and under the arching glass wall is a long narrow bed of cactus garden. As old Barney welcomes you into the main room, the three ferociously friendly German shepherds who have met your car as it entered the gates come leaping through a plastic hoop in the door and go churning around your legs, snapping and tugging at a Frisbee until they jump through the hoop again to race on the lawn. The entire day is passed against this ebb and flow of romping animals and people.

In the country Rosset strikes you as being utterly without pretensions. He lives like a big kid in a clubhouse. Obviously, he wants to go out and play, but you have to ask him a couple of questions first. Will films like *I Am Curious* affect the country's morals? Sure, he says, the films steam up the culture and persuade many people that there is nothing wrong with acting out their fantasies. It's an age of exploration. Doesn't he see danger in such a sudden breakthrough, possibly in the form of boomeranging guilt and anxiety? Sure he does, but that's not his problem. His job is to promote freedom; if people louse it up when they get it, that's their worry.

Then with the big grin that he wears constantly on this day, he's off through the house door and into a parked jeep, beckoning you to follow in your car. His gravely handsome son Peter, a young Viking, jumps in beside his father and the three dogs follow and the jeep goes careening out the gates with dogs barking and craning in every direction. He leads you down ever narrower and rougher roads until you're riding along a trail that winds through dozens of acres of untended land covered with groves of scrub pine. Disembarking at an isolated ranch house, Rosset tells you that he's just bought this land, the biggest chunk of undeveloped real estate in the whole area, and plans to keep it as a wilderness. Then he runs off to fire a retrieving gun fitted up with a wooden decoy for the dogs, and you run too, and pretty soon you and the blond boy and the panting dogs and old Barney the smut peddler are romping on a sunny hillside like a gaggle of innocent children.

Life, 1969

The Bed in the Lab

Human *Sexual Response* by William H. Masters and Virginia E. Johnson (Little, Brown, 1966)—which is being offered as the most important contribution to this well-worked field since the Kinsey Report—would have been more appropriately titled "Sexual Body Mechanics." For what is presented here as a scientific treatment of the intimate workings of the sexual impulse is, in fact, a drastic reduction of the human to the mechanical with consequent distortions of the meaning of sexual experience.

Though the authors are loath to provide more than the barest minimum of information about their experimental methods, it is clear that the technique of investigation consisted in staging sexual events in the laboratory and then observing the results with every available instrument from the electrocardiogram to the color motion-picture camera. The activities studied included: "manual and mechanical manipulation, natural coition with the female partner in supine, superior, or knee-chest position and, for many female study subjects, artificial coition in supine and knee-chest positions." Artificial coition involved the use of a plastic dildo:

The equipment can be adjusted for physical variations in size, weight, and vaginal development. The rate and depth of penile thrust is initiated and controlled completely by the responding individual. As tension elevates, rapidity and depth of thrust are increased voluntarily, paralleling subjective demand. The equipment is powered electrically.

The implications of this remarkable instrument are raised forcibly by what is probably the most startling single statement to emerge from the literature of sex since Freud's attribution of perverse sexual tendencies to children. With their usual *sang-froid,* the authors write:

Understandably, the maximum physiologic intensity of orgasmic response subjectively reported or objectively recorded has been achieved by self-regulated mechanical or auto-manipulative techniques. The next highest level of erotic intensity has resulted from partner manipulation, again with established or self-regulated methods, and the lowest intensity of target-organ response was achieved during coition.

For the layman, at least, this will prove to be the principal finding of a study based on eleven years' work with over 600 subjects and comprising "10,000 complete cycles of sexual response." To evaluate this finding, one needs to pay attention not only to the scientists' data, but also to the methods with which they reached it. That many thousands of people will read the book without making this critical distinction is the strongest argument against making such works available to the general public. This issue was raised with the publication of the Kinsey study; it becomes even more acute here.

For if Kinsey erred in claiming to represent the behavior of the "human male," when, in fact, he was only describing the behavior of some thousands of North American males, think of the false implications of the present study, which claims to describe one of the most basic biologic processes by a sampling of a few hundred of each sex. If Kinsey's sample was less than fully representative sociologically, how much less representative is this study's "research population," which was recruited from the "academic community associated with a large university-hospital complex." In other words, virtually all the subjects were white, middle-class, well-educated, the majority between the ages of twenty-one and forty. The results provide an interesting comment on the "academic community," but this is hardly a cross-section of the population, much less a fair sample of humanity.

A more serious failing is the almost complete exclusion of psychological data. (The authors promise a future volume of "psychological evaluation.") About the screening of subjects, we are told only that important considerations were "willingness to participate, facility of sexual responsiveness, and ability to communicate finite details of sexual reaction." One gathers that many people were attracted by the hope of improving their sexual technique or enjoying the opportunity for anonymous and irresponsible sexual relations.

It could be argued that the study's concentration on the physiology of sex makes the social and psychological identity of its subjects a matter of small importance. But to say this is to assume what should have been proved. To a greater degree perhaps than any other physiological processes, sexual responses fuse the most rudimentary and the most sophisticated functions of the human organism; consequently, their analysis creates enormous problems for those who would draw a line between mind and body. *Human Sexual Response*—apart from the anatomical description of tissues, organs, glands, and the chemical analysis of secretions and exudates—deals almost entirely with processes that are initiated and controlled by complex neurological stimuli that are in turn associated with the higher centers of consciousness. The possibilities here for significant variations arising from individual, social or cultural causes are so great that they cannot be ignored.

By far the most serious problem of methodology is raised by the laboratory setting in which the observations were made. Here there would appear to be an inversion of scientific method: instead of the researchers adjusting their methods to the phenomena being investigated, the subjects were obliged to adapt themselves to the demands of the recording apparatus. This indifference to the integrity of sexual experience arises from the basic and abiding assumption of the whole study: namely, that there is such a thing as "the human sexual response," that it is an autonomous physiological process leading up to and away from orgasm, and that once it is set in motion, it always functions in much the same manner. Having set out with this idea, the scientists selected those people best able to demonstrate it, created an artificial situation in which it was clear that this was what was expected from them, and carefully isolated this activity from every other factor that might complicate or confuse it. The result is an extreme simplification of sexual responses. Sex is viewed merely as an array of discrete physiological reactions describable in quantitative terms. It is no wonder that having reduced sex to mechanism, the scientists found that its needs were best satisfied by one of their own instruments.

The gravest criticism of this study, therefore, is that by abstracting its subject to such an extreme degree and by omitting so much ancillary data, it becomes very difficult to know what value to place on the findings or how to fit them back into reality. Rather than debate the soundness of its conclusions—a task best left to specialists—one may grant these conclusions a certain tentative validity and then go on to ask what they offer us that is novel or suggestive.

As regards physiology, the findings are, considering the drastic methods employed, disappointingly obvious. In fact, were it not for medical jargon, which has the power to invest the familiar with an aura of the recondite, one's most common reaction would be amusement at the scientist's laborious efforts to demonstrate the obvious. It hardly re-

quires eleven years of study to discover that sexual
excitement produces "hyperventilation" (fast breathing),
"tachycardia" (racing heart), "myotonia" (muscular tension), and "vasocongestion" (swollen veins). Nor will it
surprise anyone to learn that the sexual cycle consists of
four stages: "excitement," "plateau," "orgasm" and "resolu-
tion." For scientists the statistical expression of these familiar processes will doubtless have value; for the layman, the
charts and tables will have little meaning.

The authors of *Human Sexual Response* resemble the
compilers of the Kinsey Report in their concern for everyone's sexual well-being. They believe that every healthy
person from eighteen to eighty has the right to and the capacity for a daily orgasm. They deliberately emphasize the
similarities between the sexual responses of men and women.
They try to dispel the fear of impotency in old age. When
they come to the disquieting topic of genital size, they stress
the consoling fact that a small penis may enlarge to a relatively greater degree than a large one, and treat actual size
only by the most extreme indirections.

Yet despite these efforts to reassure and prove helpful, the
study reveals some serious discrepancies between the sexual
patterns of men and women, as well as the distressing details
of genital "involution" in older people. The female capacity
for repeated and prolonged orgasm is not matched by the
male one. After reading that the aged male's ejaculation is
apt to be a mere "seepage," that the "steroid-starved post-
menopausal" female has vaginal walls that are "tissue-paper-
thin," one wishes that we could return to the wisdom of an
earlier time that accepted physical decline and sought com-
pensations in pursuits that transcend the physical.

The modern fixation on youth demands, however, that
every vestige of this idealized age be preserved as long as
possible. The study is in this regard typical of its day.
Everywhere we look today we see fresh signs of sexual regression. If one adds up the strongest notes of the current
scene—increasing homosexuality, rampant exhibitionism and

voyeurism, fun-and-games rationalizations for promiscuity, masturbatory dances, sadism, and the enormous proliferation of sexual fantasy—all these things bespeak the frustration of mature love and the falling back on more primitive levels of sexual gratification which require only a minimum of emotional involvement with others.

Perhaps, then, what most people will regard as the most implausible finding of *Human Sexual Response* is actually its one profound truth. Perhaps a genuinely prophetic imagination is declaring itself in the book's most indelible image, that of woman mating with herself by means of a machine.

Book Week, 1966

The New Repression

WHILE *I am Curious* (*Yellow*) wraps lines of edgy ticket buyers around the Cinema Rendezvous and various Village cockpits prepare to show sexual intercourse flat-out on their stages, a renowned sociologist reports that one American male out of every six is homosexual. While the sexual "rights" of adolescents and college students are recognized through cohabitory dormitories and the average age of wedlock drops a few months each year, another sociologist reports that mutually recognized infidelity has become the acknowledged pattern of marriage among younger Americans. While the whole country shucks off its traditional inhibitions and indulges in sprees of sexual behavior that would once have been branded debauchery, the nation's overworked psychiatrists sit patiently from morn till night listening to endless tales of missed orgasms, guilty infidelities and the mysterious loss of "affect."

On the one hand, there is more apparent sexual freedom than ever before; on the other, there is more apparent sexual disturbance, neurosis and perversion than ever before. A

366

profound and perplexing paradox occurs to an observer of our sex mores, and that is the fact that the behavioral freedom that has long been desired and urged by doctors, psychoanalysts and social reformers is being rapidly achieved, but this sexual revolution is not being accompanied by the predicted happiness and joy that seemed a logical result of throwing off our inherited taboos.

So we are compelled to ask, "Is this sexual revolution what it seems to be?" Is it a genuine revolution freeing us from the inhibiting dualism of Judeo-Christian morality, freeing us to believe, as did the Greeks, that the life of the body is just as important as the life of the mind, banishing the guilt and shame associated traditionally with openly expressed sexuality, particularly in unconventional forms? Is it, in fact, a revolution at all—or is it merely the illusion of freedom, carte blanche for every conceivable form of experiment that does not so much remove a repression as drive it deeper? The professed goal of the current upheaval in sex mores is appealing as a utopian idea, but in setting out to achieve it merely by flattening barriers without taking into account the immense amount of anxiety and disorientation that accompanies any basic change in human behavior, we may be merely burying our inhibitions instead of eradicating them.

What the current sexual revolution comes down to is twofold. First, there is a casting off of old restrictions against the display, enactment or discussion of sexual behavior, so that we live in the midst of a steady and ever-increasing bombardment of sexual stimuli, the net effect of which is to constantly provoke and check arousal until a state of general indifference—the cool beyond sex—is reached. The second and doubtless more significant feature of the sexual revolution is that the traditional moral code—explicit, clear-cut, well understood—and the traditional punishments are being swept aside. The combination of these two factors more and more leaves the individual alone to maintain a precarious balance between his heightened sense of possibilities and his confused notions of what is safe and right.

Far from opening the doors to sexual freedom, the current trend leads straight into the mazes of psychic repression. We are free to act as boldly as we please, but instead of carrying into our actions the full charge of our souls, enjoying or suffering to the full extent of our involvement, we must play it safe and act without feeling. When such situations multiply until they become the rule of life, the individual's emotional core develops a dense protective shield; even when he wants to, he can never let go. Worse still is the fact that this whole process goes forward beneath the surface of awareness. Repression is internal, unconscious, pervasive in its operation; it is easily assimilated to the individual's habitual life style. Instead of experiencing conflicts and accepting ambiguous situations, the victim is both sheltered and deadened by apathy.

With feelings and behavior sundered, there arises a dangerous dissociation of sexual sensibility. Unsatisfying experiences accumulate and with them the urgency for sexual release mounts; this cycle prompts a search for a greater number and variety of sexual encounters. And as the behavior becomes more extravagant, the repressions clamp their protective hold even tighter. The eventual result must be either an explosion of baffled emotion or the zombie-like state of those hippies, hipsters and haw-haw aristocrats who, having tried everything, are now pure stone.

The sexual revolution's major contributions to sexual security have been the pill, penicillin and permissiveness. Yet, according to the findings of the psychoanalysts, what people fear most is not pregnancy, disease and censure but sex itself —or, more accurately, the loss of control that is the essence of intense sexual experience. The traditional answer to this most basic of sexual anxieties is the development of close, trusting, deeply responsive relationships, in or outside of marriage. Today, however, these relationships are forestalled or undercut by the very conditions of our so-called freedom. We are free to do everything but settle down.

As the cycle of the new repression works itself out, the combination of increasingly reckless behavior, mounting frustration and the loss of faith in other people produces a powerful undertow of sexual *involution*. Drawing his sex back into himself, the individual seeks sources of satisfaction that engage his fantasies but remain firmly under his control. Certainly, one of the basic questions raised by the current flood of peephole pornography is whether sex today is not often masturbatory even when it involves a partner. The difference between a man and a machine is great; yet both may be put to the same use. Similarly, the current image of the desirable female, from *Playboy*'s papermates to the lingerie ads in *The New York Times*, is that of a sleek new sexual appliance—often matched with a shiny new automobile.

If men have reduced women in their imaginations to subservient sexual toys, the women have found an apt revenge. They are preparing to dispense with men altogether. The recent *I Am Curious (Yellow)* is not the first serious movie to exhibit sexual intercourse, nor is it the most daring. About two years ago a film was made and shown in the United States that concentrated on the sex life of another ordinary, representative modern woman. She was shown in the most revealing detail slowly coming to climax. This film was much more graphic than the drab Swedish production; for one thing, it was in Technicolor. The camera was locked in a tight close-up, so close the audience could actually see the woman's skin changing color from bright pink to scarlet to a stippled burgundy as she came nearer and nearer to orgasm. Best of all, she was not at the mercy of some brutal and faithless man. The result: her climax was the most satisfying experience of sex that she had ever had.

The woman was, of course, one of the 10,000 subjects of the Masters report, published as *Human Sexual Response*. Her mate was a power-driven plastic penis. Though this contraption has not turned up yet in the windows of Hammacher Schlemmer, a discreet sales campaign directed at "people who live alone" might earn a fortune. The inventors could even consider adding an attachment for artificial insemination.

New York, 1969

Filth Fascination

DURING THE SUMMER of 1967 as the public health officials of San Francisco braced themselves against a threatened wave of epidemics—everything from typhus and cholera on down through hepatitis and venereal disease to a mass invasion of bedbugs and crab lice—the American public looked on aghast at the gigantic filth-in and stink-through of the Haight-Ashbury. Nobody really cared if the kids flaunted the moral code with orgies, gang bangs, prostitution and theft, nor if they blew their minds with pot, hash, meth and smack, nor if they got lost, forever separated from their families, displaced persons in self-made concentration camps —*"I don't care what they do; I just wish they'd take a bath."* Thus spoke the voice of America.

An Italian journalist, a small, immaculate, highly refined man, visited New York recently and took out one night a very good-looking young woman. When he brought her home—to the East Village—he found a huge dog stalking around in her apartment. Entering the bedroom, they discovered that the dog had defecated on top of the bed. A repulsive sight. But it didn't disgust the girl, who turned to her friend, saying, "Let's get naked and do it right in this stuff." He left reeling.

A salesgirl in a sophisticated midtown shop was talking to a fashion stylist, when the visitor said, "Got to get to the john—whoops! Did it in my pants."
"That's terrible."
"Don't be silly, everybody does it nowadays."

The first installment of Norman Mailers *An American Dream* is a psychotic merry-go-round: from an abyss of apathy and self-loathing, the hero climbs to the manic peak of wife-slaughter. Then, suddenly, he is seized with an onrush of irresistible amoral energy. Hurtling downstairs, he enters the maid's room and rapes her anally. Returning to his wife's corpse, he finds she has evacuated her bowels. Tenderly, he wipes her clean.

Back in real life—the Hell's Angels perform their initiation rites: "The ceremony varies from one chapter to another but the main feature is always the defiling of the initiate's new uniform. A bucket of dung and urine will be collected during the meeting, then poured on the newcomer's head in a solemn baptismal." (Hunter S. Thompson, *Hell's Angels*)

The prohibition against filth is the deepest taboo in our culture. Stronger than the restrictions on sex and aggression, it goes all the way back to the rise of monotheism and the elaborate hygienic laws of the Old Testament. The rival gods of Jehovah, having been defeated and overthrown, were hurled on the dung heap, outlawed along with blood and excrement. Then the link between the dirty and diabolic was strengthened by Christianity. As Norman O. Brown reminds us in *Life Against Death*, the Devil is a black and filthy creature whose appearance is accompanied by foul smells. "Hieronymus Bosch," he writes, "enthrones Satan on a privy, from which the souls that have passed out of his anus drop into the black pit." The worship of the Devil culminates in an orgy of filth: the host for the Black Mass is prepared by kneading on the buttocks of the Queen Witch "a mixture of the most repulsive material, feces, menstrual blood, urine and offal of various kinds." The culmination of this perverted fascination with filth is the demon-fearing, witch-burning Puritan theocracy of New England, where cleanliness and godliness become symbolically inseparable and indistinguishable.

The taboo on filth has been enforced so rigorously in modern times that the subject is virtually unspeakable. Apart from the abstruse speculations of Freud and his followers on "anality" as a stage in childhood, the topic of cultural attitudes toward excrement has been scrupulously avoided even by anthropologists and sociologists. In an age of superabundant academic research into every nook and corner of human experience, the standard work on the scatological is the same today as it was eighty years ago. *Scatologic Rites of All Nations*, a compilation of information drawn together from a thousand sources by a one-time captain in the Indian Wars, John G. Bourke, is not only an old study: it is virtually inaccessible. Stamped "Not for General Perusal," the book can be obtained today in New York only from behind the locked steel grill of the 42nd Street Library's Rare Book Room.

Even a glance at the crowded pages of *Scatologic Rites* reveals the extreme importance of filth in ancient and primitive civilizations. Excrement was an essential resource of medicine, magic, divination, witchcraft and even the preparation of foods. So numerous and basic were the uses of filth that it seems obvious that primitive man regarded his wastes as valuable substances—as do infants and animals today. Current attitudes in the civilized world, therefore, are really an inversion of primitive human nature.

Nowhere has the terror of filth as an enemy of the civilized life struck deeper than in modern America. Our compulsive cleanliness and fear of dirt have made us laughingstocks all over the world. The spectacle of millions of Americans taking off every year for the cultural capitals of the West with arms aching from inoculations, luggage bulging with soaps and toilet paper, is obviously funny, but no more ridiculous than the germ warfare conducted at home and celebrated in thousands of ads for detergents, deodorizers, mouthwashes and floral-scented sprays. At the head of the legions of cleanliness and godliness, modern America has placed its grandaddy general, Dwight D. Eisenhower, alias Mr. Clean.

Excesses in one direction always beget answering extravagances. As the incidents set out at the beginning of this article suggest, cracks are starting to appear in our hard white armor. Youth is fascinated today by the image of an ultimately funky, hairy, raunchy, down-on-all-fours style of existence. Rock music celebrates such a return to the Ur-slime with its dirty, raucous, noise-polluted texture, its hot, grunting, flatulant basses and the sounds of electric organs whose notes burble slowly to the surface through heavy sonic slop. The language of the young reeks with scatologic references, ranging from satiric Lenny-Bruceisms through the fondled vocabulary of the Southern Negro to the dirty twisted scrawls on the widely published walls of downtown queer bars. When one visits the inner citadel of youth culture, the Hashberry or the East Village, what impresses him most is the dirt, the omnipresent litter, the scabrous look of decaying tenements. The hippie pads are incredibly squalid. They are flophouses, really, with the floors covered with dirty, stained, torn mattresses, the walls blackened and broken, the bathtub long since torn loose and hurled out the window in a symbolic act of taking possession.

These dirty appearances are not misleading; in fact, they are fusty symbols of the new cultural values embodied in much avant-garde art. What they imply is made explicit in the excremental sculptures of Sam Goodman, molded from brown polyethylene plastic in familiar tubular and cake shapes; Robert Whitman's film triptych, the center panel a shot of a turd launching into a toilet bowl; the garbage- and offal-stuffed car at the recent Riverside Museum ex- hibit; the animal organs crammed in nylon slings at the slaughterhouse show of several years ago. The masterpiece of the downtown theater, last year's *Gorilla Queen,* offers the densest scatologic texture ever exposed on a public stage: the costumes had the "nappy" look of an old drag queen's wardrobe; the language was shockingly dirty ("I'd eat the cheese out of a dead monkey's jockstrap") and the action entailed perverse spectacles, like eight apes urinating on a recumbent girl.

To dismiss the current absorption in filth as merely a quirk of the hippie mentality, however, would be a mistake. A fervid mysticism of filth flares forth from the most con- temporary modern authors. Filth is lyrically celebrated by Jean Genet, laconically crystalized by William Burroughs— homosexual writers both, to no one's surprise. Almost inevi- tably homosexual sensibility entails a coming to terms with the intertwining of the erotic and anal, offering especially urgent exemplification of the Yeatsian phrase, "Love has pitched his mansion in the place of excrement." The novels of Genet are paens of excremental sensibility, colloidal sus- pensions in which float glinting bits of filth, sperm, sweat, hair and urine. Describing how he would lie in his prison cot, he writes:

> . . . above all the odor of my farts, which is not the odor of my shit, a loathesome odor, so much so that here again, I bury myself beneath the covers and gather in my cupped hands my crushed farts which I carry to my nose. They open to me hidden treasures of happi- ness. I inhale. I suck in. I feel them almost solid going down through my nostrils.

Genet's rhapsodic solipsism simply exaggerates a familiar truth: that the filth taboo does not extend in full force to the individual's own excrement—a fact underscored by many vulgar witticisms.

Even beyond the worlds of the alienated—the youth, the homosexual, the artist—the American middle class, even at its most elegant and decorous, is beginning to flirt with filth. In a recent issue of *Vogue*, that great blonde beast Veruschka appeared with her face covered with a layer of brown goo that made her look like a greasy African queen. The exquisite Catherine Deneuve is shown, in one episode of the visually lovely *Belle de Jour*, being spattered from head to foot with black bull dung. One awaits the appearance of *Candy* to see how faithfully its makers will render the scene in which the heroine is seduced standing in a toilet bowl.

The current obsession with filth has as many explanations as there are examples to illustrate it: rebellion, regression, homosexuality. For young people brought up on a tight schedule of morning tooth-brushing, nightly bathing, clean underwear every day, fresh sheets every week, the defiant lapse into filth is an act of social sabotage. For the children of permissiveness—the gate never slammed on infancy— filth is redolent of the nursery, with its familiar odors and excremental sensations. One could invoke the whole gamut of overworked psychosocial causes which are cited every day to explain each new bizarre feature of our freaky civilization. Yet Freud himself would have been hard-pressed to find a wholly satisfying explanation for such an astonishing phenomenon. Indeed, if we could have his view, it might prove very similar to those expressed by your Aunt Minnie or Uncle Schmul. Ask them about such goings-on, and they'll wrap it all up for you in one indignant word—"animals!" Well, here is Sigmund Freud, seated on the throne of Mosaic wisdom, speaking about the relation of dirt to culture: "Dirtiness of any kind seems to us incompatible with civilization. . . . Indeed, we are not surprised by the idea of setting up the use of soap as an actual yardstick of civilization." In other words, "*I don't care what they do; I just wish*—" Yes, doctor—so do we.

Index

DESPERADOS
The Roots of Country Rock
John Einarson
304 pp., 31 b/w photos
0-8154-1065-4
$19.95

COLONEL TOM PARKER
The Curious Life of Elvis Presley's
Eccentric Manager
James L. Dickerson
320 pp., 35 b/w photos
0-8154-1088-3
$28.95

LIVING WITH THE DEAD
Twenty Years on the Bus with
Garcia and the Grateful Dead
Rock Scully with David Dalton
408 pp., 31 b/w photos
0-8154-1163-4
$17.95

HE'S A REBEL
Phil Spector—Rock and Roll's
Legendary Producer
Mark Ribowsky
368 pp., 35 b/w photos
0-8154-1044-1
$18.95

LENNON IN AMERICA
1971–1980, Based in Part
on the Lost Lennon Diaries
Geoffrey Giuliano
320 pp., 50 b/w photos
0-8154-1073-5
$27.95 cloth
0-8154-1157-X
$17.95 paperback

ROCK 100
The Greatest Stars of
Rock's Golden Age
David Dalton and Lenny Kaye
with a new introduction
288 pp., 195 b/w photos
0-8154-1017-4
$19.95

GOIN' BACK TO MEMPHIS
A Century of Blues, Rock 'n' Roll,
and Glorious Soul
James L. Dickerson
284 pp., 58 b/w photos
0-8154-1049-2
$16.95

MICK JAGGER
Primitive Cool
Updated Edition
Chris Sandford
352 pp., 56 b/w photos
0-8154-1002-6
$16.95

FAITHFULL
An Autobiography
Marianne Faithfull
with David Dalton
320 pp., 32 b/w photos
0-8154-1046-8
$16.95

DEPECHE MODE
A Biography
Steve Malins
288 pp., 24 b/w photos
0-8154-1142-1
$17.95

ANY OLD WAY YOU CHOOSE IT
Rock and Other Pop Music, 1967–1973
Expanded Edition
Robert Christgau
360 pp.
0-8154-1041-7
$16.95

HARMONICAS, HARPS, AND HEAVY BREATHERS
The Evolution of the People's Instrument
Updated Edition
Kim Field
368 pp., 32 b/w photos
0-8154-1020-4
$18.95

TURNED ON
A Biography of Henry Rollins
James Parker
280 pp., 10 b/w photos
0-8154-1050-6
$17.95

CHER
If You Believe
Mark Bego
376 pp., 50 b/w photos
0-8154-1153-7
$25.95 cloth

MADONNA
Blonde Ambition
Updated Edition
Mark Bego
368 pp., 57 b/w photos
0-8154-1051-4
$18.95

BACKSTAGE PASSES
Life on the Wild Side with David Bowie
Angela Bowie with Patrick Carr
368 pp., 36 b/w photos
0-8154-1001-8
$17.95

ROCK SHE WROTE
Women Write About Rock, Pop, and Rap
Edited by Evelyn McDonnell and Ann Powers
496 pp.
0-8154-1018-2
$16.95

LOU'S ON FIRST
A Biography of Lou Costello
Chris Costello with Raymond Strait
257 pp., 31 b/w photos
0-8154-1083-2
$17.95

THE ART PEPPER COMPANION
Writings on a Jazz Original
Edited by Todd Selbert
200 pp., 12 b/w photos, 4 color photos
0-8154-1067-0
$30.00 cloth

SUMMER OF LOVE
The Inside Story of LSD, Rock & Roll, Free Love and High Times in the Wild West
Joel Selvin
392 pp., 23 b/w photos
0-8154-1019-0
$15.95